Mastering SQL and Database

From Basics to Expert Proficiency

Contents

Introduction

The purpose of this book, "Mastering SQL and Database: From Basics to Expert Proficiency," is to provide a comprehensive guide to understanding and mastering SQL and database concepts. Databases are foundational to any modern computing system, offering a structured way to store, manage, and query data efficiently.

SQL, or Structured Query Language, is the standard language for interacting with relational databases. This book aims to equip readers with the skills needed to write efficient SQL queries, design robust database schemas, and manage database systems effectively. With a clear structure and detailed explanations, this text will address both fundamental concepts and advanced topics.

The initial chapters will introduce you to the basics of databases and SQL. You will learn what databases are, the different types of databases available, and the history and evolution of SQL. Basic database concepts and database management systems (DBMS) will also be discussed to lay a solid foundation.

Following that, you will delve into the basics of SQL queries. This includes understanding SQL syntax, data types, writing simple queries, filtering and sorting data, using aggregate functions, and managing data through insertion, updating, and deletion of records.

Once the foundational knowledge is established, the book will explore more advanced SQL queries. Topics such as subqueries, nested queries, common table expressions (CTEs), window functions, and advanced join techniques will be covered in detail. Understanding these advanced topics will significantly enhance your ability to handle complex data retrieval and manipulation.

Database design and normalization are crucial aspects of creating efficient and scalable databases. You will learn about different data models, entity-relationship diagrams, and normalization forms from the first normal form (1NF) to the Boyce-Codd normal form (BCNF). Practical considerations for denormalization and design for scalability will also be discussed.

Working with multiple tables is another fundamental aspect addressed in this book. You will learn different types of joins, including inner, left, right, and full outer joins, as well as cross joins and self joins. Subqueries and their applications will also be thoroughly examined.

Database transactions and concurrency are vital for maintaining data integrity and consistency. This book will cover transaction control commands, isolation levels, locking mechanisms, and deadlock resolution. Best practices for handling long-running transactions will be provided alongside case studies.

Optimizing database performance through indexing and query optimization is essential for maintaining efficient operations. You will learn about different types of indexes, strategies for their use, understanding execution plans, and optimizing various types of SQL queries.

The book will also guide you through stored procedures, triggers, and user-defined functions. Detailed instructions on creating, executing, and managing these database objects will be provided, along with best practices.

Database security and user management are paramount to protecting sensitive data. Topics will include user authentication, access control, data encryption, auditing, compliance, and backup strategies. The book will detail comprehensive security practices and offer case studies.

Lastly, the book will explore NoSQL databases and their integration with SQL systems. It covers the various types of NoSQL databases, their use cases, and how they differ from traditional SQL databases. Integration strategies and polyglot persistence will also be discussed to provide a well-rounded understanding of modern database systems.

By the end of this book, readers will have the knowledge and skills necessary to design, implement, and manage robust database systems using both SQL and NoSQL technologies. This book aims to serve as an invaluable resource for students, developers, and database administrators seeking to deepen their understanding of database management and SQL.

Chapter 1

Introduction to Databases and SQL

This chapter provides a fundamental understanding of databases and SQL. It begins by defining what a database is and discusses various types of databases. The chapter introduces SQL, outlining its history and evolution. Basic database concepts and the role of Database Management Systems (DBMS) are presented. An overview of relational databases and a primer on SQL's structure and syntax are included. Practical instructions on setting up an initial database and connecting to it, along with an exploration of various database clients and tools, conclude this chapter.

1.1 What is a Database?

A database is an organized collection of data stored and accessed electronically. Databases are designed to store, retrieve, manage, and manipulate data efficiently and securely. The key components of a database include the data itself, the database management system (DBMS), and the application programs that access and interact with the database.

A database typically structures information into tables, columns, and rows to facilitate organized data storage and retrieval. This tabular representation allows for efficient querying and manipulation using Structured Query Language (SQL). Data within a database can be of various types, including text, numbers, dates, and binary data, enabling diverse applications ranging from simple record keeping to complex data analytics.

Several attributes define an effective database system:

1. **Consistency:** Ensuring data integrity and accuracy.
2. **Concurrency:** Allowing multiple users to access data simultaneously without conflicts.
3. **Durability:** Protecting data against system failures and ensuring data persists over time.
4. **Isolation:** Holding transactions separate from each other to prevent interference.

The primary components of a database environment include:

1. Data: The actual information stored in the database. This constitutes records, files, and other forms of data that the database manages and makes available for retrieval and manipulation.

2. Database Management System (DBMS): A suite of tools and software that facilitates the creation, management, and interaction with databases. Some well-known DBMS software includes MySQL, PostgreSQL, Microsoft SQL Server, and Oracle Database.

3. Database Schema: The blueprint of the database, detailing the structure of the database like tables, columns, data types, and relationships between the data entities.

4. Queries: Commands executed within SQL to perform various operations on the data such as retrieval (SELECT), insertion (INSERT), updating (UPDATE), and deletion (DELETE) of data.

Consider the following SQLite example to illustrate a basic database structure:

```
CREATE TABLE Students (
    StudentID INTEGER PRIMARY KEY,
    FirstName TEXT,
    LastName TEXT,
    DateOfBirth TEXT,
    EnrollmentDate TEXT
);
```

```
INSERT INTO Students (FirstName, LastName, DateOfBirth, EnrollmentDate)
VALUES ('John', 'Doe', '1995-05-15', '2023-01-12');

SELECT * FROM Students;
```

The SQL commands above create a table named *Students* with columns for 'StudentID', 'FirstName', 'LastName', 'DateOfBirth', and 'EnrollmentDate'. The 'INSERT INTO' statement adds one student record to the *Students* table, and the 'SELECT *' statement retrieves and displays all records from the table.

```
StudentID | FirstName | LastName | DateOfBirth | EnrollmentDate
---------------------------------------------------------------
1         | John      | Doe      | 1995-05-15  | 2023-01-12
```

Types of Data in Databases:

Data stored in databases can be broadly classified into several types:

1. **Structured Data:** Easily searchable data organized in a fixed format such as tables (e.g., SQL databases).
2. **Unstructured Data:** Data without a predefined data model or organization (e.g., text documents, images).
3. **Semi-structured Data:** Data that does not conform to a rigid structure but contains tags or markers to separate data elements (e.g., XML, JSON).

Types of Database Models:

Databases are classified into different models based on their structures and use cases:

1. **Relational Databases:** Utilize tabular structure and SQL for data manipulation (e.g., MySQL, PostgreSQL).
2. **NoSQL Databases:** Designed for specific data models other than tabular relations, such as key-value pairs, document-based storage, column-family stores, and graph databases (e.g., MongoDB, Cassandra, Neo4j).
3. **Hierarchical Databases:** Structure data in a tree-like format, with parent-child relationships (e.g., IBM Information Management System).

4. **Network Databases:** Use a graph structure to handle complex relational data, allowing multiple relationships (e.g., Integrated Data Store).

5. **Object-Oriented Databases:** Store data in the form of objects, similar to object-oriented programming (e.g., db4o, ObjectDB).

Understanding these fundamental aspects of databases forms the foundational knowledge necessary for deeper exploration of database design, management, and optimization, essential for mastering SQL and database technologies.

1.2 Types of Databases

Databases come in various forms, each suited to different types of tasks and applications. Understanding the types of databases is essential for choosing the right database for specific needs. Broadly, databases can be classified into six main categories: relational databases, NoSQL databases, object-oriented databases, graph databases, hierarchical databases, and network databases.

Relational Databases: Relational databases are the most common type of database in use today. They are founded on the relational model proposed by E.F. Codd in 1970. In a relational database, data is organized into tables (also called relations), which consist of rows and columns. Each row represents a unique record, and each column represents a field or attribute of the record. Tables can be linked to each other through foreign keys, allowing for complex querying and data manipulation.

Relational databases use Structured Query Language (SQL) for defining and manipulating data. Some popular relational database systems include MySQL, PostgreSQL, Oracle Database, and Microsoft SQL Server. Relational databases are well-suited for applications requiring complex queries and transactions, such as financial systems, customer relationship management systems, and e-commerce platforms.

NoSQL Databases: NoSQL databases, or "Not Only SQL" databases, are designed to handle a wide variety of data models, including key-value pairs, document storage, wide-column stores, and graph storage. These databases emerged in response to the limitations of relational databases, particularly in terms of scalability and flexibility.

- **Key-Value Stores**: These databases use a simple key-value pair for storage. They are highly performant and can handle large amounts of data quickly. Examples include Redis and Amazon DynamoDB. - **Document Stores**: These databases store data in document format, often using JSON or BSON. They are ideal for storing semi-structured data. Examples include MongoDB and CouchDB. - **Wide-Column Stores**: These databases store data in tables, but unlike relational databases, they allow for a dynamic number of columns. They are designed for high throughput and large data volume. Examples include Apache Cassandra and HBase. - **Graph Databases**: These databases are designed to represent data with complex relationships. They use graph structures with nodes, edges, and properties to store data. Examples include Neo4j and Amazon Neptune.

NoSQL databases are particularly useful for applications that require horizontal scaling, like social media platforms, real-time analytics, and big data applications.

Object-Oriented Databases: Object-oriented databases store data in the form of objects, similar to object-oriented programming languages. Each object is an instance of a class, and the database can store methods that can be used to manipulate the object's data. These databases support complex data types and can model real-world entities more naturally than relational databases.

Object-oriented databases integrate seamlessly with object-oriented programming languages, making them a preferred choice for applications that require complex data representations, such as computer-aided design (CAD) systems, telecommunications, and software engineering repositories. Examples include ObjectDB and db4o.

Graph Databases: Graph databases are specialized databases designed to store and query data in terms of nodes, edges, and properties. Nodes represent entities, edges represent relationships between entities, and properties provide additional information about the nodes and edges. Graph databases are based on graph theory and are optimized for traversing relationships.

Graph databases excel in applications where relationships and connections are first-class citizens, such as social networks, recommendation engines, and fraud detection systems. Their ability to efficiently handle complex, interconnected data makes them ideal for tasks that demand high-performance graph traversals. Examples include Neo4j, JanusGraph, and OrientDB.

Hierarchical Databases: Hierarchical databases organize data in a tree-like structure, where each record has a single parent and one or more children. This parent-child relationship is known as a hierarchy. These databases are best suited for applications with a clear hierarchical relationship, such as organizational structures, file systems, and XML data storage.

Hierarchical databases offer fast access to data through predefined paths, making them efficient for read-heavy operations. However, their rigid schema can be limiting when dealing with complex or evolving data relationships. Examples include IBM's Information Management System (IMS) and Windows Registry.

Network Databases: Network databases are similar to hierarchical databases but with a more flexible model. In network databases, records can have multiple parent and child records, forming a graph-like structure. This many-to-many relationship allows for more complex data modeling compared to hierarchical databases.

Network databases, governed by the CODASYL (Conference on Data Systems Languages) standard, are adept at handling many-to-many relationships and are used in applications where such relationships are frequent, such as telecommunications and networking systems. Examples include Integrated Data Store (IDS) and IDMS (Integrated Database Management System).

Choosing the right type of database is critical for the efficiency and scalability of an application. Understanding the strengths and limitations of each type will aid in making informed decisions tailored to specific data management needs.

1.3 Introduction to SQL

Structured Query Language (SQL) is a standardized programming language specifically designed for managing and manipulating relational databases. It facilitates various database operations which encompass querying, updating, inserting, and deleting data. Despite its origins dating back to the 1970s, SQL remains a cornerstone in database management, thanks to its powerful, yet straightforward syntax.

SQL can be classified as both a Data Definition Language (DDL) and a Data Manipulation Language (DML). The DDL components of SQL allow database administrators to define the schema, or structure, of a database by specifying tables, columns, data types, and relationships. Examples of DDL commands include CREATE, ALTER, and DROP. On the other hand, DML is concerned with the manipulation of data within the existing schema, including operations such as SELECT, INSERT, UPDATE, and DELETE.

To illustrate the syntax and structure of SQL, consider a practical example where a sample database is constructed and utilized.

```
CREATE DATABASE SampleDB;
USE SampleDB;
CREATE TABLE Employees (
    EmployeeID INT PRIMARY KEY,
    FirstName VARCHAR(50),
    LastName VARCHAR(50),
    BirthDate DATE,
    Position VARCHAR(50)
);

INSERT INTO Employees (EmployeeID, FirstName, LastName, BirthDate, Position)
VALUES (1, 'John', 'Doe', '1980-05-15', 'Software Engineer'),
       (2, 'Jane', 'Smith', '1985-11-22', 'Data Analyst'),
       (3, 'Emily', 'Johnson', '1990-02-14', 'Project Manager');

SELECT * FROM Employees;
```

In this example, the CREATE DATABASE statement initiates the creation of a new database named SampleDB. Following this, the USE command switches the working context to SampleDB, allowing subsequent SQL commands to operate within the specified database.

The CREATE TABLE command then defines a new table, Employees, with columns tailored to store employee data. Each column's data type is specified; for example, FirstName and LastName are defined as variable character strings (VARCHAR) of up to 50 characters, while BirthDate is a date type (DATE). The EmployeeID column is designated as the primary key, ensuring that each employee record is unique.

The INSERT INTO statement populates the Employees table with initial data entries. Multiple records are inserted in a single command, each encapsulated within parentheses and separated by commas.

Finally, the SELECT statement retrieves all records from the Employees table. Running this command yields the following output:

```
EmployeeID  FirstName  LastName  BirthDate   Position
1           John       Doe       1980-05-15  Software Engineer
2           Jane       Smith     1985-11-22  Data Analyst
3           Emily      Johnson   1990-02-14  Project Manager
```

Understanding the basic SQL operations serves as a foundation for mastering more complex queries and database manipulations. As SQL is deeply ingrained in relational database management, proficiency in its syntax and functions is indispensable for database professionals.

SQL is also known for its declarative nature, allowing users to specify *what* they want to retrieve or update without dictating *how* to accomplish it. This property significantly simplifies database manipulation tasks, abstracting the underlying procedural complexity from the user.

Moreover, modern SQL extends its capabilities to incorporate features for transaction control, such as BEGIN, COMMIT, and ROLLBACK, ensuring data integrity and consistency within a multi-user database environment. Transaction control commands are essential for maintaining atomicity, consistency, isolation, and durability (ACID) properties, which are fundamental principles in database management.

As the reach of SQL expands, so does the repertoire of SQL dialects—variations of SQL tailored for specific Database Management Systems (DBMS), such as MySQL, PostgreSQL, Oracle SQL, and Microsoft SQL Server. While the core syntax and functionality remain consistent across these implementations, certain dialect-specific features and extensions facilitate enhanced performance and additional capabilities tailored to the respective systems.

The forthcoming sections will delve deeper into SQL's structure and syntax, examining advanced querying techniques, data manipulation strategies, and best practices for efficient database management. This exploration will be complemented by practical exercises designed to solidify the reader's comprehension and proficiency in SQL.

1.4 History and Evolution of SQL

Structured Query Language (SQL) stands as a significant milestone in the evolution of database management and querying. Initially conceptualized as a means to interact with relational databases, SQL has undergone numerous adaptations and expansions, growing into the comprehensive language employed in diverse database environments today.

The inception of SQL can be traced back to the early 1970s when IBM researchers, Donald D. Chamberlin and Raymond F. Boyce, were working on a project known as System R at IBM's San Jose Research Laboratory. This project aimed to demonstrate the practicality of Edgar F. Codd's relational database model, a theoretical framework proposed in

Codd's seminal 1970 paper titled "A Relational Model of Data for Large Shared Data Banks". Codd's model advocated for organizing data into tables (relations) to minimize redundancy and dependency, ensuring data integrity and simplifying management.

Chamberlin and Boyce's efforts resulted in the creation of a new language initially termed SEQUEL (Structured English Query Language). SEQUEL allowed users to describe and manage data stored in the relational database without necessitating detailed programming knowledge. However, due to trademark issues with an existing acquaintance, the name was changed to SQL, which has since become the standard nomenclature.

IBM debuted SQL in commercial products with the release of SQL/DS in 1981 and DB2 in 1983. These pioneering implementations cemented SQL's status as the language for relational database management, influencing other contemporary and subsequent database systems. Around the same era, Relational Software, Inc. (now Oracle Corporation) released Oracle V2, which also prominently featured SQL, enhancing its adoption and standardization.

The formal standardization process for SQL began in the mid-1980s. In 1986, the American National Standards Institute (ANSI) adopted SQL as the standard for relational database query language, designating it ANSI SQL. Subsequently, the International Organization for Standardization (ISO) endorsed this standard in 1987, marking it as ISO SQL. These standards aimed to ensure the uniformity and interoperability of SQL implementations across various database systems.

Since its initial standardization, SQL has undergone periodic revisions and enhancements, addressing the evolving requirements of data management, integration, and analytics. Key milestones in the evolution of SQL standards include:

- **SQL-89 (SQL1)**: The initial ANSI SQL standard, formally establishing fundamental constructs such as SELECT, INSERT, UPDATE, DELETE, and transactional commands like COMMIT and ROLLBACK.
- **SQL-92 (SQL2)**: An extensive revision introducing new features like integrity constraints, set operators (UNION, INTERSECT, EXCEPT), data type extensions (DATE, TIME, TIMESTAMP), and enhanced join operations including OUTER JOIN.
- **SQL:1999 (SQL3)**: Expanding SQL's capabilities with object-

relational features, User-Defined Types (UDTs), table inheritance, recursive queries, and procedural extensions through persistent stored modules.

- **SQL:2003**: Introducing window functions (OVER), the XML data type, and the MERGE statement to facilitate more complex and efficient querying and data manipulation.
- **SQL:2006**: Addressing XML-related extensions to support the SQL/XML standard, reflecting the increasing importance of semi-structured and hierarchical data.
- **SQL:2008**: Enhancing previous standards with new temporal data specifications, language features like the TRUNCATE statement, and further XML integration.
- **SQL:2011**: Introducing enhanced temporal data support through system-versioned tables, thus facilitating temporal queries.
- **SQL:2016**: Incorporating JSON (JavaScript Object Notation) support, recognizing the widespread use of JSON in modern web and mobile applications.

SQL's adaptability and extensive feature set have made it a cornerstone in data management across multiple industries and applications. The language's ability to interface with vast datasets, perform complex queries, and maintain consistency and integrity has positioned it as an indispensable tool in the modern data-centric world.

Many relational database management systems (RDBMS) implement SQL with proprietary extensions to differentiate their platforms while maintaining core SQL compatibility. Major RDBMS platforms such as Oracle, Microsoft SQL Server, MySQL, PostgreSQL, and SQLite exhibit variations in their SQL implementations, yet all adhere to the baseline standards for interoperability.

```
-- Example SQL query demonstrating the usage of SQL features
SELECT p.ProductName, SUM(od.Quantity) AS TotalQuantity
FROM Orders AS o
JOIN OrderDetails AS od ON o.OrderID = od.OrderID
JOIN Products AS p ON od.ProductID = p.ProductID
WHERE o.OrderDate BETWEEN '2021-01-01' AND '2021-12-31'
GROUP BY p.ProductName
ORDER BY TotalQuantity DESC;
```

The output of this query would list product names along with the total quantity ordered within the year 2021, ordered by the total quantity in descending order. Below is a hypothetical formatted outcome of this query to display the practical application:

```
+-----------------+--------------+
| ProductName     | TotalQuantity |
+-----------------+--------------+
| Widget A        | 3,450        |
| Gadget B        | 2,980        |
| Doohickey C     | 2,500        |
+-----------------+--------------+
```

This foundational understanding of SQL's history and evolution underscores the language's significance and enduring relevance in the realm of data management.

1.5 Basic Database Concepts

At the core of understanding databases is grasping the fundamental concepts that form the foundation of database systems. This section will delve into key terms and principles, such as data, information, database schema, tables, records, fields, and keys. Familiarity with these concepts is essential for effective database design, usage, and management.

Data and Information:

Data refers to raw, unprocessed facts that need to be transformed into meaningful and actionable insights. Information, on the other hand, is processed data that provides value and context. For example, "John, 28, New York" is a set of data points; when organized in a specific manner, such as in a table, it becomes informative.

Database Schema:

A schema is a blueprint or architecture that defines the structure of a database. It outlines how data is organized, including tables, columns, data types, constraints, and relationships among different tables. Schemas are crucial for maintaining integrity and consistency within a database.

Tables:

Tables, also known as relations, are fundamental structures in relational databases. Each table contains rows and columns, where columns represent fields (attributes) and rows represent records (tuples). Tables are used to store and organize data in a structured format.

```
CREATE TABLE Employees (
```

```
    EmployeeID INT PRIMARY KEY,
    FirstName VARCHAR(50),
    LastName VARCHAR(50),
    BirthDate DATE,
    Position VARCHAR(100)
);
```

The above SQL statement creates a table named Employees with columns for employee ID, first name, last name, birth date, and position. Each row in this table would represent a unique employee.

Records:

A record, also known as a tuple, is a single, complete set of related data fields. Each record in a table corresponds to a row. For instance, a record in the Employees table could be:

EmployeeID	FirstName	LastName	BirthDate	Position
1	John	Doe	1990-01-01	Software Eng

Fields:

Fields, or attributes, are the columns in a table. Each field contains a specific type of data such as integer, string, or date. Fields define the nature of data stored in a table.

```
FirstName: VARCHAR(50)
LastName: VARCHAR(50)
BirthDate: DATE
Position: VARCHAR(100)
```

Primary Keys:

Primary keys are unique identifiers for records within a table. A primary key ensures that each record can be uniquely identified, preventing duplicate records. In the Employees table, EmployeeID serves as the primary key.

```
ALTER TABLE Employees
ADD CONSTRAINT PK_EmployeeID PRIMARY KEY (EmployeeID);
```

Foreign Keys:

Foreign keys establish relationships between tables, ensuring data integrity and enabling complex queries. A foreign key in one table corresponds to a primary key in another table, creating a link between these tables.

```
CREATE TABLE Projects (
    ProjectID INT PRIMARY KEY,
    ProjectName VARCHAR(100),
    EmployeeID INT,
    FOREIGN KEY (EmployeeID) REFERENCES Employees(EmployeeID)
);
```

In this example, the Projects table contains a foreign key EmployeeID that references the primary key in the Employees table. This enables the Projects table to link each project to a specific employee.

Understanding these basic concepts is essential for designing, implementing, and managing relational databases. By comprehensively understanding the structure and components of databases, users can efficiently organize data, maintain integrity, and perform complex queries with ease. The subsequent sections will build upon these foundational concepts, delving deeper into advanced database design and SQL manipulation techniques.

1.6 Database Management Systems (DBMS)

A Database Management System (DBMS) is software designed to store, retrieve, define, and manage data in a database. It serves as an intermediary between the end user and the database, ensuring that data is consistently organized and remains easily accessible. The primary functionalities of a DBMS include data storage, retrieval, update, and administration of databases. In essence, a DBMS handles the complexities of managing large amounts of data, enabling users to focus on higher-level tasks.

Key Functions of a DBMS

- **Data Definition:** The DBMS provides a Data Definition Language (DDL) for defining the database schema. Users can create, modify, and delete schema objects like tables, indexes, and views using specific DDL commands. For example, to create a table in SQL, you might use the following command:

```
CREATE TABLE Employees (
    EmployeeID int,
    FirstName varchar(255),
    LastName varchar(255),
    BirthDate date,
    HireDate date
);
```

- **Data Storage:** A DBMS stores data in a structured format, ensuring efficient space utilization and quick access. Data is typically stored on disk in the form of tables, and the DBMS provides mechanisms to maintain the integrity and reliability of this data over time.

- **Data Retrieval:** Utilizing a Query Language, like SQL, users can extract specific information from large datasets. A simple query to retrieve all employees hired after a certain date might look like this:

```
SELECT * FROM Employees
WHERE HireDate > '2020-01-01';
```

- **Data Update:** A DBMS ensures that data can be updated efficiently while maintaining consistency. Updates can include inserting new data, modifying existing data, or deleting data. Here is an example of an update operation:

```
UPDATE Employees
SET LastName = 'Smith'
WHERE EmployeeID = 1;
```

- **Data Security:** DBMSs enforce security through user authentication and authorization mechanisms. They ensure that only authorized users can access or manipulate data. This includes defining roles and permissions, enabling secure multi-user environments.

- **Data Integrity:** To maintain data accuracy and consistency, DBMSs enforce integrity constraints. These constraints include primary keys, foreign keys, unique constraints, and check constraints. For example, to ensure that each employee has a unique EmployeeID:

```
ALTER TABLE Employees
ADD CONSTRAINT PK_Employee PRIMARY KEY (EmployeeID);
```

- **Transaction Management:** A DBMS ensures that all database transactions are processed reliably and adhere to ACID (Atomicity, Consistency, Isolation, Durability) properties. This allows multiple users to interact with the database concurrently without compromising data integrity.

- **Backup and Recovery:** DBMSs provide mechanisms for regularly backing up data and recovering it in case of disasters or data corruption. These features are critical for the preservation and continuity of operations.

- **Concurrency Control:** To handle multiple users accessing the database simultaneously, a DBMS employs concurrency control methods to prevent conflicts and ensure that transactions are processed in a thread-safe manner.

Components of a DBMS

- **Database Engine:** This core service stores, processes, and secures data. It interprets and executes SQL commands, managing data retrieval and manipulation efficiently.
- **Database Schema:** The schema defines the logical structure of the database, including tables, relationships, and constraints. It serves as a blueprint for how data is stored and organized.
- **Query Processor:** The query processor interprets and executes SQL queries. It optimizes query performance by determining the most efficient ways to execute requests.
- **Transaction Manager:** This component ensures that all database transactions adhere to ACID properties, managing conflicts and maintaining a consistent database state.
- **Storage Manager:** Responsible for managing how data is stored on disks, including the organization of files and indexes. It handles data storage, retrieval, and update operations.
- **Metadata Manager:** This component manages metadata, which is data about data. Metadata includes information about table definitions, indexes, constraints, and user permissions.
- **Authorization Manager:** Ensures that database security policies are enforced. It controls user access to data and database objects based on defined permissions and roles.
- **Backup and Recovery Manager:** Facilitates the backup of database data and provides recovery mechanisms to restore data in the event of a failure.

Types of DBMS Architectures

- **Centralized DBMS:** A centralized DBMS stores all the data in a single location, such as a mainframe computer or a server. This architecture simplifies data management but can become a bottleneck as user demand increases.

- **Distributed DBMS:** In a distributed DBMS, data is stored across multiple locations or computing devices. This architecture enhances performance, availability, and reliability but requires complex synchronization and data distribution strategies.
- **Client-Server DBMS:** This architecture separates the client application, which queries the database, from the server, which processes the queries and manages the data. It balances resource utilization between the client and server, improving performance and scalability.
- **Cloud DBMS:** Cloud-based DBMSs utilize cloud computing resources to provide scalable, on-demand database services. They offer flexibility, lower upfront costs, and reduce the need for physical infrastructure, supporting varied workloads and high availability.

Example implementations and outputs of DBMS functionalities can be observed in industrial-strength DBMS software like MySQL, PostgreSQL, Oracle Database, and Microsoft SQL Server. Each provides extensive tools and features adhering to the described principles and mechanisms.

The essence of a DBMS lies in its ability to provide structured, secure, and efficient data management, underpinning numerous applications—from simple personal databases to complex, high-transaction enterprise systems. This makes it a cornerstone technology in the realm of modern computing.

1.7 Relational Database Concepts

Relational databases are the cornerstone of modern data management systems. The framework of relational databases is founded on relational algebra, an abstraction introduced by Edgar F. Codd in 1970. This section delves deeply into the principles, terminology, and structural elements that define relational databases.

At its core, a relational database is a collection of relations, where a relation is commonly referred to as a table. Each table consists of rows and columns. The formal term for a row is a *tuple*, whereas columns are known as *attributes*.

Tables and Schemas

Every relational database contains multiple tables, each precisely defined by a schema. A schema specifies the table structure, including the table name and the attributes, along with their respective data types. The attributes are listed within parentheses separated by commas. An example of a table schema definition for an 'Employee' table is as follows:

$$\text{Employee}(\text{EmployeeID}, \text{Name}, \text{Department}, \text{Salary})$$

In this schema:

- EmployeeID is a unique identifier for each employee and often serves as the table's primary key.
- Name represents the employee's full name.
- Department indicates the department to which the employee belongs.
- Salary denotes the employee's salary.

Each row in the 'Employee' table would represent an individual employee's information, conforming to the schema's structure.

Primary Keys and Unique Constraints

A primary key is an attribute or a combination of attributes that uniquely identifies each tuple in a relation. The primary key ensures that no two rows have identical values in the primary key column(s), thus enforcing the uniqueness constraint. For example, in the 'Employee' table, EmployeeID could serve as the primary key since each employee has a unique identifier.

Primary key constraints are implemented within SQL during table creation. For instance, the SQL command to create the 'Employee' table with a primary key is:

```
CREATE TABLE Employee (
    EmployeeID INT PRIMARY KEY,
    Name VARCHAR(100),
    Department VARCHAR(100),
    Salary DECIMAL(10, 2)
);
```

Foreign Keys and Referential Integrity

A foreign key is an attribute in one table that links to the primary key of another table, creating a relationship between the two tables. Foreign keys are crucial for maintaining referential integrity, ensuring that the relationships between tables remain consistent.

Consider a second table called Department that defines each department:

$$\text{Department}(\text{DepartmentID}, \text{DeptName})$$

The Employee table can include a foreign key that references the DepartmentID in the Department table:

```
CREATE TABLE Department (
    DepartmentID INT PRIMARY KEY,
    DeptName VARCHAR(100)
);

ALTER TABLE Employee
ADD CONSTRAINT FK_Department
FOREIGN KEY (Department) REFERENCES Department(DepartmentID);
```

This foreign key constraint ensures that each value in the Employee table's Department column corresponds to a valid DepartmentID in the Department table.

Normalization

Normalization is a database design process that organizes columns (attributes) and tables (relations) to minimize data redundancy. The primary objective is to ensure that each piece of data is stored only once. There are several normal forms, each with specific rules to follow:

- **First Normal Form (1NF)**: Ensures that all columns in a table contain atomic, indivisible values. Each column must hold a single value, and each row must be unique.

- **Second Normal Form (2NF)**: Meets all 1NF criteria and ensures that all non-key attributes are fully functionally dependent on the primary key.

- **Third Normal Form (3NF)**: Meets all 2NF criteria and ensures that all attributes are directly dependent on the primary key, eliminating transitive dependency.

- **Boyce-Codd Normal Form (BCNF)**: A stricter version of 3NF that addresses specific anomalies by ensuring that every determinant is a candidate key.

Consider a table that initially stores data about employees and their projects as follows:

EmployeeProject(EmployeeID, ProjectID, EmployeeName, StartDate, DeptID, DeptName)

To apply normalization, we start with 1NF by ensuring atomicity, then proceed to 2NF and 3NF by creating separate tables for employees, projects, and departments.

The resulting tables might look like this:

```
CREATE TABLE Employee (
    EmployeeID INT PRIMARY KEY,
    EmployeeName VARCHAR(100)
);

CREATE TABLE Project (
    ProjectID INT PRIMARY KEY,
    ProjectName VARCHAR(100)
);

CREATE TABLE EmployeeProject (
    EmployeeID INT,
    ProjectID INT,
    StartDate DATE,
    PRIMARY KEY (EmployeeID, ProjectID),
    FOREIGN KEY (EmployeeID) REFERENCES Employee(EmployeeID),
    FOREIGN KEY (ProjectID) REFERENCES Project(ProjectID)
);

CREATE TABLE Department (
    DeptID INT PRIMARY KEY,
    DeptName VARCHAR(100)
);

ALTER TABLE Employee
ADD DeptID INT,
ADD FOREIGN KEY (DeptID) REFERENCES Department(DeptID);
```

Relational Operations

Relational databases use a set of operations to manipulate data. These operations form the foundation of SQL queries. The primary operations include:

- **SELECT**: Retrieves data from one or more tables.
- **JOIN**: Combines rows from two or more tables based on a related column.
- **INSERT**: Adds new rows to a table.
- **UPDATE**: Modifies existing data within a table.
- **DELETE**: Removes existing rows from a table.

An example of a SELECT statement that retrieves employee names alongside their department names is:

```
SELECT Employee.EmployeeName, Department.DeptName
FROM Employee
JOIN Department ON Employee.DeptID = Department.DeptID;
```

The JOIN clause combines the Employee and Department tables based on the common attribute DeptID, demonstrating the practical use of relational concepts.

Understanding these relational database concepts is key to mastering SQL and effectively designing, querying, and managing relational databases.

1.8 SQL Structure and Syntax

SQL, which stands for Structured Query Language, is the standard language for interacting with relational databases. It is essential to understand its structure and syntax to effectively manage and manipulate data. SQL commands are typically divided into several categories, including Data Definition Language (DDL), Data Manipulation Language (DML), Data Control Language (DCL), and Transaction Control Language (TCL).

Data Definition Language (DDL) commands are used to define, modify, and delete database objects such as tables, indexes, and views. The primary DDL commands include CREATE, ALTER, and DROP.

```
CREATE TABLE Employees (
    EmployeeID int NOT NULL,
    FirstName varchar(255) NOT NULL,
    LastName varchar(255) NOT NULL,
    BirthDate date,
    PRIMARY KEY (EmployeeID)
);
```

The CREATE TABLE statement initializes a new table called Employees with an integer EmployeeID as the primary key, and text columns for FirstName, LastName, and a date for BirthDate.

```
ALTER TABLE Employees
ADD Email varchar(255);
```

The ALTER TABLE statement adds a new column named Email to the Employees table.

```
DROP TABLE Employees;
```

The DROP TABLE statement deletes the Employees table from the database.

Data Manipulation Language (DML) commands are employed to insert, update, delete, and retrieve data. Key DML commands include INSERT, UPDATE, DELETE, and SELECT.

```
INSERT INTO Employees (EmployeeID, FirstName, LastName, BirthDate)
VALUES (1, 'John', 'Doe', '1980-01-01');
```

The INSERT INTO statement adds a new record to the Employees table with specified values.

```
UPDATE Employees
SET Email = 'john.doe@example.com'
WHERE EmployeeID = 1;
```

The UPDATE statement modifies existing data. Here, it sets the Email of the employee with EmployeeID = 1.

```
DELETE FROM Employees
WHERE EmployeeID = 1;
```

The DELETE FROM statement removes the record with EmployeeID = 1 from the Employees table.

```
SELECT FirstName, LastName FROM Employees;
```

The SELECT statement retrieves data. This example fetches the FirstName and LastName columns from the Employees table.

Data Control Language (DCL) commands manage access permissions. The primary commands are GRANT and REVOKE.

```
GRANT SELECT, INSERT ON Employees TO 'user';
```

The GRANT statement provides the specified user with SELECT and INSERT permissions on the Employees table.

```
REVOKE INSERT ON Employees FROM 'user';
```

The REVOKE statement removes the previously granted INSERT permission from the user.

Transaction Control Language (TCL) commands handle transaction management, ensuring data integrity. The primary commands include COMMIT, ROLLBACK, and SAVEPOINT.

```
COMMIT;
```

The COMMIT statement saves all the changes made during the transaction, making them permanent.

```
ROLLBACK;
```

The ROLLBACK statement undoes all the changes made during the current transaction.

```
SAVEPOINT Savepoint1;
-- some operations
ROLLBACK TO Savepoint1;
```

The SAVEPOINT sets a point within the transaction to which you can later roll back. The ROLLBACK TO statement undoes changes up to the specified save point, without affecting preceding operations.

SQL syntax also encompasses various clauses and operators essential for constructing complex queries. Common clauses include WHERE, ORDER BY, GROUP BY, and HAVING.

```
SELECT * FROM Employees
WHERE BirthDate > '1990-01-01';
```

The WHERE clause filters records. Here, it selects employees born after January 1, 1990.

```
SELECT * FROM Employees
ORDER BY LastName ASC;
```

The ORDER BY clause sorts results. This example orders employees by their last names in ascending order.

```
SELECT COUNT(EmployeeID), BirthDate
FROM Employees
GROUP BY BirthDate;
```

The GROUP BY clause groups rows that have the same values in specified columns and allows aggregate functions like COUNT to be applied.

```
SELECT COUNT(EmployeeID), BirthDate
FROM Employees
GROUP BY BirthDate
HAVING COUNT(EmployeeID) > 1;
```

The HAVING clause filters groups formed by the GROUP BY clause. In this instance, it finds birth dates shared by more than one employee.

Understanding SQL's structured format and its various commands is fundamental to employing relational databases effectively. Mastery of these elements lays the groundwork for more complex data manipulations, optimizations, and sophisticated database interactions.

1.9 Setting Up Your First Database

Setting up your initial database involves a series of precise steps that ensure you create a robust foundation for future operations. This section will delve into these steps meticulously, providing you with the knowledge to confidently establish your first database using SQL.

Firstly, you need to choose a Database Management System (DBMS). Popular options include MySQL, PostgreSQL, SQLite, and Microsoft SQL Server. For this tutorial, we will use MySQL due to its widespread use and comprehensive feature set.

Installing MySQL MySQL can be installed on various operating systems, including Windows, macOS, and Linux. Installation procedures differ slightly between these systems, but the overall process is similar:

- **Windows**: Download the MySQL installer from the official MySQL website. Follow the on-screen instructions to complete the installation process, ensuring you include the MySQL server, MySQL Workbench, and MySQL command line tools.
- **macOS**: Use Homebrew to install MySQL by executing the following command in your terminal:

  ```
  brew install mysql
  ```

  After installation, start the MySQL server using:

  ```
  brew services start mysql
  ```

- **Linux**: Utilize the package manager specific to your distribution. For instance, on Debian-based systems like Ubuntu, run the following commands:

  ```
  sudo apt update
  sudo apt install mysql-server
  ```

  Ensure the MySQL service is active with:

```
sudo systemctl start mysql
```

Securing Your MySQL Installation Post installation, securing your MySQL instance is paramount. MySQL offers a security script to perform essential configuration steps.

Invoke the security script with:

```
sudo mysql_secure_installation
```

Follow the prompts to implement security enhancements such as setting a root password, removing anonymous users, disallowing remote root login, and removing test databases.

Creating a Database and User After securing the installation, you can proceed to create a database and a user with appropriate privileges. Start by logging into the MySQL server as root:

```
mysql -u root -p
```

Enter the password for the root user as prompted.

Next, create a database with a meaningful name:

```
CREATE DATABASE my_first_database;
```

Create a new user and grant them privileges to operate on the database:

```
CREATE USER 'db_user'@'localhost' IDENTIFIED BY 'secure_password';
GRANT ALL PRIVILEGES ON my_first_database.* TO 'db_user'@'localhost';
FLUSH PRIVILEGES;
```

You can verify the creation and privileges assigned using:

```
SHOW DATABASES;
SHOW GRANTS FOR 'db_user'@'localhost';
```

Connecting to the New Database With the database and user established, you can connect to the database using any MySQL client. The two common interfaces are MySQL's command line tool and MySQL Workbench.

Using the command line, connect with:

```
mysql -u db_user -p my_first_database
```

Enter the user's password when prompted. You should now see the MySQL prompt, indicating successful connection:

```
mysql>
```

Alternatively, you can use MySQL Workbench by configuring a new connection with the appropriate credentials in its user interface.

Initial Table Creation Once connected, you can create tables to store data. For example, creating a simple table to store user information:

```
CREATE TABLE users (
    id INT AUTO_INCREMENT PRIMARY KEY,
    username VARCHAR(50) NOT NULL,
    email VARCHAR(100) NOT NULL,
    created_at TIMESTAMP DEFAULT CURRENT_TIMESTAMP
);
```

You can verify the table's creation with the following command:

```
SHOW TABLES;
```

The expected output should list the 'users' table:

```
+----------------------+
| Tables_in_my_first_database |
+----------------------+
| users                |
+----------------------+
```

Populating the table with initial data can be accomplished with:

```
INSERT INTO users (username, email) VALUES ('test_user', 'user@example.com');
```

Verify the data insertion using:

```
SELECT * FROM users;
```

The output should reflect the inserted record:

```
+----+-----------+-----------------+---------------------+
| id | username  | email           | created_at          |
+----+-----------+-----------------+---------------------+
|  1 | test_user | user@example.com | 2023-05-18 12:34:56 |
+----+-----------+-----------------+---------------------+
```

Through these steps, you have effectively set up a MySQL environment, created a database, defined a user, connected to the database, and constructed an initial table with sample data. This foundational work enables you to perform more advanced database operations in subsequent sections.

1.10 Connecting to a Database

Establishing a connection to a database is an essential step for executing SQL queries and managing data. The connection typically involves a Database Management System (DBMS), a database client or tool, and appropriate credentials. This section covers the procedures for connecting to a database using different clients, command-line interfaces, and programming languages, emphasizing practical implementations.

A standard connection string format includes the database type, server address, database name, username, and password. For instance, connecting to a PostgreSQL database may use a connection string formatted as follows:

```
postgresql://username:password@hostname:port/database_name
```

- **username**: Your database username.
- **password**: Your database password.
- **hostname**: The server's address (e.g., localhost or a remote server's IP).
- **port**: The port number (default for PostgreSQL is 5432).
- **database_name**: The specific database to connect to.

Using a Command-Line Interface (CLI) Most DBMS offer a native command-line tool. For PostgreSQL, the psql command-line interface can be used to connect to and interact with the database. Example command to connect:

```
psql -h hostname -p port -U username -d database_name
```

Upon executing the command, the tool will prompt for a password if a password is required for authentication. Once connected, the CLI provides an interactive prompt to execute SQL commands directly. Sample session:

```
postgres=# SELECT version();
                         version
------------------------------------------------------------
 PostgreSQL 12.4 (Ubuntu 12.4-1.pgdg18.04+1) on x86_64
(1 row)
```

Connecting Using Database Clients Graphical User Interface (GUI) database clients simplify the process of connecting to databases and executing queries. Popular database clients include pgAdmin for PostgreSQL, MySQL Workbench for MySQL, and DBeaver, a universal database client. Connecting using pgAdmin involves the following steps:

- Open pgAdmin and navigate to the "Servers" section.
- Right-click and select "Create" → "Server".
- Fill in the connection details in the "General" and "Connection" tabs, including server name, hostname, port, username, and password.
- Click "Save" to establish the connection.

Once connected, you can interact with the database using the client's interface to execute SQL queries, view schema, and manage database objects.

Connecting Programmatically Database connections are frequently managed programmatically within applications. This section demonstrates how to connect to a PostgreSQL database using Python's psycopg2 library. The following code snippet shows a basic connection:

```
import psycopg2

try:
    connection = psycopg2.connect(
        user="username",
        password="password",
        host="hostname",
        port="port",
        database="database_name"
    )
    cursor = connection.cursor()
    cursor.execute("SELECT version();")
    record = cursor.fetchone()
    print("You are connected to - ", record, "\n")

except (Exception, psycopg2.Error) as error:
    print("Error while connecting to PostgreSQL", error)

finally:
    if connection:
        cursor.close()
        connection.close()
        print("PostgreSQL connection is closed")
```

This code performs the following operations:

- Imports the psycopg2 library.
- Establishes a connection to the database using the connection parameters.
- Creates a cursor object to execute SQL commands.
- Executes a simple query to retrieve the PostgreSQL version.
- Handles exceptions to catch any connection errors.
- Ensures that the cursor and connection are closed properly in a cleanup step.

Configuration and Environment Variables For security and convenience, database connection details are often managed via configuration files or environment variables. This practice prevents hardcoding sensitive information in your source code. An example using Python's os module to read environment variables is shown below:

```
import os
import psycopg2

try:
    connection = psycopg2.connect(
        user=os.getenv("DB_USERNAME"),
        password=os.getenv("DB_PASSWORD"),
```

```
        host=os.getenv("DB_HOST"),
        port=os.getenv("DB_PORT"),
        database=os.getenv("DB_NAME")
    )
    cursor = connection.cursor()
    cursor.execute("SELECT version();")
    record = cursor.fetchone()
    print("You are connected to - ", record, "\n")

except (Exception, psycopg2.Error) as error:
    print("Error while connecting to PostgreSQL", error)

finally:
    if connection:
        cursor.close()
        connection.close()
        print("PostgreSQL connection is closed")
```

In this example:

- Environment variables such as DB_USERNAME, DB_PASSWORD, DB_HOST, DB_PORT, and DB_NAME store the connection parameters.
- Python's os.getenv() method retrieves these values to establish the database connection.

Accurate configuration settings are essential for successful database connections. Reviewing DBMS documentation and client configuration guides will assist in resolving any connectivity issues.

Understanding the process to connect to databases is fundamental for effective database management. The ability to use various tools and methods ensures flexibility and efficiency in various scenarios and application contexts.

1.11 Database Clients and Tools

Database clients and tools are essential for efficiently managing and interacting with your databases. A database client provides an interface through which users can connect to a database to perform tasks such as creating, reading, updating, and deleting data (CRUD operations). Various tools facilitate database design, query generation, performance monitoring, and administration.

A database client can either be a command-line interface (CLI) or a graphical user interface (GUI). Each type has its advantages and suited use cases, which we will explore alongside some popular examples.

- **Command-Line Interfaces (CLI)**:
  Command-line interfaces require users to input commands in a text-based format. CLIs are lightweight, typically faster, and provide a higher level of control, which makes them ideal for scripting and automation.

  - psql: This is the CLI for PostgreSQL. It is widely used for running scripts, performing day-to-day tasks, and executing SQL queries directly from the terminal.

    ```
    psql -h hostname -U username -d database
    ```

  - mysql: The MySQL CLI enables users to interact with MySQL databases.

    ```
    mysql -h hostname -u username -p
    ```

- **Graphical User Interfaces (GUI)**:
  GUIs offer a user-friendly, visual interaction paradigm, which can be especially helpful for users who prefer not to work with command-line syntax. They often include tools for database administration, query building, and visualizing database schema.

  - pgAdmin: An open-source administration and development platform for PostgreSQL. It provides a comprehensive web-based interface to interact with PostgreSQL databases, manage user roles, and perform regular administrative tasks.

    ```
    pgadmin4
    ```

  - MySQL Workbench: This is a unified visual tool for database architects, developers, and DBAs. It provides various features such as designing, developing, and administrating MySQL databases.

    ```
    mysql-workbench
    ```

- **Database Design Tools**:
  These tools help in creating and visualizing the structure of a database, managing complex relationships between tables, and ensuring referential integrity.

  - ER/Studio: A comprehensive data modeling tool that provides powerful visual design capabilities for database structures.

- dbForge Studio for SQL Server: An integrated environment for SQL Server development, management, administration, data reporting, and analysis.

Besides, there are cloud-based tools and services provided by major cloud providers such as Amazon Web Services (AWS), Microsoft Azure, and Google Cloud Platform (GCP). These are designed to handle large-scale databases, offer extensive functionality, and ensure high availability and scalability.

- **AWS Management Console**:
  This is a web-based interface for managing AWS resources. For databases, it offers services like Amazon RDS, which supports multiple database engines (e.g., MySQL, PostgreSQL, Oracle).

```
aws rds create-db-instance --db-instance-identifier mypgdb \\
--db-instance-class db.t2.micro --engine postgres --master-username username \\
--master-user-password password --allocated-storage 20
```

- **Azure Data Studio**:
  A lightweight and extensible database management tool that provides a modern experience for managing SQL Server on-premises and in the cloud.

```
mssql-scripter -S servername.database.windows.net -d database \\
-U username -P password --query "SELECT * FROM table"
```

Performance monitoring tools are also integral in the maintenance of database systems. These tools help database administrators (DBAs) identify and resolve issues impacting performance, such as long-running queries, hardware bottlenecks, and inefficient indexing.

- **New Relic**:
  A powerful application performance management (APM) solution that provides deep insights into database performance. It can be integrated with various database engines to monitor application and database interactions.

```
newrelic-install install
```

- **SolarWinds Database Performance Analyzer (DPA)**:
  This tool provides database performance monitoring, anomaly detection, and tuning advisories for various database systems like SQL Server, Oracle, and MySQL. It helps DBAs pinpoint performance issues and optimize query execution.

```
swis-gateway start
```

Choosing the right set of tools depends on the specific needs of the project and the database being used. What remains consistent is the importance of these tools in ensuring efficient database management, promoting productivity, and maintaining data integrity and performance.

Chapter 2

SQL Basics: Understanding Queries

This chapter covers the fundamental components of SQL syntax and data types. It guides readers through writing their first SQL queries and explores the basics of the SELECT statement. Techniques for filtering data using WHERE clauses, sorting results with ORDER BY, and limiting output with LIMIT and OFFSET are introduced. An explanation of aggregate functions and the GROUP BY clause is provided, along with handling NULL values. The chapter also includes instructions on inserting, updating, and deleting data in tables.

2.1 Introduction to SQL Syntax

Structured Query Language (SQL) serves as the standard language for interacting with relational database management systems (RDBMS). It is utilized for querying, updating, and managing data, and the syntax is structured to facilitate these tasks with precision and clarity. In this section, we will meticulously examine the fundamental components that constitute SQL syntax, providing essential knowledge required to write and comprehend SQL queries efficiently.

SQL syntax is constructed from a combination of keywords, identifiers, operators, and punctuation.

- **Keywords:** Reserved words that have predefined meanings in SQL. Examples include SELECT, FROM, WHERE, INSERT, UPDATE, and DELETE. These keywords are case-insensitive, meaning SELECT and select are interpreted identically by SQL.
- **Identifiers:** Names given to database objects such as tables, columns, indexes, and databases. Identifiers typically follow naming rules that may vary based on the SQL dialect but generally include alphanumeric characters and can often be enclosed in double quotes or backticks to allow for spaces or special characters.
- **Operators:** Symbols that specify operations to be performed. Examples include arithmetic operators (+, -, *, /), comparison operators (=, <>,<, >, <=, >=), and logical operators (AND, OR, NOT).
- **Punctuation:** Symbols used to delimit queries and components within queries. Common punctuation includes commas (,) to separate column names, semicolons (;) to terminate statements, and parentheses (()).

A foundational SQL query structure involves the SELECT statement, which is used to retrieve data from one or more tables. The basic form of a SELECT statement is as follows:

```
SELECT column1, column2, ...
FROM table_name;
```

This syntax indicates that the query will return the specified columns from the given table. Each component plays a distinct role:

- The SELECT keyword specifies the action of retrieving data.
- The column list (e.g., column1, column2, ...) specifies which columns' data should be fetched.
- The FROM keyword indicates the source table from which to retrieve the data.

SQL also allows for more complex queries through various clauses and keywords that refine data retrieval, as detailed in subsequent sections. However, it is crucial to understand the basic syntax to build upon this foundation.

Let's consider an example to illustrate a simple SELECT query:

```
SELECT first_name, last_name
FROM employees;
```

Assuming we have a table named employees with columns first_name and last_name, this query will retrieve and display the first name and last name of each employee in the table. The execution of this query might produce the following result:

```
first_name | last_name
-----------|-----------
John       | Doe
Jane       | Smith
Bob        | Johnson
```

Next, we delve into the WHERE clause, which filters the retrieved data based on specified conditions. Integrating the WHERE clause into a SELECT statement allows you to query data fulfilling certain criteria. The basic form is:

```
SELECT column1, column2, ...
FROM table_name
WHERE condition;
```

Remember, conditions can include various operators and expressions, enabling powerful and granular data filtering. For example, to retrieve only employees with the last name 'Doe':

```
SELECT first_name, last_name
FROM employees
WHERE last_name = 'Doe';
```

This query returns:

```
first_name | last_name
-----------|-----------
John       | Doe
```

Understanding the syntax foundation is imperative as we transition into more advanced querying techniques, including filtering, sorting, and aggregating data. Mastery of SQL syntax sets the stage for writing robust and efficient queries tailored to specific data needs.

2.2 Data Types in SQL

SQL (Structured Query Language) is a powerful tool for managing and manipulating relational databases. One of the foundational aspects of SQL is understanding the different data types available. SQL data types define the kind of data that can be stored in a table column. Knowing the appropriate data type to use is crucial for database efficiency, data integrity, and optimal performance.

1. Numeric Data Types

Numeric data types are used for storing numerical values. SQL provides several options based on whether the data includes integer values or real numbers with floating points.

- INT, INTEGER: These are used for storing whole numbers. The storage size may vary, but typically they can hold values in the range -2,147,483,648 to 2,147,483,647 (4 bytes).
- SMALLINT: Smaller range integer data type, generally used for values between -32,768 to 32,767 (2 bytes).
- BIGINT: Used for very large integer values. It typically can store values from -9,223,372,036,854,775,808 to 9,223,372,036,854,775,807 (8 bytes).
- DECIMAL, NUMERIC: Fixed precision and scale numbers. The syntax is DECIMAL(p, s) where p denotes the precision (total number of digits) and s represents the scale (number of digits to the right of the decimal point).
- FLOAT, REAL, DOUBLE PRECISION: Floating-point numbers. The precision can vary, and these types are generally used when the range of values is large and precision is less critical.

2. Character String Data Types

Character string data types are used to store text. SQL distinguishes between fixed-length and variable-length strings.

- CHAR(n), CHARACTER(n): Fixed-length character strings with a specified length n. If the input string is shorter than n, it is padded with spaces.
- VARCHAR(n), CHARACTER VARYING(n): Variable-length character strings, where n defines the maximum length. Unlike CHAR, VARCHAR strings are not padded with spaces.
- TEXT: An unlimited-length string that can store large amounts of text data. Not all database systems support this type.

3. Binary Data Types

Binary data types store binary data, such as images, files, or other media.

- BINARY(n): Fixed-length binary data.
- VARBINARY(n): Variable-length binary data. The n parameter defines the maximum length.
- BLOB (Binary Large Object): Used for large binary data. It's useful for storing media files, except in databases that specifically limit the BLOB size.

4. Date and Time Data Types

Date and time data types store date and time information.

- DATE: Stores only the date in the form YYYY-MM-DD.
- TIME: Stores only the time in the form HH:MM:SS.
- TIMESTAMP: Stores both date and time, in the form YYYY-MM-DD HH:MM:SS.
- INTERVAL: Represents a duration of time, often used in date and time arithmetic.

5. Boolean Data Type

The boolean data type stores logical values.

- BOOLEAN: Typically stored as TRUE or FALSE. Some SQL implementations also recognize 1 as TRUE and 0 as FALSE.

6. Enumerated Types

Enumerated types are user-defined data types with a set of named values.

- ENUM: A string object with a value chosen from a list of permitted values. Commonly used to ensure data integrity by restricting the values that can be stored in a column.

7. UUID

UUID (Universally Unique Identifier) is a 128-bit number used to uniquely identify information in a database.

- UUID: Stores a UUID, which is a standardized 128-bit format for a globally unique identifier.

Understanding and properly using SQL data types allows for structured data storage that maintains data integrity and optimizes query performance. Each data type has its own storage requirements and constraints, making it essential to choose the appropriate type for the data's nature and expected operations.

Below is an example of SQL code demonstrating the declaration of various columns with different data types:

```
CREATE TABLE example_table (
    id SERIAL PRIMARY KEY,
    username VARCHAR(50),
    password CHAR(64),
    email TEXT,
    birthdate DATE,
    created_at TIMESTAMP,
    balance DECIMAL(10, 2),
    is_active BOOLEAN,
    profile_picture BLOB
);
```

2.3 Writing Your First SQL Query

The initial step to becoming proficient in SQL is to write your first query. Understanding how to construct basic queries is crucial as it forms the foundation for more advanced SQL concepts and operations.

Setting Up the Environment

Before you can write and execute SQL queries, ensure you have access to an SQL environment. This environment could be a local database setup using software like MySQL, PostgreSQL or SQL Server, or an online platform such as db-fiddle or SQL Fiddle.

The Basic Structure of an SQL Query

An SQL query typically follows a simple structure:

```
SELECT columns
FROM table
WHERE conditions;
```

We will elaborate on each component in detail.

Selecting Columns

The SELECT statement specifies the columns to retrieve from the database. For instance:

```
SELECT first_name, last_name
FROM employees;
```

This query selects the first_name and last_name columns from the employees table.

To select all columns, use the wildcard *:

```
SELECT *
FROM employees;
```

From Clause

The FROM clause determines the table from which to retrieve the data. It's essential that the table exists in the database, and the table name should be correctly specified. Multiple tables can be involved in a single query using various types of joins, which will be explored in later chapters.

Where Clause

The WHERE clause is used to filter records. For example:

```
SELECT first_name, last_name
FROM employees
WHERE department = 'Sales';
```

This query returns only the employees whose department is 'Sales'.

Executing the Query

Once a query is written, it must be executed to obtain the result. Depending on your environment, this can be done by pressing the "Run" or "Execute" button, or by typing a command (such as pressing F5 in some SQL editors).

Sample Database

Consider a sample database for an online bookstore. One of the tables, books, may have the following columns: book_id, title, author, price, and publication_year.

We can practice our first queries on this table.

Example Queries

1. To retrieve the titles and authors of all books in the store:

```
SELECT title, author
FROM books;
```

2. To find books published after the year 2015:

```
SELECT title, author, publication_year
FROM books
WHERE publication_year > 2015;
```

3. To select the title and price of all books with a price less than $20:

```
SELECT title, price
FROM books
WHERE price < 20;
```

4. To list all columns for books authored by 'Jane Austen':

```
SELECT *
FROM books
WHERE author = 'Jane Austen';
```

Understanding Query Results

The result of a query, known as a result set, is typically displayed in a tabular format, with rows representing records and columns representing fields.

Executing the first example query would yield:

```
| Title                    | Author      |
|--------------------------|-------------|
| Pride and Prejudice      | Jane Austen |
| To Kill a Mockingbird    | Harper Lee  |
| The Great Gatsby         | F. Scott ... |
| ......................... |
```

Consistently practicing writing and running SQL queries solidifies the understanding of different query components and their interactions. Each run reinforces comprehension, helping to identify mistakes and refine query techniques. As queries become more complex, maintaining clarity in writing and debugging becomes paramount.

Understanding the syntax and structure of simple SQL queries serves as the baseline from which more intricate data manipulations arise, enabling data professionals to perform robust and efficient database operations.

2.4 SELECT Statement Basics

The SELECT statement is the cornerstone of SQL and serves as the primary means of retrieving data from a database. It allows users to specify precisely what data to fetch from one or more tables, offering flexibilities such as filtering, sorting, and joining data. The basic syntax of a SELECT statement can be expressed as follows:

```
SELECT column1, column2, ...
FROM table_name;
```

Here, column1, column2, ... are the columns from which we wish to retrieve data, and table_name is the table containing those columns. For example, consider a table named employees with columns id, name, and position. To retrieve data from all columns in this table, we could write:

```
SELECT id, name, position
FROM employees;
```

To retrieve all columns without specifying them individually, SQL provides a shorthand by using the asterisk (*) symbol:

```
SELECT *
FROM employees;
```

This command retrieves every column in the employees table for all rows. In practice, it's often more efficient and readable to specify only the needed columns.

We shall now delve into some detailed use cases and variations of the SELECT statement.

Renaming Columns Using AS Clause

Columns in the result set can be given temporary names or aliases using the AS clause. This can be especially useful when columns are derived from expressions or when their original names are not intuitive. For instance:

```
SELECT id AS employee_id, name AS employee_name, position
FROM employees;
```

Here, id is renamed to employee_id and name to employee_name in the result set. Executing this query produces output similar to:

```
+-------------+---------------+----------+
| employee_id | employee_name | position |
+-------------+---------------+----------+
| 1           | John          | Manager  |
| 2           | Jane          | Analyst  |
| ...         | ...           | ...      |
+-------------+---------------+----------+
```

Distinct Values with DISTINCT

To avoid duplicate values in the result set, the DISTINCT keyword can be employed. This is often necessary when a column includes repeated values and only unique entries are desired. For instance, to list distinct positions held by employees:

```
SELECT DISTINCT position
FROM employees;
```

The outcome displays each position only once, ignoring any duplicates.

```
+----------+
| position |
+----------+
| Manager  |
| Analyst  |
| Clerk    |
| ...      |
+----------+
```

Conditional Selection Using WHERE Clause

The WHERE clause introduces conditional selection, refining which rows are included based on certain criteria. It is paramount for filtering data. For example, to find employees who are managers:

```
SELECT id, name, position
FROM employees
WHERE position = 'Manager';
```

This command selects only those rows where the position column equals 'Manager':

```
+----+------+-----------+
| id | name | position  |
+----+------+-----------+
| 1  | John | Manager   |
| 5  | Alice| Manager   |
| ...| ...  | ...       |
+----+------+-----------+
```

Combining Conditions with AND, OR, and NOT

Multiple conditions can be combined using AND, OR, and NOT logical operators. For instance, to find employees who are either managers or analysts and whose names start with 'J':

```
SELECT id, name, position
FROM employees
WHERE (position = 'Manager' OR position = 'Analyst')
AND name LIKE 'J%';
```

The LIKE operator here is used with the percent sign (%) wildcard to denote names that begin with 'J'. The output may appear as follows:

```
+----+------+-----------+
| id | name | position  |
+----+------+-----------+
| 1  | John | Manager   |
| 2  | Jane | Analyst   |
+----+------+-----------+
```

Sorting Results Using ORDER BY

The ORDER BY clause arranges the result set according to one or more columns. By default, the order is ascending (ASC), but it can be explicitly set to descending (DESC). For instance, to sort employees by name in descending order:

```
SELECT id, name, position
FROM employees
ORDER BY name DESC;
```

The result set appears as:

```
+----+-------+----------+
| id | name  | position |
+----+-------+----------+
| 4  | Zoe   | Clerk    |
| 3  | Xavier| Manager  |
| 2  | Jane  | Analyst  |
| 1  | John  | Manager  |
+----+-------+----------+
```

Limiting Results with LIMIT

The LIMIT clause restricts the number of rows returned by the query. This is particularly useful for pagination or when working with large datasets. For example, to fetch the first 3 employees:

```
SELECT id, name, position
FROM employees
```

```
LIMIT 3;
```

The query yields:

```
+----+------+----------+
| id | name | position |
+----+------+----------+
| 1  | John | Manager  |
| 2  | Jane | Analyst  |
| 3  | Alice| Clerk    |
+----+------+----------+
```

SQL Functions in SELECT

SQL supports various functions that can be used within the SELECT statement to perform calculations and manipulate data. For instance:

```
SELECT COUNT(id) AS total_employees
FROM employees;
```

This query counts the number of employees in the table and returns:

```
+-----------------+
| total_employees |
+-----------------+
| 10              |
+-----------------+
```

SQL functions like SUM(), AVG(), MAX(), and MIN() can similarly be used to perform arithmetic computations on numerical data.

These foundational elements of the SELECT statement enable a wide spectrum of data retrieval capabilities, from basic selections to complex queries, empowering users to efficiently interact with and extract meaningful insights from databases.

2.5 Filtering Data with WHERE

The WHERE clause is an essential component of SQL that allows for conditional selection of rows from a table based on specified criteria. This clause refines query results by filtering out rows that do not meet the criteria defined within the WHERE condition. It is typically used in conjunction with the SELECT, UPDATE, and DELETE statements.

Consider the basic syntax of a SELECT statement incorporating the WHERE clause:

```
SELECT column1, column2, ...
FROM table_name
```

```
WHERE condition;
```

The condition in the WHERE clause can include various operators and expressions, such as comparison operators, logical operators, and special operators. Let us delve into the different aspects of the WHERE clause.

Comparison Operators

Comparison operators are used to compare the values in a specified column with a particular value or expression. Here are some of the most commonly used comparison operators:

- =: Equal to
- <>, !=: Not equal to
- >: Greater than
- <: Less than
- >=: Greater than or equal to
- <=: Less than or equal to

For instance, to retrieve all employees with a salary greater than 50000, the query would be:

```
SELECT employee_id, first_name, last_name, salary
FROM employees
WHERE salary > 50000;
```

Logical Operators

Logical operators are utilized to combine multiple conditions in a WHERE clause. These operators include:

- AND: Returns true if both conditions are true
- OR: Returns true if either condition is true
- NOT: Inverts the result of the condition

To retrieve employees who have a salary greater than 50000 and belong to the 'IT' department, the query can be written as:

```
SELECT employee_id, first_name, last_name, department, salary
FROM employees
WHERE salary > 50000 AND department = 'IT';
```

In another example, to retrieve employees who either have a salary greater than 50000 or work in the 'HR' department, the following query would be used:

```
SELECT employee_id, first_name, last_name, department, salary
FROM employees
WHERE salary > 50000 OR department = 'HR';
```

Special Operators

Special operators extend the capability of the WHERE clause by allowing more complex conditions. Some of the frequently used special operators include BETWEEN, IN, LIKE, and IS NULL.

The BETWEEN operator selects a range of values:

```
SELECT employee_id, first_name, last_name, salary
FROM employees
WHERE salary BETWEEN 40000 AND 60000;
```

The IN operator specifies multiple possible values for a column:

```
SELECT employee_id, first_name, last_name, department, salary
FROM employees
WHERE department IN ('IT', 'HR', 'Finance');
```

The LIKE operator is used for pattern matching. The wildcard characters are % (percent) for zero or more characters, and _ (underscore) for a single character:

```
SELECT employee_id, first_name, last_name
FROM employees
WHERE first_name LIKE 'J%';
```

The IS NULL operator checks for NULL values:

```
SELECT employee_id, first_name, last_name, commission_pct
FROM employees
WHERE commission_pct IS NULL;
```

Combining Logical and Special Operators

Complex conditions often involve a combination of comparison, logical, and special operators. Here is an example that retrieves employees with a salary between 40000 and 60000, who are in the 'IT' or 'HR' departments:

```
SELECT employee_id, first_name, last_name, department, salary
FROM employees
WHERE (salary BETWEEN 40000 AND 60000)
  AND department IN ('IT', 'HR');
```

Order of Evaluation

SQL evaluates multiple conditions in a WHERE clause based on the precedence of operators. The logical operators have the following precedence order:

- NOT
- AND
- OR

To control the order of evaluation when combining multiple logical operators, use parentheses to group conditions. Consider the following query which illustrates this concept:

```
SELECT employee_id, first_name, last_name, department, salary
FROM employees
WHERE (department = 'IT' OR department = 'HR')
  AND salary > 50000;
```

The conditions within the parentheses are evaluated first, followed by the AND condition.

In practice, the effective use of the WHERE clause is pivotal in querying and managing data efficiently. Readers are encouraged to practice constructing diverse conditions to leverage the full potential of the WHERE clause in SQL.

2.6 Sorting Results with ORDER BY

The ORDER BY clause in SQL is essential for sorting the result set of a query according to one or multiple columns. As a frequently used SQL command, ORDER BY allows for meaningful and organized presentation of data, ensuring readability and facilitating subsequent data analysis operations. The syntax integration of the ORDER BY clause within a SELECT statement is straightforward but can exhibit varying nuances based on use-case complexity.

```
SELECT column1, column2, ...
FROM table_name
ORDER BY column1 [ASC|DESC], column2 [ASC|DESC], ...;
```

The ORDER BY clause follows the selection of columns and the base specification of the table within a query. It sorts the results on the basis of specified columns, whereby each column can be sorted in ascending (ASC) or descending (DESC) order. If no explicit order is defined, SQL implicitly sorts the result set in ascending order by default.

Consider a practical example where a table named employees contains the following columns: employee_id, first_name, last_name, and hire_date. To retrieve a list of employees sorted by their last names in ascending order, the query would be:

```
SELECT employee_id, first_name, last_name, hire_date
FROM employees
ORDER BY last_name ASC;
```

This query output presents a list of employees sorted alphabetically by their last names:

```
employee_id first_name last_name hire_date
------------------------------------------
4           John       Adams     2021-03-15
2           Alice      Brown     2019-11-22
3           Charlie    Davis     2020-06-01
1           Bob        Evans     2018-08-10
```

To sort the result set in descending order by the hire date, ensuring that the most recently hired employees appear first, the query would be slightly modified:

```
SELECT employee_id, first_name, last_name, hire_date
FROM employees
ORDER BY hire_date DESC;
```

The execution of this query would order the employee records starting from the most recent hire:

```
employee_id first_name last_name hire_date
------------------------------------------
4           John       Adams     2021-03-15
3           Charlie    Davis     2020-06-01
2           Alice      Brown     2019-11-22
1           Bob        Evans     2018-08-10
```

It is feasible and often necessary to sort the result set by multiple columns, applying distinct sorting orders to each. For instance, to arrange employees first by their last name in ascending order and then by first name in descending order in cases of matching last names, the query is designed as:

```
SELECT employee_id, first_name, last_name, hire_date
FROM employees
ORDER BY last_name ASC, first_name DESC;
```

The results will be accurately sorted using the stipulated order criteria for both columns:

```
employee_id first_name last_name hire_date
------------------------------------------
4           John       Adams     2021-03-15
2           Alice      Brown     2019-11-22
1           Bob        Evans     2018-08-10
3           Charlie    Davis     2020-06-01
```

When querying database structures where null values (NULL) are present, it's crucial to understand how SQL treats these values during sorting operations. By default, NULLs are sorted as the lowest possible values in ascending order and the highest in descending order. Therefore, a column comprised entirely of numerical values and NULLs sorted in ascending order places all NULLs before any numerical values.

For example, if a column salary in the employees table contains NULL values, and we sort by this column, the query and its result could be exhibited as follows:

```
SELECT employee_id, first_name, last_name, salary
FROM employees
ORDER BY salary ASC;
```

```
employee_id first_name last_name salary
----------------------------------------
2           Alice      Brown     NULL
1           Bob        Evans     NULL
3           Charlie    Davis     55000
4           John       Adams     70000
```

In contrast, utilizing the DESC order for the salary column inversely places the NULLs at the end of the result set.

```
SELECT employee_id, first_name, last_name, salary
FROM employees
ORDER BY salary DESC;
```

```
employee_id first_name last_name salary
----------------------------------------
4           John       Adams     70000
3           Charlie    Davis     55000
2           Alice      Brown     NULL
1           Bob        Evans     NULL
```

Understanding and employing these sorting mechanisms effectively is fundamental to constructing well-ordered SQL queries that enhance data's interpretability and accessibility. Proper usage of the ORDER BY clause forms an indispensable component of SQL proficiency.

2.7 Using LIMIT and OFFSET

In many applications, retrieving large datasets all at once might not be feasible due to performance constraints or the specific requirements of pagination in user interfaces. SQL provides two crucial clauses—LIMIT and OFFSET—to facilitate controlled data retrieval. These clauses can be particularly useful in scenarios where you need to fetch a specified number of rows from a table or skip a certain number of rows before starting the retrieval process.

The LIMIT Clause: The LIMIT clause restricts the number of rows returned by a query. It is especially helpful in situations where the dataset is large, and only a subset of the data is required. The basic syntax for the LIMIT clause is as follows:

```
SELECT column1, column2, ...
FROM table_name
LIMIT number_of_rows;
```

Here, number_of_rows specifies how many rows to return.

Example: To retrieve the first 5 rows from the employees table:

```
SELECT *
FROM employees
LIMIT 5;
```

This query fetches the first 5 rows in the employees table. The LIMIT clause is typically used in combination with the ORDER BY clause to ensure predictable results, especially if the table does not have a primary key or unique identifier.

The OFFSET Clause: Sometimes, it is necessary to skip a certain number of rows before starting to return rows from the query. This is where the OFFSET clause comes into play. The OFFSET clause is used to specify the number of rows to skip before starting to return rows from the query. The basic syntax for the OFFSET clause is:

```
SELECT column1, column2, ...
FROM table_name
LIMIT number_of_rows
OFFSET row_offset;
```

Here, row_offset specifies the number of rows to skip before beginning to retrieve rows.

Example: To retrieve 5 rows after skipping the first 10 rows from the employees table:

```
SELECT *
FROM employees
LIMIT 5
OFFSET 10;
```

This query skips the first 10 rows and then fetches the next 5 rows from the employees table.

Using LIMIT with OFFSET: The combination of LIMIT and OFFSET is commonly used for pagination. Pagination is essential for displaying small chunks of data on web pages instead of loading entire datasets. This approach improves performance and user experience.

Example: To implement pagination where each page displays 10 rows of the employees table, and you want to fetch the second page of results:

```
SELECT *
FROM employees
LIMIT 10
OFFSET 10;
```

This query skips the first 10 rows and then retrieves the next 10 rows.

In applications, these clauses can be dynamically set according to the user's interaction. For instance, in a web application, OFFSET might be calculated as (page_number - 1) * page_size, where page_number is the current page selected by the user, and page_size is the number of rows per page.

```
-- Fetch data for page 3 with 10 rows per page
SELECT *
FROM employees
LIMIT 10
OFFSET 20; -- OFFSET is (3-1)*10 = 20
```

This query retrieves rows 21 to 30 from the employees table, effectively showing the third page of results if each page contains 10 rows.

Considerations: When using LIMIT and OFFSET, it is vital to understand their performance implications, especially on large tables. Both clauses operate by scanning the table and, combined with the lack of indexing, might lead to inefficient queries as the database engine skips rows. Proper indexing and query optimization are necessary to mitigate performance issues.

Combining LIMIT and OFFSET with other SQL features, such as indexes, partitions, and optimized queries, ensures efficient data retrieval. Proper usage helps in creating scalable applications capable of handling large datasets and improving user experience through efficient data pagination and retrieval mechanisms.

2.8 Aggregate Functions and GROUP BY

Aggregate functions are essential components in SQL that enable performing computations on a set of values to return a single value. This section introduces the various aggregate functions available in SQL and demonstrates how to effectively use the GROUP BY clause to organize data into groups, enabling meaningful summary analyses.

Aggregate functions include COUNT(), SUM(), AVG(), MIN(), and MAX(). Each of these functions serves a distinct purpose:

- COUNT(): Returns the number of rows matching a specified criterion.
- SUM(): Calculates the total sum of numeric values.
- AVG(): Computes the average of numeric values.
- MIN(): Identifies the minimum value in a set of values.
- MAX(): Identifies the maximum value in a set of values.

Below is an example query that demonstrates the use of these aggregate functions. Consider a table named sales that tracks each sale's amount and accompanying information:

```
SELECT
    COUNT(*) AS total_sales,
    SUM(amount) AS total_amount,
    AVG(amount) AS average_amount,
    MIN(amount) AS minimum_amount,
    MAX(amount) AS maximum_amount
FROM
    sales;
```

```
+-------------+--------------+----------------+--------------+--------------+
| total_sales | total_amount | average_amount | minimum_amount | maximum_amount |
+-------------+--------------+----------------+--------------+--------------+
|           5 |         1500 |            300 |          200 |         400 |
+-------------+--------------+----------------+--------------+--------------+
```

In this example, the COUNT(*) function counts the number of sales records, SUM(amount) calculates the total sales amount, AVG(amount) computes the average sales amount, MIN(amount) finds the smallest sales amount, and MAX(amount) finds the largest sales amount.

The GROUP BY clause is crucial when using aggregate functions on a dataset that needs to be grouped by one or more columns. This facilitates summarizing data for each unique value of the specified column(s). Consider a modified version of the sales table that includes a region column:

```
SELECT
    region,
    COUNT(*) AS total_sales,
    SUM(amount) AS total_amount,
    AVG(amount) AS average_amount,
    MIN(amount) AS minimum_amount,
    MAX(amount) AS maximum_amount
FROM
    sales
GROUP BY
    region;
```

region	total_sales	total_amount	average_amount	minimum_amount	maximum_amount
East	2	600	300	200	400
West	3	900	300	200	400

In this query, records from the sales table are grouped by the region column. Aggregate functions are then applied to each group. The result provides a consolidated view of sales data for each region.

Additionally, the HAVING clause allows filtering groups based on certain conditions, analogous to the WHERE clause used for filtering rows. The HAVING clause is generally used in conjunction with the GROUP BY clause. For instance, to only include regions with a total sales amount greater than 800:

```
SELECT
    region,
    COUNT(*) AS total_sales,
    SUM(amount) AS total_amount,
    AVG(amount) AS average_amount,
    MIN(amount) AS minimum_amount,
    MAX(amount) AS maximum_amount
FROM
    sales
GROUP BY
    region
HAVING
    total_amount > 800;
```

region	total_sales	total_amount	average_amount	minimum_amount	maximum_amount
West	3	900	300	200	400

This query groups the sales table by region and then filters those groups to only include those where the total_amount exceeds 800.

Careful application of aggregate functions and the GROUP BY clause enhances the analytical capability within SQL, enabling detailed summaries and filtered data analysis. This integration facilitates efficient data summarization and extensive insight generation from large datasets.

2.9 Working with NULL Values

In the context of SQL, NULL is a special marker used to indicate that a data value does not exist in the database. Unlike empty strings or zero values, NULL represents the absence of any data value, meaning that the attribute has not been assigned any value. Understanding how to handle NULL values effectively is crucial for accurate data manipulation and retrieval.

NULL values can appear in various scenarios. For example, when data is first inserted and some columns are left unspecified, those columns may default to NULL. Or, certain fields may have optional values that, if not provided, would result in NULL entries.

```
CREATE TABLE employees (
    employee_id INT PRIMARY KEY,
    first_name VARCHAR(50),
    last_name VARCHAR(50),
    manager_id INT
);

INSERT INTO employees (employee_id, first_name, last_name)
VALUES (1, 'John', 'Doe');

INSERT INTO employees (employee_id, first_name, last_name, manager_id)
VALUES (2, 'Jane', 'Smith', NULL);
```

In the employees table, notice that John Doe does not have a manager assigned, resulting in a NULL value for the manager_id column.

When performing queries that involve NULL values, it is important to use the IS NULL and IS NOT NULL operators rather than the equality operators. This is because NULL is not equivalent to any value, including itself.

```
SELECT employee_id, first_name, last_name
FROM employees
WHERE manager_id IS NULL;
```

The above query retrieves all employees who do not have a manager assigned. Conversely, to find employees who do have a manager:

```
SELECT employee_id, first_name, last_name
FROM employees
WHERE manager_id IS NOT NULL;
```

When performing comparisons that involve NULL values, standard operators like = and <> (not equal) do not yield useful results. For instance:

```
SELECT *
FROM employees
WHERE manager_id = NULL;
```

No rows will be returned because NULL does not compare as equal to any value. Instead, we must use the IS NULL operator.

Aggregate functions also interact with NULL values in specific ways. Functions like COUNT, SUM, AVG, MAX, and MIN typically ignore NULL values in their calculations. For instance:

```
SELECT COUNT(manager_id) AS num_managed_employees
FROM employees;

SELECT AVG(manager_id) AS avg_manager_id
FROM employees;
```

The COUNT function above counts only those rows where manager_id is not NULL. Aggregates such as SUM and AVG behave similarly by excluding NULL values from their calculations.

To handle NULL values more effectively, SQL provides the COALESCE function and the IFNULL (or equivalent) function. COALESCE returns the first non-NULL value from a list of expressions, while IFNULL returns the second argument if the first is NULL.

```
SELECT employee_id, COALESCE(manager_id, 'No Manager') AS
    effective_manager_id
FROM employees;

SELECT employee_id, IFNULL(manager_id, 'No Manager') AS effective_manager_id
FROM employees;
```

These functions are useful for ensuring that NULL values are handled gracefully, avoiding potential issues in various applications.

NULL values are an integral part of SQL, representing missing or unknown data. Properly using these functions and operators ensures accurate query results and effective database management.

2.10 Inserting Data into Tables

The INSERT statement in SQL serves as the primary method for adding new rows of data into a table. It is crucial to understand the syntax and functionality of this statement to interact efficiently with relational databases. The basic structure of the INSERT statement involves specifying the target table and the values to be inserted.

Basic Syntax:

```
INSERT INTO table_name (column1, column2, column3, ...)
VALUES (value1, value2, value3, ...);
```

In this syntax, table_name represents the name of the table where data is to be inserted. The parentheses following the table name specify the column names where corresponding values will be inserted. The VALUES clause contains the values to be inserted into those columns, respectively.

Consider the following example:

```
INSERT INTO employees (first_name, last_name, hire_date)
VALUES ('John', 'Doe', '2023-01-15');
```

In this example, a new row is added to the employees table. The values for the first_name, last_name, and hire_date columns are specified in the VALUES clause.

Inserting Multiple Rows: SQL allows inserting multiple rows in a single INSERT statement by providing additional sets of values in the VALUES clause. These sets of values are separated by commas.

```
INSERT INTO employees (first_name, last_name, hire_date)
VALUES ('John', 'Doe', '2023-01-15'),
       ('Jane', 'Smith', '2023-02-20'),
       ('Emily', 'Johnson', '2023-03-10');
```

This statement inserts three new rows into the employees table.

Inserting Data into All Columns: If values are provided for all columns of a table, the column list can be omitted from the INSERT statement. However, the order of the values must correspond exactly to the order in which the columns are defined in the table.

```
INSERT INTO employees
VALUES ('Alice', 'Wang', '2023-04-05', 'HR');
```

Here, a new row is added to the employees table, assuming it has columns first_name, last_name, hire_date, and department in that specific order.

Using INSERT with SELECT: The INSERT statement can be combined with a SELECT statement to insert data returned by a query into a table.

```
INSERT INTO employees_archive (first_name, last_name, hire_date)
SELECT first_name, last_name, hire_date
FROM employees
WHERE hire_date < '2023-01-01';
```

This statement copies all rows from the employees table, where the hire_date is before January 1, 2023, into the employees_archive table.

Handling NULL Values: If the value for a particular column is not specified in the INSERT statement and the column allows NULL values, SQL will insert NULL into that column by default. Otherwise, the database will generate an error.

```
INSERT INTO employees (first_name, last_name)
VALUES ('Michael', 'Brown');
```

Assuming the hire_date column is allowed to be NULL, this statement inserts a new row with NULL as the hire_date.

Using Default Values: Many databases allow setting default values for columns, which can be used when the INSERT statement does not provide a value for those columns. If a default value is specified for a column, it will be used when data is inserted through INSERT without specifying a value.

```
CREATE TABLE departments (
    dept_id INT PRIMARY KEY,
    dept_name VARCHAR(100) NOT NULL,
    created_date DATE DEFAULT CURRENT_DATE
);

INSERT INTO departments (dept_id, dept_name)
VALUES (1, 'Research and Development');
```

In the example above, a new row is inserted into the departments table. Since created_date has a default value of the current date, it will be filled automatically.

Understanding the INSERT statement is fundamental for populating tables with data. Practicing these variations will solidify the application and breadth of SQL commands necessary for effective database management and operations.

2.11 Updating Data in Tables

Updating data within SQL tables is a fundamental operation that allows for modification of existing records to reflect changes in the underlying dataset. The SQL UPDATE statement is used for this purpose. This section provides in-depth insights, syntax structures, and practical examples to ensure a clear understanding of how to perform updates on SQL tables.

The primary structure of an UPDATE statement consists of specifying the table to be updated, identifying the columns to be modified, and providing the new values. Additionally, it is essential to include the WHERE clause to pinpoint specific records; omitting this clause results in updating all rows in the table, which is often not the desired outcome. The basic syntax for the UPDATE statement is as follows:

```
UPDATE table_name
SET column1 = value1, column2 = value2, ...
WHERE condition;
```

Here, table_name denotes the name of the table to be updated, column1, column2, etc., represent the columns to be updated, and value1, value2, etc., are the new values to be assigned to these columns. The WHERE clause specifies the condition that must be met for a row to be updated.

Consider a table named employees with the following records:

```
+----+------------+-----------+--------+
| id | first_name | last_name | salary |
+----+------------+-----------+--------+
|  1 | John       | Doe       | 50000  |
|  2 | Jane       | Smith     | 60000  |
|  3 | Adam       | Johnson   | 55000  |
+----+------------+-----------+--------+
```

Suppose we need to increase the salary of the employee with id = 1 by 10,000 units. The UPDATE statement for this operation would be:

```
UPDATE employees
SET salary = 60000
WHERE id = 1;
```

After executing this statement, the table employees will be updated as follows:

```
+----+------------+-----------+--------+
| id | first_name | last_name | salary |
+----+------------+-----------+--------+
|  1 | John       | Doe       | 60000  |
|  2 | Jane       | Smith     | 60000  |
|  3 | Adam       | Johnson   | 55000  |
+----+------------+-----------+--------+
```

To ensure more complex updates, multiple columns can be changed at once. For instance, if we need to update both the first_name and salary for the employee with id = 3, we can modify the query as follows:

```
UPDATE employees
SET first_name = 'Eve', salary = 58000
WHERE id = 3;
```

This query will update the record, yielding the following table state:

```
+----+------------+-----------+--------+
| id | first_name | last_name | salary |
+----+------------+-----------+--------+
|  1 | John       | Doe       | 60000  |
|  2 | Jane       | Smith     | 60000  |
|  3 | Eve        | Johnson   | 58000  |
+----+------------+-----------+--------+
```

Additionally, complex conditions can be used in the WHERE clause to update multiple rows based on specific criteria. For example, to increase the salary of all employees whose current salary is below 60000, the query is structured as follows:

```
UPDATE employees
SET salary = salary + 5000
WHERE salary < 60000;
```

Executing this statement will modify the table to:

```
+----+------------+-----------+--------+
| id | first_name | last_name | salary |
+----+------------+-----------+--------+
|  1 | John       | Doe       | 65000  |
|  2 | Jane       | Smith     | 60000  |
|  3 | Eve        | Johnson   | 63000  |
+----+------------+-----------+--------+
```

Updating values based on conditions ensures precise control over the data modification process. Additionally, one must take heed of potential pitfalls, such as forgetting the WHERE clause, which otherwise would result in all rows being updated indiscriminately.

The UPDATE statement can also be utilized with subqueries to set a column's value based on another query. For instance, to set the salary of the employee with first_name = 'Jane' to the average salary of all employees, you could use:

```
UPDATE employees
```

```
SET salary = (SELECT AVG(salary) FROM employees)
WHERE first_name = 'Jane';
```

This powerful combination of UPDATE with subqueries enables conditional and dynamic data modifications aligned with live or computed dataset characteristics.

2.12 Deleting Data from Tables

Deleting data from tables is a crucial aspect of database management. It allows the removal of rows that are no longer necessary or relevant for the dataset. In SQL, the DELETE statement is used for this purpose. Understanding how to effectively and safely delete data is essential for maintaining the integrity and performance of the database.

Basic DELETE Statement

The basic syntax for the DELETE statement is straightforward. It targets specified rows in a table and removes them. Consider the following example:

```
DELETE FROM table_name
WHERE condition;
```

Here, table_name is the name of the table from which you want to delete data, and condition specifies which rows should be deleted. If the WHERE clause is omitted, all rows in the table will be deleted, but the table itself will remain intact.

```
DELETE FROM employees
WHERE employee_id = 123;
```

In this example, the row where employee_id equals 123 will be removed from the employees table.

Deleting All Rows

To delete all rows from a table, you may write the DELETE statement without a WHERE clause. However, this action is drastic and should be performed with caution due to its irreversible nature:

```
DELETE FROM employees;
```

Executing the above command will delete all records in the employees table. It is critical to use this statement carefully and potentially follow up with a check to ensure there are no unintended deletions.

Using TRUNCATE for Faster Deletion

An alternative to the DELETE statement when removing all rows is the TRUNCATE command, which deletes all rows in a table more efficiently. Unlike DELETE, TRUNCATE does not generate individual row deletions, but rather deallocates the data pages used by the table:

```
TRUNCATE TABLE employees;
```

The TRUNCATE command is faster but also has some limitations, such as it cannot be used when a foreign key constraint references the table.

Deleting Rows with Joins

Sometimes, it's necessary to delete rows based on conditions that involve multiple tables. This can be achieved using JOIN operations within the DELETE statement. For example:

```
DELETE e
FROM employees e
JOIN departments d ON e.department_id = d.department_id
WHERE d.department_name = 'Sales';
```

In this case, the statement joins the employees table with the departments table and deletes rows from the employees table where the department name is 'Sales'.

Transaction Control and Deleting Data

When deleting data, it is often essential to do so within a transaction. Transactions provide a way to ensure that a sequence of operations is performed atomically – either all the operations are completed successfully, or none of them are. This can be particularly useful when deleting data to ensure that you can roll back changes if something goes wrong.

```
START TRANSACTION;

DELETE FROM employees WHERE employee_id = 123;

-- If everything is correct
COMMIT;

-- In case of any error
ROLLBACK;
```

By starting a transaction with START TRANSACTION, you can then execute the DELETE statement. If everything is as expected, you commit the transaction with COMMIT. If an issue arises, you can revert all changes made during the transaction using ROLLBACK.

Cascading Deletes

In relational databases, there are scenarios where deleting a row requires the deletion of related rows in other tables. This is managed through foreign key constraints with the ON DELETE CASCADE option. If a foreign key in a child table has this option, deleting a row in the parent table will automatically trigger the deletion of the related rows in the child table.

Consider the following example where departments is the parent table and employees is the child table:

```
CREATE TABLE departments (
  department_id INT PRIMARY KEY,
  department_name VARCHAR(255)
);

CREATE TABLE employees (
  employee_id INT PRIMARY KEY,
  department_id INT,
  FOREIGN KEY (department_id) REFERENCES departments(department_id)
  ON DELETE CASCADE
);
```

When a row in departments is deleted, all rows in employees that reference the deleted department_id will also be removed.

Best Practices for Deleting Data

- **Backup Data:** Always ensure that important data is backed up before performing any deletion operations.
- **Use Transactions:** Utilize transactions to group delete operations, allowing for rollback if an error occurs.
- **Review WHERE Clauses:** Verify the conditions in WHERE clauses to prevent unintentional deletions.
- **Test on a Subset:** Test deletion commands on a subset of data before performing full-scale deletions.
- **Log Deletions:** Maintain a log of deleted records for auditing and recovery purposes.

Implementing these practices will help maintain data integrity and ensure that deletions are executed safely and effectively.

Chapter 3

Advanced SQL Queries

This chapter delves into complex SQL query techniques, including subqueries, nested queries, and common table expressions (CTEs). It explores the use of CASE statements, window functions, and advanced join techniques. The chapter also covers set operations such as UNION, INTERSECT, and EXCEPT, materialized views, and handling complex data types like JSON and XML. Additionally, it addresses managing hierarchical data and implementing full-text search capabilities.

3.1 Subqueries and Nested Queries

Subqueries, also known as inner queries or nested queries, are essential constructs in SQL for performing complex queries by embedding one query within another. A subquery can be placed in various clauses, including the SELECT, FROM, WHERE, and HAVING clauses. The fundamental principle of subqueries is to retrieve data that will be used by the main query, also known as the outer query.

A subquery should always be enclosed within parentheses. Subqueries can be classified into multiple types based on their use and return values. The most common types are scalar subqueries, which return a single value; row subqueries, which return a single row; and table subqueries, which return a result set that can contain multiple rows and columns.

The following sections will detail each type, including their construction, execution, and practical applications.

To illustrate the use of subqueries, we will use a hypothetical database containing two tables: 'Employees' and 'Departments'.

The schema for these tables is as follows:

```
CREATE TABLE Employees (
    EmployeeID INT PRIMARY KEY,
    FirstName VARCHAR(50),
    LastName VARCHAR(50),
    DepartmentID INT,
    Salary DECIMAL(10, 2)
);

CREATE TABLE Departments (
    DepartmentID INT PRIMARY KEY,
    DepartmentName VARCHAR(50)
);
```

Scalar Subqueries

A scalar subquery returns a single value. These are commonly used in the SELECT clause to provide a calculated column or in the WHERE clause to filter results based on a computed value.

Example: Retrieve all employees whose salary is above the average salary of the entire company.

```
SELECT FirstName, LastName, Salary
FROM Employees
WHERE Salary > (SELECT AVG(Salary) FROM Employees);
```

This query computes the average salary of all employees using the subquery '(SELECT AVG(Salary) FROM Employees)'. The outer query then compares each employee's salary against this average to filter out the employees with salaries above the average.

Row Subqueries

A row subquery returns a single row of values. Such subqueries can often be used with operators that compare rows, like 'IN', 'NOT IN', or the row constructor '=(...)'.

Example: Retrieve the department details for the department with the highest average salary.

```
SELECT DepartmentID, DepartmentName
FROM Departments
WHERE DepartmentID = (SELECT DepartmentID
                      FROM Employees
                      GROUP BY DepartmentID
                      ORDER BY AVG(Salary) DESC
```

```
            LIMIT 1);
```

The subquery '(SELECT DepartmentID FROM Employees GROUP BY DepartmentID ORDER BY AVG(Salary) DESC LIMIT 1)' finds the 'DepartmentID' with the highest average salary. The outer query then retrieves the details of this department.

Table Subqueries

Table subqueries return a result set of one or more rows and columns. These are generally used in the FROM clause to provide a derived table or in the WHERE clause with the 'EXISTS' operator.

Example: List all employees who work in a department with more than five employees.

```
SELECT E.FirstName, E.LastName, E.DepartmentID
FROM Employees E
WHERE E.DepartmentID IN (
    SELECT DepartmentID
    FROM Employees
    GROUP BY DepartmentID
    HAVING COUNT(*) > 5);
```

Here, the subquery selects 'DepartmentID's from the 'Employees' table, grouping by 'DepartmentID', and filters groups having a count greater than five. The outer query then uses these results to display employees within those departments.

Correlated Subqueries

Correlated subqueries reference columns from the outer query in the subquery, making their execution dependent on the outer query. Each row processed by the outer query can produce a different result for the subquery.

Example: Retrieve employees whose salary is higher than the average salary in their respective department.

```
SELECT E.FirstName, E.LastName, E.Salary
FROM Employees E
WHERE E.Salary > (
    SELECT AVG(E2.Salary)
    FROM Employees E2
    WHERE E2.DepartmentID = E.DepartmentID);
```

In this case, for each employee in the outer query, the subquery '(SELECT AVG(E2.Salary) FROM Employees E2 WHERE E2.DepartmentID = E.DepartmentID)' calculates the average salary of the current employee's department.

Using Subqueries in the FROM Clause

Subqueries in the FROM clause act as derived tables or inline views. They can help in complex query decomposition by breaking down a problem into more manageable parts.

Example: Retrieve departments along with the number of employees and the average salary, based on departments having more than three employees.

```
SELECT D.DepartmentName, T.EmployeeCount, T.AverageSalary
FROM Departments D
JOIN (
    SELECT DepartmentID, COUNT(*) AS EmployeeCount, AVG(Salary) AS
        AverageSalary
    FROM Employees
    GROUP BY DepartmentID
    HAVING COUNT(*) > 3
) T
ON D.DepartmentID = T.DepartmentID;
```

In this example, the subquery creates a derived table 'T' containing department IDs, employee counts, and average salaries for departments with more than three employees. The outer query then joins this derived table with 'Departments' to produce the final result.

These examples highlight the flexibility and power of subqueries to enhance the functionality and readability of SQL queries. Understanding and mastering the use of subqueries is crucial for efficient database querying and management.

3.2 Using CASE Statements

The CASE statement is a versatile and powerful component of SQL that allows conditional logic to be applied within queries. It can be used for various purposes such as creating computed columns, transforming data, and achieving complex aggregations. The CASE statement functions in a manner similar to if-else statements in procedural programming languages.

The general syntax for a CASE statement is as follows:

```
CASE
    WHEN condition_1 THEN result_1
    WHEN condition_2 THEN result_2
    ...
    ELSE result_n
END
```

In this structure: - Each WHEN clause is followed by a condition. If this condition evaluates to TRUE, the query returns the corresponding THEN value. - The ELSE clause is optional. If none of the specified conditions are TRUE, the ELSE clause value is returned. If the ELSE clause is omitted, NULL is returned by default in the case that no conditions are met.

Consider the following example where a CASE statement is used to categorize employees based on their salary:

```
SELECT employee_id,
       employee_name,
       salary,
       CASE
           WHEN salary < 40000 THEN 'Low'
           WHEN salary BETWEEN 40000 AND 70000 THEN 'Medium'
           WHEN salary > 70000 THEN 'High'
           ELSE 'Unknown'
       END AS salary_category
FROM employees;
```

In this query, the CASE statement assigns a category to each employee based on their salary: - Salaries less than 40000 are categorized as 'Low'. - Salaries between 40000 and 70000 are categorized as 'Medium'. - Salaries greater than 70000 are categorized as 'High'. - Any other salaries (including NULL) are categorized as 'Unknown'.

Using CASE statements, you can also simplify and enhance the readability of your complex queries. Here is an example where CASE statements are used for more intricate computations:

```
SELECT order_id,
       order_date,
       total_amount,
       CASE
           WHEN total_amount < 100 THEN 'Small Order'
           WHEN total_amount BETWEEN 100 AND 1000 THEN 'Regular Order'
           WHEN total_amount > 1000 THEN 'Large Order'
       END AS order_size,
       CASE
           WHEN EXTRACT(MONTH FROM order_date) IN (11, 12) THEN 'Winter'
           WHEN EXTRACT(MONTH FROM order_date) IN (6, 7, 8) THEN '
               Summer'
           ELSE 'Other Season'
       END AS order_season
FROM orders;
```

Key points in this example include: - Two CASE statements are utilized to determine both the order size and the season based on the total_amount and order_date. - The first CASE statement categorizes the orders into 'Small Order', 'Regular Order', and 'Large Order' based on the total_amount. - The second CASE statement determines whether the order was placed in 'Winter', 'Summer', or 'Other Season'.

CASE statements can also be nested to address more complex conditional logic. Here is an example demonstrating nested CASE statements:

```
SELECT product_id,
       product_name,
       price,
       CASE
           WHEN category = 'Electronics' THEN
               CASE
                   WHEN price < 500 THEN 'Budget'
                   WHEN price BETWEEN 500 AND 1500 THEN 'Standard'
                   ELSE 'Premium'
               END
           WHEN category = 'Clothing' THEN
               CASE
                   WHEN price < 50 THEN 'Budget'
                   WHEN price BETWEEN 50 AND 200 THEN 'Standard'
                   ELSE 'Premium'
               END
           ELSE 'Other Category'
       END AS price_range_category
FROM products;
```

In this query: - The outer CASE statement checks the category of the product (e.g., 'Electronics' or 'Clothing'). - Inside each branch of this outer CASE statement, another CASE statement categorizes the price accordingly.

Finally, CASE statements can be leveraged in ORDER BY and GROUP BY clauses to influence the ordering and grouping of results:

```
SELECT department,
       SUM(salary) AS total_salary,
       CASE
           WHEN department IN ('HR', 'Admin') THEN 'Support'
           WHEN department IN ('Sales', 'Marketing') THEN 'Revenue'
           ELSE 'Other'
       END AS department_type
FROM employees
GROUP BY department_type;
```

In this example:

- - The CASE statement groups departments into 'Support', 'Revenue', and 'Other'.
- - The GROUP BY clause groups the results by these derived categories rather than the original department names.

The flexibility of CASE statements makes them indispensable for handling conditional logic within SQL queries, offering significant enhancements to data transformation and analysis capabilities. Their utility extends from simple categorization to intricate, nested conditions, allowing for robust and dynamic query development.

3.3 Common Table Expressions (CTEs)

Common Table Expressions (CTEs) allow for the creation of temporary result sets that can be referenced within a SELECT, INSERT, UPDATE, or DELETE statement. These expressions provide a way to simplify complex queries by breaking them down into more manageable parts and can offer improved readability and maintainability of SQL code.

A CTE is defined using the WITH keyword, followed by a query that creates the temporary result set. This temporary result set exists only for the duration of the execution of the outer query. The basic syntax of a CTE is as follows:

```
WITH cte_name (column1, column2, ...)
AS
(
    SELECT column1, column2, ...
    FROM table
    WHERE condition
)
SELECT *
FROM cte_name;
```

Simple Example:

Consider a scenario where we have a table named employees with columns employee_id, first_name, last_name, department, and salary. We want to find all employees in the 'Sales' department who earn more than $50,000.

```
WITH high_earning_sales AS
(
    SELECT employee_id, first_name, last_name, salary
    FROM employees
    WHERE department = 'Sales' AND salary > 50000
)
SELECT *
FROM high_earning_sales;
```

Executing this query would produce the result set of high earners in the Sales department:

```
employee_id first_name last_name salary
------------------------------------------
1           John       Doe       60000
2           Jane       Smith     70000
```

Referencing Multiple CTEs:

CTEs can also be chained together by separating each CTE with a comma. This allows for complex queries to be broken down into multiple, more understandable parts.

```
WITH sales_dept AS
(
    SELECT employee_id, first_name, last_name, salary
    FROM employees
    WHERE department = 'Sales'
),
high_earners AS
(
    SELECT employee_id, first_name, last_name, salary
    FROM sales_dept
    WHERE salary > 50000
)
SELECT *
FROM high_earners;
```

Here, the first CTE, sales_dept, extracts employees from the Sales department, and the second CTE, high_earners, filters those employees to find only those earning more than $50,000. The result will be the same as in the previous example.

Recursive CTEs:

Recursive CTEs are a powerful feature that allows a CTE to reference itself. This is useful for hierarchical data structures such as organizational charts or bill of materials.

The basic syntax for a recursive CTE includes an anchor member and a recursive member. The anchor member is the initial query, while the recursive member is a query that references the CTE itself.

```
WITH RECURSIVE cte_name (column1, column2, ...)
AS
(
    -- Anchor member
    SELECT column1, column2, ...
    FROM table
    WHERE condition

    UNION ALL

    -- Recursive member
    SELECT column1, column2, ...
    FROM table
    INNER JOIN cte_name
    ON table.column = cte_name.column
)
```

```
SELECT *
FROM cte_name;
```

Example of Recursive CTE:

Consider an employees table with a manager_id column that references the employee_id of the manager. To find the hierarchy starting from an employee with a specific ID:

```
WITH RECURSIVE employee_hierarchy AS
(
    -- Anchor member: start with the specified employee
    SELECT employee_id, first_name, last_name, manager_id
    FROM employees
    WHERE employee_id = 1

    UNION ALL

    -- Recursive member: find employees managed by the current employee
    SELECT e.employee_id, e.first_name, e.last_name, e.manager_id
    FROM employees e
    INNER JOIN employee_hierarchy eh
    ON e.manager_id = eh.employee_id
)
SELECT *
FROM employee_hierarchy;
```

This query builds the hierarchy starting from the employee with employee_id = 1. The anchor member retrieves the initial employee, and the recursive member retrieves direct reports, joining with the temporary result set to cascade through the hierarchy.

```
employee_id  first_name  last_name  manager_id
---------------------------------------------
1            John        Doe        NULL
2            Alice       Brown      1
3            Bob         White      2
4            Carol       Black      2
```

These examples illustrate how CTEs, including recursive CTEs, can simplify complex queries and provide better readability and maintainability. Understanding and utilizing CTEs effectively enables powerful and efficient data retrieval techniques within SQL.

3.4 Recursive Queries

Recursive queries allow us to perform operations that involve hierarchical or recursive data structures in SQL. These are particularly useful for querying hierarchical data, such as organizational structures, bill of materials (BOM), or any other data that involves parent-child relationships.

Recursive queries are achieved through Common Table Expressions (CTEs), specifically with the use of recursive CTEs.

A recursive CTE consists of two parts: the anchor member and the recursive member. The anchor member is a non-recursive term and forms the base result set. The recursive member is a query that recursively references the CTE.

Here is the basic syntax for a recursive CTE:

```
WITH RECURSIVE cte_name AS (
    -- Anchor member
    SELECT ...
    FROM ...
    WHERE ...

    UNION ALL

    -- Recursive member
    SELECT ...
    FROM cte_name
    JOIN ...
    WHERE ...
)
SELECT *
FROM cte_name;
```

Consider the example of an organizational hierarchy where each employee reports to a manager. We can represent employees in a table named employees with columns employee_id, name, manager_id.

The objective is to retrieve the hierarchy starting from a specific manager, displaying all their subordinates recursively.

```
-- Create sample employees table
CREATE TABLE employees (
    employee_id INT PRIMARY KEY,
    name VARCHAR(100),
    manager_id INT
);

-- Insert sample data
INSERT INTO employees (employee_id, name, manager_id)
VALUES
    (1, 'Alice', NULL),
    (2, 'Bob', 1),
    (3, 'Carol', 1),
    (4, 'David', 2),
    (5, 'Eve', 2),
    (6, 'Frank', 3);
```

To find the hierarchy under Alice (employee_id = 1), the following recursive CTE can be used:

```
WITH RECURSIVE EmployeeHierarchy AS (
    -- Anchor member
```

```
    SELECT employee_id, name, manager_id
    FROM employees
    WHERE manager_id IS NULL -- Root manager

    UNION ALL

    -- Recursive member
    SELECT e.employee_id, e.name, e.manager_id
    FROM employees e
    INNER JOIN EmployeeHierarchy eh ON e.manager_id = eh.employee_id
)
SELECT *
FROM EmployeeHierarchy;
```

The recursive CTE EmployeeHierarchy starts with the root manager, Alice, whose manager_id is NULL. It then recursively joins with the employees table to find all employees who report to the root manager and continues this process for the entire hierarchy.

Running this query yields the following output:

```
 employee_id | name   | manager_id
-------------+--------+------------
           1 | Alice  |       NULL
           2 | Bob    |          1
           3 | Carol  |          1
           4 | David  |          2
           5 | Eve    |          2
           6 | Frank  |          3
```

Recursive CTEs can also be used to calculate hierarchical relationships beyond simple parent-child associations. For example, consider a scenario where we wish to calculate the total number of direct and indirect reports for each manager. This can be done using the previously defined recursive CTE.

```
WITH RECURSIVE EmployeeHierarchy AS (
    -- Anchor member
    SELECT employee_id, name, manager_id, 0 AS level
    FROM employees
    WHERE manager_id IS NULL -- Root manager

    UNION ALL

    -- Recursive member
    SELECT e.employee_id, e.name, e.manager_id, eh.level + 1
    FROM employees e
    INNER JOIN EmployeeHierarchy eh ON e.manager_id = eh.employee_id
)
SELECT manager_id, COUNT(*) AS total_reports
FROM EmployeeHierarchy
GROUP BY manager_id;
```

This query segments levels of hierarchy and counts the reports at each level. The level column helps to identify the depth in the hierarchy. Running this query will give the aggregated count of employees reporting directly or indirectly to each manager.

```
manager_id | total_reports
------------+---------------
      NULL |             1
         1 |          5
         2 |          3
         3 |          1
```

Recursive queries offer significant flexibility in querying hierarchical data and provide a powerful tool for database administrators and developers dealing with complex data relationships. They extend the capability of SQL by allowing iterative processing, thus bridging the gap where traditional SQL falls short in handling data recursion.

3.5 Window Functions

Window functions in SQL provide a versatile means of performing calculations across sets of table rows that are somehow related to the current row. These functions differ fundamentally from aggregate functions, which return a single summary value for a set of input values. Instead, window functions retain the individual row data and augment it with computed values.

A window function follows this general syntax:

```
window_function([arguments]) OVER (
    [PARTITION BY partition_expression]
    [ORDER BY sort_expression]
    [frame_clause]
)
```

The key components are:

- **window_function**: The function such as ROW_NUMBER(), RANK(), LEAD(), LAG(), etc.
- **PARTITION BY**: Divides the result set into partitions to which the function is applied.
- **ORDER BY**: Sorts the rows within each partition.
- **frame_clause**: Defines the range of rows used for each calculation.

ROW_NUMBER(), RANK(), and DENSE_RANK(): These functions assign a unique number to each row based on the specified ORDER BY clause within the partition.

```
SELECT employee_id,
       salary,
       ROW_NUMBER() OVER (PARTITION BY department_id ORDER BY salary
            DESC) AS row_num,
       RANK() OVER (PARTITION BY department_id ORDER BY salary DESC) AS
            rank,
       DENSE_RANK() OVER (PARTITION BY department_id ORDER BY salary
            DESC) AS dense_rank
FROM employees;
```

The ROW_NUMBER() function generates a sequential number for each row, starting at 1 for each partition. The RANK() function also ranks rows within a partition, but unlike ROW_NUMBER(), it may leave gaps in the ranking sequence if there are ties. DENSE_RANK(), on the other hand, does not leave gaps in the ranking sequence.

LEAD() and LAG(): These functions access data from subsequent or preceding rows.

```
SELECT employee_id,
       salary,
       LEAD(salary, 1) OVER (ORDER BY salary) AS next_salary,
       LAG(salary, 1) OVER (ORDER BY salary) AS prev_salary
FROM employees;
```

In the example, LEAD() retrieves the value of salary from the next row in the result set, while LAG() retrieves the value from the previous row.

Aggregate Functions as Window Functions: Common aggregate functions like SUM(), AVG(), MIN(), and MAX() can be used as window functions to compute cumulative totals, moving averages, and other metrics.

```
SELECT employee_id,
       department_id,
       salary,
       SUM(salary) OVER (PARTITION BY department_id ORDER BY employee_id
            ROWS BETWEEN UNBOUNDED PRECEDING AND CURRENT ROW)
            AS cumulative_salary
FROM employees
ORDER BY department_id, employee_id;
```

In this query, SUM() computes the cumulative sum of salary for each department_id. The ROWS BETWEEN UNBOUNDED PRECEDING AND CURRENT ROW frame clause means that the window frame starts at the first row of the partition and ends at the current row. This produces a running total for each department.

NTILE(): This function distributes rows into a specified number of buckets or tiles and assigns a bucket number to each row.

```
SELECT employee_id,
```

```
    salary,
    NTILE(4) OVER (ORDER BY salary DESC) AS salary_quartile
FROM employees;
```

The NTILE(4) function divides the result set into four approximately equal parts (quartiles), assigning a bucket number (1 to 4) to each row according to their ranking by salary.

Frame Clauses: The frame clause further refines the subset of rows within a partition to which a window function is applied. These are defined using several options:

- **RANGE**: Considers the logical range of values.
- **ROWS**: Considers a physical set of rows.
- **GROUPS**: Considers the sets of peer groups (implemented in some SQL dialects).

Each of these may be combined with keywords such as:

- **UNBOUNDED PRECEDING**: From the start of the partition to the current row.
- **UNBOUNDED FOLLOWING**: From the current row to the end of the partition.
- **CURRENT ROW**: Only the current row.
- Integer values to specify specific rows relative to the current row, e.g., 1 PRECEDING or 1 FOLLOWING.

The integration of these components allows for sophisticated analytics and data manipulations directly within SQL queries, making window functions indispensable tools for advanced data analysis.

3.6 Advanced JOIN Techniques

Advanced SQL queries often necessitate the use of sophisticated join techniques to retrieve data from multiple tables effectively. An understanding of advanced join methods is crucial for performing complex data manipulations and deriving meaningful insights from relational databases.

Natural Join: A *natural join* is a type of join that combines tables based on columns with the same name and compatible data types. This method simplifies query writing, but it also requires caution as it implicitly matches columns without requiring explicit join conditions.

```
SELECT *
FROM Employees
NATURAL JOIN Departments;
```

In this example, the Employees and Departments tables are joined on columns that share the same name. This join condition is inferred from the schema, reducing syntactic complexity but also potentially leading to unintended results if tables have multiple common columns.

Using Aliases in Joins: Aliases create concise references to table names, improving readability and maintainability of SQL code, especially when dealing with multiple joins or self-joins.

```
SELECT e.EmployeeID, e.FirstName, e.LastName, d.DepartmentName
FROM Employees AS e
JOIN Departments AS d
ON e.DepartmentID = d.DepartmentID;
```

Here, e and d are aliases for the Employees and Departments tables respectively, making the query more compact and readable.

Self Joins: A self join occurs when a table is joined with itself. This technique is useful for querying hierarchical data or comparing rows within the same table.

```
SELECT e1.EmployeeID AS EmpID1, e1.FirstName AS FirstName1,
       e2.EmployeeID AS EmpID2, e2.FirstName AS FirstName2
FROM Employees e1, Employees e2
WHERE e1.ManagerID = e2.EmployeeID;
```

In this query, the Employees table is joined with itself to find employees and their respective managers, illustrating the utility of self joins in hierarchical queries.

Cross Join: A cross join returns the Cartesian product of two tables, generating combinations of each row of the first table with all rows in the second table. While rarely used directly due to the potentially large result set, cross joins are foundational for certain complex queries.

```
SELECT *
FROM Products
CROSS JOIN Sales;
```

This statement produces a result with every possible combination of rows from Products and Sales, leading to comprehensive pairings of data.

Lateral Join and APPLY: The LATERAL keyword or SQL Server's APPLY operator allows for calling a table-valued function once per each row of the outer query and use the output as part of the result set.

```
SELECT e.EmployeeID, e.FirstName, e.LastName,
       j.RecentProject
FROM Employees AS e
CROSS APPLY (
    SELECT TOP 1 ProjectName AS RecentProject
    FROM Projects p
    WHERE p.EmployeeID = e.EmployeeID
    ORDER BY p.ProjectDate DESC
) AS j;
```

In this example, the CROSS APPLY subquery identifies the most recent project for each employee, providing capabilities beyond typical join operations, essential for complex data extraction.

Full Outer Join: Combines the results of both left and right outer joins, returning all records when there is a match in either left or right table.

```
SELECT e.EmployeeID, e.FirstName, d.DepartmentName
FROM Employees e
FULL OUTER JOIN Departments d
ON e.DepartmentID = d.DepartmentID;
```

This query yields all employees and departments, including those without corresponding entries in the other table.

Using Non-Equi Joins: Non-equi joins involve conditions other than equality, such as greater than or less than, to relate rows between tables.

```
SELECT o.OrderID, o.OrderDate, p.ProductName
FROM Orders o
JOIN Products p
ON o.OrderDate >= p.AvailableFrom;
```

Here, the join condition is based on date comparison, demonstrating how non-equi joins can be employed for temporal data queries.

Applications of these advanced join techniques are immense, from simplifying complex data retrieval to enhancing the performance of SQL queries through optimized join strategies. Mastering these methods is instrumental for any SQL practitioner aiming to handle intricate relational data seamlessly.

3.7 Set Operations: UNION, INTERSECT, EXCEPT

In SQL, set operations allow you to combine the results of two or more queries into a single result set. These operations are significantly useful in scenarios where you need to organize data from multiple tables or queries in a meaningful way. The primary set operations available in SQL are UNION, INTERSECT, and EXCEPT. Each of these operations serves a distinct purpose and comes with its syntactical rules and use cases.

UNION: The UNION operator is used to combine the result sets of two or more SELECT queries. It removes duplicate records between the two result sets.

```
SELECT column1, column2 FROM table1
UNION
SELECT column1, column2 FROM table2;
```

If the goal is to include all records, including duplicates, the UNION ALL operator can be employed.

```
SELECT column1, column2 FROM table1
UNION ALL
SELECT column1, column2 FROM table2;
```

INTERSECT: The INTERSECT operator returns only the rows that are common to both of the result sets. This operator inherently removes duplicates from the result set, providing a list of values that appear in both queries.

```
SELECT column1, column2 FROM table1
INTERSECT
SELECT column1, column2 FROM table2;
```

EXCEPT: The EXCEPT operator returns the rows that are in the result set of the first query but not in the result set of the second query. Similar to UNION and INTERSECT, it also removes duplicates from the final result set.

```
SELECT column1, column2 FROM table1
EXCEPT
SELECT column1, column2 FROM table2;
```

When employing these set operations, it is crucial to ensure that the SELECT statements involved in the operation return the same number of columns, and the corresponding columns have compatible data types.

Example Scenarios: Consider two tables, employees_2022 and employees_2023, containing employee data for different years.

```
CREATE TABLE employees_2022 (
    id INT,
    name VARCHAR(50),
    department VARCHAR(50)
);

CREATE TABLE employees_2023 (
    id INT,
    name VARCHAR(50),
    department VARCHAR(50)
);
```

Let's say you want to find a list of all unique employees who were either in employees_2022 or employees_2023.

```
SELECT name FROM employees_2022
UNION
SELECT name FROM employees_2023;
```

Alternatively, to find employees who were present in both years:

```
SELECT name FROM employees_2022
INTERSECT
SELECT name FROM employees_2023;
```

To determine the list of employees who were in employees_2022 but not in employees_2023:

```
SELECT name FROM employees_2022
EXCEPT
SELECT name FROM employees_2023;
```

Execution and Results: Assuming the following data in the tables,

```
employees_2022:
+----+--------+-------------+
| id | name   | department  |
+----+--------+-------------+
|  1 | Alice  | HR          |
|  2 | Bob    | IT          |
|  3 | Charlie| Sales       |
+----+--------+-------------+

employees_2023:
+----+--------+-------------+
| id | name   | department  |
+----+--------+-------------+
|  2 | Bob    | IT          |
|  3 | Charlie| Sales       |
|  4 | David  | Marketing   |
+----+--------+-------------+
```

The result of the UNION query would be:

```
+--------+
| name   |
+--------+
| Alice  |
| Bob    |
| Charlie|
| David  |
+--------+
```

The result of the INTERSECT query would be:

```
+--------+
| name   |
+--------+
| Bob    |
| Charlie|
+--------+
```

The result of the EXCEPT query would be:

```
+--------+
| name   |
+--------+
| Alice  |
+--------+
```

These set operations are pivotal when dealing with large datasets that need to be merged, compared, or differentiated with high precision. Understanding how and when to use UNION, INTERSECT, and EXCEPT will greatly enhance your SQL capabilities, aiding in delivering more effective data management solutions.

3.8 Materialized Views

Materialized views are a pivotal feature in SQL that allow the precomputation and storage of complex query results. Unlike standard views, which are virtual tables created dynamically upon query execution, materialized views store the results physically. This storage mechanism results in quicker data retrieval, making them ideal for data warehousing and decision support systems where query performance is paramount.

Definition and Syntax

Creating a materialized view follows a syntax similar to that of creating a table or view. The basic syntax is as follows:

```
CREATE MATERIALIZED VIEW view_name AS
SELECT column1, column2, ...
FROM table1
WHERE condition;
```

This command constructs a materialized view named view_name that includes the result set from the specified SELECT statement.

Refreshing Materialized Views

One crucial aspect of materialized views is that they need to be refreshed to keep the data up-to-date with the underlying base tables. There are two primary options for refreshing materialized views: *complete* and *incremental* (or *fast*) refresh.

Complete Refresh: Recomputes the entire view from scratch.

```
REFRESH MATERIALIZED VIEW view_name;
```

Incremental Refresh: Updates the materialized view only with the changes made since the last refresh. For this method to be effective, the view must be defined in a way that supports incremental refresh, typically requiring materialized view logs.

```
CREATE MATERIALIZED VIEW LOG ON table_name
WITH ROWID, PRIMARY KEY, SEQUENCE (column1, column2, ...);
```

Once the materialized view log is in place, the incremental refresh can be executed using:

```
REFRESH MATERIALIZED VIEW view_name FAST;
```

Advantages and Use Cases

Materialized views offer several benefits:

- **Performance Improvement**: They significantly improve query performance by precomputing and storing complex joins, aggregations, and filtering.

- **Resource Optimization**: They reduce the load on base tables and indexes, optimizing resource utilization.

- **Data Warehousing**: Essential in data warehousing environments where real-time performance is critical for large datasets.

- **Consistency**: They ensure data consistency when the complete refresh is used post substantial data updates.

Considerations and Limitations

However, there are considerations to keep in mind:

- **Storage Overhead**: Materialized views require additional storage space for the precomputed data.

- **Maintenance Cost**: Regular maintenance through refreshing is necessary to keep data current.
- **Complexity**: Management of materialized views, especially with incremental refreshes, can add complexity to database administration.

Practical Example

Consider a database with a sales table storing daily transaction details. To optimize reporting performance, a materialized view can be created to aggregate monthly sales data.

```
CREATE MATERIALIZED VIEW monthly_sales AS
SELECT
    EXTRACT(YEAR FROM sale_date) AS year,
    EXTRACT(MONTH FROM sale_date) AS month,
    SUM(sale_amount) AS total_sales,
    COUNT(sale_id) AS total_transactions
FROM
    sales
GROUP BY
    EXTRACT(YEAR FROM sale_date),
    EXTRACT(MONTH FROM sale_date);
```

To ensure this view remains up-to-date with daily sales transactions, an incremental refresh might be more efficient. First, create a materialized view log on the sales table:

```
CREATE MATERIALIZED VIEW LOG ON sales
WITH ROWID, SEQUENCE (sale_date, sale_amount, sale_id);
```

Then, the materialized view can be refreshed incrementally:

```
REFRESH MATERIALIZED VIEW monthly_sales FAST;
```

Through this approach, the monthly_sales view will reflect recent transactions, thus yielding faster query results for monthly sales reports.

SQL Standard Compliance

Materialized views are not standardized across all SQL databases. Implementation specifics can differ, and certain features like fast refresh may not be universally supported. Thus, consult the specific database documentation for precise functionalities and limitations.

Incorporating materialized views into a database design can substantially enhance query performance and efficiency in data handling, making them an invaluable tool in the repertoire of advanced SQL techniques.

3.9 Handling Complex Data Types

Handling complex data types in SQL is essential as databases manage more sophisticated and diverse forms of data. Complex data types, which include arrays, multi-dimensional arrays, composites, and user-defined types, allow for the representation of more dynamic and structured data within a database schema. Let's explore the syntax and practical applications of these data types.

Arrays

An array is a collection of elements that allow the storage and retrieval of multiple values within a single column entry. Most SQL databases, such as PostgreSQL and Oracle, support array data types with variations in syntax. Using arrays can optimize storage and simplify queries that involve multi-valued attributes.

In PostgreSQL, an array can be defined in a table column as follows:

```
CREATE TABLE students (
    id SERIAL PRIMARY KEY,
    name VARCHAR(100),
    grades INTEGER[]
);
```

To insert data into this table, use the ARRAY keyword or list the values directly:

```
INSERT INTO students (name, grades)
VALUES ('John Doe', ARRAY[85, 90, 88]);

-- or

INSERT INTO students (name, grades)
VALUES ('Jane Doe', '{85, 90, 88}');
```

For querying array elements, PostgreSQL provides extensive support:

```
-- Retrieve students with a specific grade
SELECT name
FROM students
WHERE 90 = ANY (grades);

-- Retrieve specific element from an array
SELECT grades[1]
FROM students
WHERE name = 'John Doe';
```

Composite Types

Composite types allow the grouping of multiple fields into a single field in a table, providing a way to encapsulate related fields. For example, addressing information such as street, city, and zip code can be grouped into a composite type.

First, define a composite type:

```
CREATE TYPE address AS (
    street VARCHAR(100),
    city VARCHAR(50),
    zip_code CHAR(5)
);
```

Next, use this composite type in a table definition:

```
CREATE TABLE employees (
    id SERIAL PRIMARY KEY,
    name VARCHAR(100),
    home_address address
);
```

For inserting data into such tables:

```
INSERT INTO employees (name, home_address)
VALUES ('Alice Smith', ('123 Main St', 'Springfield', '12345'));
```

Querying composite types involves referencing individual attributes:

```
SELECT name, home_address.city
FROM employees
WHERE home_address.zip_code = '12345';
```

JSON Data Type

JSON (JavaScript Object Notation) is a widely-used format for data interchange, supported by various SQL databases like PostgreSQL, MySQL, and SQL Server, among others. JSON data types enable flexible nested structures directly within SQL tables.

In PostgreSQL, declaring a column with a JSON type:

```
CREATE TABLE books (
    id SERIAL PRIMARY KEY,
    title VARCHAR(255),
    details JSON
);
```

Insert data into the JSON column:

```
INSERT INTO books (title, details)
VALUES ('SQL Fundamentals', '{"author": "John Doe", "published_year": 2020, "
    chapters": ["Introduction", "Basics", "Advanced"]}');
```

Querying specific JSON attributes:

```
-- Retrieve book titles by author
SELECT title
FROM books
WHERE details->>'author' = 'John Doe';

-- Extract nested array elements
SELECT details->'chapters'->>0
FROM books
WHERE title = 'SQL Fundamentals';
```

XML Data Type

XML (eXtensible Markup Language) is another format for structured data interchange, supported by numerous SQL databases for handling hierarchical data.

Defining an XML type in SQL Server or PostgreSQL:

```
CREATE TABLE orders (
    id SERIAL PRIMARY KEY,
    order_info XML
);
```

Inserting data into XML columns:

```
INSERT INTO orders (order_info)
VALUES ('<order><customer>John Doe</customer><items><item>Book</item
    ><item>Pen</item></items></order>');
```

Querying data from XML fields involves XPath expressions:

```
-- Fetching the customer's name from the XML structure
SELECT order_info::xml->'order'->'customer' AS customer_name
FROM orders;
```

These examples demonstrate how complex data types enhance the flexibility and capability of SQL databases, enabling the efficient management of intricate and hierarchical data structures within conventional relational tables.

3.10 Using JSON and XML in SQL

With the increasing complexity of data and the need for versatile data representation, JSON and XML have become integral components in modern databases. Both formats allow for hierarchical data structures that are often more intuitive for certain types of data than traditional relational structures. This section explores how to interact with JSON and XML data within SQL, covering storage, retrieval, and manipulation.

Storing JSON and XML data in SQL relies on specific data types provided by most modern RDBMS (Relational Database Management Systems). For instance, PostgreSQL, MySQL, and SQL Server each offer native support for JSON, whereas XML data types are available across several databases, including Oracle and SQL Server. Below are examples of how these data types are defined and managed.

```
CREATE TABLE json_table (
    id SERIAL PRIMARY KEY,
    data JSONB NOT NULL
);

CREATE TABLE xml_table (
    id SERIAL PRIMARY KEY,
    data XML NOT NULL
);
```

Interacting with JSON data often involves functions that allow for extracting elements, transforming the JSON structure, or validating the integrity of JSON schemas. PostgreSQL's JSON functions serve as a comprehensive toolkit for these operations.

```
SELECT id, data->>'name' AS name
FROM json_table
WHERE data->>'age'::int > 30;
```

The above query demonstrates accessing JSON properties using the ->> operator to retrieve the value associated with the key 'name' and 'age'. The condition ensures we only select entries where the age is greater than 30.

Manipulating JSON often requires altering its structure or content. For example, updating a specific key-value pair within a JSON object can be achieved as shown:

```
UPDATE json_table
SET data = jsonb_set(data, '{address,city}', '"New York"')
WHERE id = 1;
```

Here, the jsonb_set function is used to modify the 'city' field under the 'address' key within the JSON object.

XML manipulation within SQL is similarly robust, employing XPath and XQuery standards for querying and modifying XML data. Below is an example of how to retrieve certain elements using XPath.

```
SELECT id,
       xml_query(data, '/person/name/text()') AS name
FROM xml_table
WHERE xml_exists('/person[age>30]', data);
```

The xml_query function extracts the name from the XML data, and the xml_exists function filters records based on the condition specified in the XPath expression.

Updates to XML data rely on similar querying capabilities. Changing a particular element is supported via the XMLQUERY and XMLMODIFY functions.

```
UPDATE xml_table
SET data = xmlquery('
    for $i in /person/address
    return copy $i modify (rename node $i/city as "town")
')
WHERE id = 1;
```

This script demonstrates renaming the 'city' node to 'town' under the 'address' element within the XML data.

Converting between data types is another common requirement, enabling the transformation of JSON to XML and vice versa. Such conversions facilitate the integration of different systems and data workflows.

```
SELECT
    id,
    xmlelement(name "person",
        xmlforest(
            (data->>'name') as "name",
            (data->>'age') as "age",
            (data->>'address') as "address"
        )
    ) AS xml_data
FROM json_table;
```

The XMLelement and XMLforest functions transform JSON fields into an equivalent XML structure, allowing for cross-format compatibility.

Integrating JSON and XML into SQL environments enhances the ability to handle complex, hierarchical data efficiently. Through the use of specialized functions and operations, RDBMS can manage heterogeneous data with ease, advancing data storage and retrieval capabilities beyond traditional relational models.

3.11 Managing Hierarchical Data

Hierarchical data refers to data that is structured in a tree-like format, where each record has a parent-child relationship with one or more other records. In relational databases, managing hierarchical data can pose specific challenges due to the inherently flat nature of tables. To effectively manage and query hierarchical data, several techniques and strategies are commonly used.

One widely used method for representing hierarchical data is the adjacency list model. This model uses a table to store each node of the hierarchy, with each record referencing its parent node. Consider the following example of an employees table:

```
CREATE TABLE employees (
    employee_id INT PRIMARY KEY,
    employee_name VARCHAR(50),
    manager_id INT
);
```

Here, employee_id uniquely identifies each employee, employee_name stores the employee's name, and manager_id references the employee_id of the employee's manager. This allows the hierarchical relationships to be represented, as each employee points to their manager.

To retrieve a hierarchical structure using the adjacency list model, recursive queries (often implemented using Common Table Expressions, or CTEs) are employed. The following SQL query illustrates how to use a recursive CTE to retrieve the hierarchy of employees:

```
WITH RECURSIVE EmployeeHierarchy AS (
    SELECT
        employee_id,
        employee_name,
        manager_id,
        1 AS level
    FROM employees
    WHERE manager_id IS NULL

    UNION ALL

    SELECT
        e.employee_id,
        e.employee_name,
        e.manager_id,
        eh.level + 1
    FROM employees e
    INNER JOIN EmployeeHierarchy eh ON e.manager_id = eh.employee_id
)
SELECT
    employee_id,
    employee_name,
    manager_id,
    level
FROM EmployeeHierarchy
ORDER BY level, employee_name;
```

In this query, the recursive CTE EmployeeHierarchy starts by selecting the root node(s) where manager_id is NULL. It then recursively joins the employees table to itself, increasing the level by 1 for each subsequent level of the hierarchy. The final result is ordered by level and employee_name.

Another approach to managing hierarchical data is the nested set model. This model stores the hierarchy as a set of nested intervals rather than explicitly storing parent-child relationships. In the nested set model, each node is assigned two values, lft and rgt, which represent the nested intervals. Consider the following modification to the employees table:

```
CREATE TABLE employees (
    employee_id INT PRIMARY KEY,
    employee_name VARCHAR(50),
    lft INT,
    rgt INT
);
```

The lft and rgt columns are used to encode the hierarchical structure. For example, an employee with $\text{lft} = 1$ and $\text{rgt} = 10$ would have subordinates with lft and rgt values between 1 and 10. The advantage of the nested set model is that hierarchical queries can be performed efficiently using simple range queries. Consider the following example to retrieve all descendants of a given employee:

```
SELECT
    employee_id,
    employee_name
FROM employees
WHERE lft BETWEEN 2 AND 9;
```

In this query, the range values 2 and 9 would typically be dynamically determined based on the employee of interest. This approach allows for efficient querying of the entire subtree without the need for recursive joins.

In addition to these strategies, modern databases offer support for managing hierarchical data using proprietary features. For instance, PostgreSQL provides the ltree data type, which is designed for hierarchical data management. This data type stores labels of data in a hierarchical tree structure, allowing for efficient querying and indexing.

Consider the following example of using the ltree extension in PostgreSQL:

```
CREATE EXTENSION ltree;

CREATE TABLE employees (
    employee_id INT PRIMARY KEY,
    employee_name VARCHAR(50),
    path ltree
);
```

```
INSERT INTO employees (employee_id, employee_name, path) VALUES
(1, 'CEO', '1'),
(2, 'CTO', '1.2'),
(3, 'CFO', '1.3'),
(4, 'Engineer', '1.2.4'),
(5, 'Accountant', '1.3.5');

SELECT
    employee_id,
    employee_name
FROM employees
WHERE path @> '1.2';
```

In this example, the path column uses the ltree data type to store hierarchical paths. The query retrieves all employees under the CTO by using the @> operator, which checks if a path is a descendant of another path.

Ultimately, selecting the appropriate method for managing hierarchical data depends on the specific requirements and capabilities of the database system being used. Each method—whether the adjacency list model, nested set model, or proprietary features—offers distinct advantages and tradeoffs in terms of ease of maintenance, query performance, and complexity.

```
employee_id | employee_name
------------+--------------
2           | CTO
4           | Engineer
```

3.12 Full-Text Search

Full-text search (FTS) refers to various techniques used in database systems to search for and retrieve instances of specific text patterns within text data. When dealing with large textual data, traditional searching methods, such as the use of the LIKE operator, can be inefficient and inadequate. Full-text search addresses these limitations by enabling sophisticated and performance-optimized search capabilities.

FTS typically involves a few key components: indexing the text data, storing the index, and querying the index. The system creates an index from the text data to facilitate rapid searching. This index allows the database engine to quickly locate the positions and occurrences of specific text patterns.

Creating Full-Text Indexes:

To create a full-text index, the text data needs to be indexed, meaning the words and word positions are stored in a way that makes retrieval efficient. This often involves several steps, including tokenization, normalization, and storing the results in an inverted index.

For example, in SQL Server, a full-text index can be created as follows:

```
-- Create a full-text catalog
CREATE FULLTEXT CATALOG MyCatalog AS DEFAULT;

-- Create a full-text index on a specific table and column
CREATE FULLTEXT INDEX ON MyTable(MyColumn)
KEY INDEX PK_MyTable
WITH STOPLIST = SYSTEM;
```

In this example, the CREATE FULLTEXT CATALOG command creates a catalog for storing the full-text index. The CREATE FULLTEXT INDEX command is then used to create the actual index on the column MyColumn of the table MyTable, using the primary key PK_MyTable as the unique identifier.

Querying Full-Text Indexes:

Once a full-text index is in place, querying it is relatively straightforward. Most SQL databases provide specific querying capabilities for full-text indexed data. For instance, using SQL Server again, the CONTAINS function allows for querying the full-text index:

```
-- Search for a single word
SELECT *
FROM MyTable
WHERE CONTAINS(MyColumn, 'searchterm');

-- Search for multiple words
SELECT *
FROM MyTable
WHERE CONTAINS(MyColumn, 'word1 AND word2');

-- Search for an exact phrase
SELECT *
FROM MyTable
WHERE CONTAINS(MyColumn, '"exact phrase"');
```

The CONTAINS function is used to match against the full-text index. The above queries demonstrate searching for a single term, multiple terms with logical operators (e.g., AND, OR), and exact phrases.

Ranked Searches and Relevance:

An important feature of full-text search is the ability to rank search results by relevance. Depending on the database system, the ranking can be automated or customizable. For example, in SQL Server, the FREETEXTTABLE function can return a ranking score with the results.

```
-- Perform a full-text search with ranking
SELECT *
FROM FREETEXTTABLE(MyTable, MyColumn, 'search term');
```

The FREETEXTTABLE function returns a table with the rows that match the search term, including a column for the ranking score. This helps in prioritizing search results based on their relevance to the query term.

Languages and Inflectional Forms:

Full-text search systems often provide support for multiple languages and can handle inflectional forms of words. This means they can match variations of a word (e.g., "run", "running", "ran") and can be configured for specific linguistic rules.

Stopwords and Noise Words:

Stopwords, also known as noise words, are common words that are often excluded from the full-text index because they do not contribute to the search's accuracy or utility. Examples include "and", "the", "is", etc. The management of stopwords can be configured to optimize the index's efficiency and relevance.

In SQL Server, you can create a list of stopwords or use the system default. Customizing stopwords can be done as follows:

```
-- Create a stop list
CREATE FULLTEXT STOPLIST MyStoplist;

-- Add words to the stop list
ALTER FULLTEXT STOPLIST MyStoplist
ADD 'example';
```

Best Practices:

To ensure the efficiency and accuracy of full-text search, consider the following best practices:

- Regularly update and rebuild full-text indexes to keep them optimized as data changes.
- Customize stopwords based on the specific domain and typical user queries.
- Use appropriate linguistic and language settings for multilingual data.
- Analyze search term patterns and adjust indexes and configurations accordingly.

Effective full-text search implementation can significantly enhance the performance and user experience of search capabilities within a database, enabling powerful and scalable text querying and retrieval.

Chapter 4

Database Design and Normalization

This chapter introduces key principles of database design, including data models and Entity-Relationship (ER) diagrams. It explains how to define entities, attributes, and relationships, and discusses the importance of primary and foreign keys. The chapter guides readers through the normalization process, covering the first to Boyce-Codd normal forms. It also addresses denormalization and performance considerations, designing for scalability, and includes practical case studies in database design.

4.1 Introduction to Database Design

Database design is a fundamental aspect of database management that involves the conceptualization, modeling, and structuring of data in a database. The primary objective of database design is to create a logical and efficient schema that accurately represents the data, relationships, and constraints required by the information system. An effective database design improves data integrity, reduces redundancy, and optimizes performance, thereby ensuring the reliability and scalability of the database system.

Database design begins with a thorough understanding of user requirements and business rules. These requirements are typically gathered through interviews, surveys, document analysis, and observation. Once the requirements are clear, the next step is to model the data using formal techniques, such as Entity-Relationship (ER) diagrams, which facilitate the visualization of entities, attributes, and relationships.

In the context of database design, an **entity** represents a real-world object or concept that is distinguishable from other objects. Examples of entities include 'Customer', 'Order', 'Product', and 'Employee'. Each entity is characterized by a set of **attributes**, which are properties or characteristics of the entity. For instance, a 'Customer' entity may have attributes such as 'CustomerID', 'Name', 'Address', and 'PhoneNumber'.

Entities are related to one another through **relationships**. A relationship describes an association between two or more entities. For example, a 'Customer' may place an 'Order', or an 'Employee' may belong to a 'Department'. Relationships can have different cardinalities (one-to-one, one-to-many, or many-to-many) and may also possess attributes. It is essential to identify and accurately represent these relationships to ensure the integrity and usability of the database.

Once entities and relationships are defined, the next step is to assign **primary keys** to entities. A primary key is a unique identifier for each record in an entity. It ensures that each record can be uniquely distinguished from all other records. For example, 'CustomerID' might serve as the primary key for the 'Customer' entity. Similarly, **foreign keys** are used to establish and enforce links between entities. A foreign key in one entity refers to the primary key of another entity, thus creating a reference between the records.

To illustrate the concepts of database design, consider the example of a simple e-commerce application. The primary entities might include 'Customer', 'Order', and 'Product'. Their attributes could be as follows:

- **Customer**: CustomerID (primary key), Name, Address, Email, PhoneNumber

- **Order**: OrderID (primary key), OrderDate, CustomerID (foreign key), TotalAmount

- **Product**: ProductID (primary key), ProductName, Description, Price, StockQuantity

The relationships in this scenario could include:

- **Customer-Order** (one-to-many): A customer can place multiple orders, but each order is placed by a single customer. The 'CustomerID' in the 'Order' entity serves as a foreign key referencing the 'Customer' entity's primary key.
- **Order-Product** (many-to-many): An order can contain multiple products, and a product can appear in multiple orders. This many-to-many relationship can be represented using an intermediary entity, 'OrderDetail', with attributes such as 'OrderDetailID' (primary key), 'OrderID' (foreign key), 'ProductID' (foreign key), and 'Quantity'.

In the SQL schema, these relationships can be represented as:

```
CREATE TABLE Customer (
    CustomerID INT PRIMARY KEY,
    Name VARCHAR(255),
    Address VARCHAR(255),
    Email VARCHAR(255),
    PhoneNumber VARCHAR(50)
);

CREATE TABLE Product (
    ProductID INT PRIMARY KEY,
    ProductName VARCHAR(255),
    Description TEXT,
    Price DECIMAL(10, 2),
    StockQuantity INT
);

CREATE TABLE Orders (
    OrderID INT PRIMARY KEY,
    OrderDate DATE,
    CustomerID INT,
    TotalAmount DECIMAL(10, 2),
    FOREIGN KEY (CustomerID) REFERENCES Customer(CustomerID)
);

CREATE TABLE OrderDetail (
    OrderDetailID INT PRIMARY KEY,
    OrderID INT,
    ProductID INT,
    Quantity INT,
    FOREIGN KEY (OrderID) REFERENCES Orders(OrderID),
    FOREIGN KEY (ProductID) REFERENCES Product(ProductID)
);
```

The creation of these tables in SQL not only defines the structure of the database but also enforces referential integrity through primary and foreign key constraints. This ensures that relationships between entities are maintained correctly, preventing data anomalies such as orphaned records and inconsistent data entries.

Normalization is a critical process in database design that involves organizing data to minimize redundancy and dependence. It is achieved through a series of rules or normal forms, starting with the First Normal Form (1NF) and progressing to more advanced forms like Boyce-Codd Normal Form (BCNF). Normalization aims to ensure that the database structure is free from undesirable anomalies such as insertion, update, and deletion anomalies. This systematic approach provides a blueprint for creating robust databases that support efficient data retrieval and manipulation.

While normalization is essential for maintaining data integrity and quality, it is equally important to consider performance implications. Highly normalized databases may result in complex queries and increased join operations, potentially leading to performance bottlenecks. Conversely, denormalization techniques, such as combining tables or introducing redundancy, can improve query performance at the expense of data integrity. Balancing normalization with performance considerations is crucial in achieving an optimal database design.

In summary, the design of a database is a multifaceted process that requires a comprehensive understanding of data requirements, careful modeling of entities and relationships, and judicious application of normalization principles. This foundation enables the creation of a well-structured and efficient database system that meets the needs of users and applications effectively.

4.2 Understanding Data Models

Understanding data models is crucial for effective database design. Data models are abstract representations of the data and the relationships between them within a database. They serve as a blueprint for constructing physical databases that support data storage, retrieval, and management efficiently. Common data models include the hierarchical, network, relational, and object-oriented models, each with particular benefits and use cases.

The hierarchical model organizes data in a tree-like structure where each record has a single parent and any number of children, reflecting a one-to-many relationship. This model is akin to a file system's directory structure. However, its limitation is inability to handle many-to-many relationships efficiently.

The network model allows more complex relationships through graph structures, where entities are nodes, and relationships are edges. It supports many-to-many relationships via records and sets, providing greater flexibility than the hierarchical model. However, it can be more challenging to navigate and manage, especially with large-scale data.

The relational model, the most widely used data modeling approach, represents data using tables (relations). Each table consists of rows (tuples) and columns (attributes). Relations are expressed through primary and foreign keys, ensuring data integrity and facilitating complex queries. This model's simplicity and mathematical foundation make it powerful and flexible, catering to virtually any application domain.

The object-oriented model integrates object-oriented programming principles into database design. Entities are represented as objects, encapsulating both data and behaviors (methods). This model is ideal for applications requiring tight integration between the database and application logic, particularly in fields with complex data and relationships.

```
CREATE TABLE Students (
    StudentID INT PRIMARY KEY,
    FirstName VARCHAR(50),
    LastName VARCHAR(50),
    DateOfBirth DATE
);
```

This SQL statement creates a table named Students, encapsulating a relational model's characteristics. Each column represents an attribute, while each row would represent an individual student record.

Entities, attributes, and relationships are fundamental concepts across all data models. Entities are objects or things of interest, such as a student, course, or department. Attributes are properties or details about entities, such as a student's name, course duration, or department head. Relationships describe how entities interact or are associated, such as a student enrolling in a course or a course being offered by a department.

Graphical representations, such as Entity-Relationship (ER) diagrams, help visualize data models, shedding light on entities, attributes, and relationships. This visual approach simplifies conceptualizing the database's structure, especially when dealing with intricate schemas.

```
+-------------+
|  Students   |
+-------------+
| StudentID   |
| FirstName   |
| LastName    |
| DateOfBirth |
+-------------+
       |
      \|/
+-------------+           +-------------+
|  Enrolls    |           |  Courses    |
+-------------+           +-------------+
| CourseID    |<---------->| CourseID    |
| StudentID   |           | CourseName  |
| Grade       |           | Credits     |
+-------------+           +-------------+
```

In this simple ER diagram, two tables Students and Courses are linked via an associative entity Enrolls, capturing many-to-many relationships between students and courses. Each course may have multiple students enrolled, and a student may enroll in multiple courses.

Data integrity ensures the accuracy and consistency of data within a database. Relational models achieve this through keys and constraints. Primary keys uniquely identify records within a table, while foreign keys establish and enforce linkages between tables, preserving referential integrity. For instance, StudentID in the Enrolls table should match a valid StudentID in the Students table, preventing orphan records.

Normalization is the process of organizing data to minimize redundancy and dependency. It involves decomposing tables to achieve higher normal forms, each with specific rules for eliminating anomalies. Starting with the First Normal Form (1NF), which ensures atomicity of data, normalization progresses through Second Normal Form (2NF), Third Normal Form (3NF), and beyond, each addressing particular types of redundancy and dependency issues.

```
-- Non-normalized table
CREATE TABLE StudentCourse (
    StudentID INT,
    StudentName VARCHAR(50),
    CourseID INT,
    CourseName VARCHAR(50)
);

-- Normalized tables achieving 1NF to 3NF
CREATE TABLE Students (
    StudentID INT PRIMARY KEY,
    StudentName VARCHAR(50)
);

CREATE TABLE Courses (
    CourseID INT PRIMARY KEY,
    CourseName VARCHAR(50)
);
```

```
CREATE TABLE Enrollments (
    EnrollmentID INT PRIMARY KEY,
    StudentID INT,
    CourseID INT,
    FOREIGN KEY (StudentID) REFERENCES Students(StudentID),
    FOREIGN KEY (CourseID) REFERENCES Courses(CourseID)
);
```

In this normalization example, an initial non-normalized table StudentCourse is decomposed into three normalized tables: Students, Courses, and Enrollments, achieving up to the Third Normal Form (3NF). This removes redundancy and establishes clear relationships.

Understanding data models equips database designers with the necessary tools to model real-world problems accurately, ensuring efficient, scalable, and maintainable databases. It forms the foundation for implementing robust systems that can adapt to evolving data requirements and business needs.

4.3 Entity-Relationship (ER) Diagrams

Entity-Relationship (ER) diagrams are a critical tool in database design. They provide a graphical representation of entities, attributes, and relationships within a database, thereby serving as a blueprint for constructing a relational database.

An **entity** in an ER diagram is an object or thing about which data is stored. Entities can represent anything from a physical object like a person or a product to a concept such as an event or a transaction. Each entity is represented by a rectangle containing the entity's name.

Attributes are characteristics or properties of an entity. For instance, the entity Student might have attributes such as Student_ID, Name, Date_of_Birth, and Major. In ER diagrams, attributes are depicted as ellipses connected to their respective entities.

There are different types of attributes:

- **Simple (or atomic) attributes**: These are indivisible and represent a single value, like Name or Date_of_Birth.
- **Composite attributes**: These can be divided into smaller subparts, which represent more basic attributes with independent meanings. For example, an attribute Name could be further divided into First_Name, Middle_Initial, and Last_Name.

- **Derived attributes**: These are attributes whose values can be calculated or derived from other attributes, such as Age derived from $\mathrm{Date\_of\_Birth}$.

Relationships illustrate how entities interact with one another. They are indicated by diamond shapes in ER diagrams. Relationships can be one-to-one (1:1), one-to-many (1:M), or many-to-many (M:N).

Cardinality specifies the number of instances of one entity that can or must be associated with each instance of another entity. For example, in a *course registration system*, an entity $\mathrm{Student}$ can enroll in multiple instances of the entity Course, representing a one-to-many relationship. Additionally, each Course might have multiple $\mathrm{Students}$ enrolled, characterizing a many-to-many relationship.

The **Participation** constraint, also known as the mandatory or optional sense in relationships, specifies whether all or only some entity instances participate in a relationship. There are two types of participation:

- **Total participation**: Every instance of the entity must participate in at least one instance of the relationship.

- **Partial participation**: Some instances of the entity can exist without being connected to instances of the relationship.

ER Diagram Notation and Symbols

The following symbols are used in ER diagrams:

- **Rectangles**: Represent entities.

- **Ellipses**: Represent attributes.

- **Diamonds**: Represent relationships.

- **Lines**: Link attributes to entities and entities to relationships.

Example:

```
+-------------+
|  Student    |
+-------------+
      |
      |
      |
  +------+
  | Name |
  +------+
      |
      |
      |
+------+
|Student_ID|
+------+
```

Example of an ER Diagram

Consider the scenario of a university database maintaining information about students, courses, and instructors.

Entities:

- Student (Attributes: Student_ID, Name, Date_of_Birth, Major)
- Course (Attributes: Course_ID, Course_Name, Credits)
- Instructor (Attributes: Instructor_ID, Name, Department)

Relationships:

- Enrolls (Associates Student and Course)
- Teaches (Associates Instructor and Course)

The ER diagram can be represented as follows:

```
        +-------------+
        |  Student   |
        +-------------+
            /     \
           /       \
    +------+         +-------+
    | Name |         | Student_ID |
    +------+         +-------+
       |              |
       |              |
       |              |
+-------------+        +--------+
|Date_of_Birth|          | Major |
+-------------+        +--------+
           \
            \Enrolls
             \
          +--------------+
          |  Course     |
          +--------------+
             /     \
            /       \
       +-------+     +---------+
       |Course_ID|    |Course_Name|
       +-------+     +---------+
          |           |
          |           |
          |           |
       +----------+      +---------+
       |Credits   |       | Teaches |
       +----------+        /     \
                          /       \
        +------------+  +-------------+
        |Instructor  |  |Instructor  |
        +------------+  +-------------+
            /     \
           /       \
     +--------+    +------+
     |Name    |    |Instructor_ID|
     +--------+/   +------+
           \    \
          +------+
          |Department|
          +------+
```

In this ER diagram, the rectangles represent the entities, the ellipses represent their attributes, and the diamonds represent the relationships between them. The lines connecting attributes to entities and entities to relationships indicate the associations.

Understanding ER diagrams is an essential skill for database design. They not only help in visualizing the structure of the database but also ensure that the relationships and constraints among the data are well-defined. Crafting a robust ER diagram is the first step towards developing an efficient and effective database system.

4.4 Defining Entities, Attributes, and Relationships

Entities, attributes, and relationships form the foundational constructs of database design within the Entity-Relationship (ER) model. Understanding these concepts enables the accurate representation of real-world scenarios in a database, ensuring data integrity, consistency, and efficiency.

An **entity** represents any object or concept that can have data stored about it. This could be a tangible object (like a book, car, or person) or an intangible concept (such as a department, project, or event). Each entity is a distinct object within the domain of the database system being designed.

An **attribute** is a property or characteristic of an entity. In systems design, attributes describe the entity's properties, providing granular details that are necessary to uniquely identify or contextualize the entity. Examples include a person's name, a book's ISBN, or a car's VIN. Attributes possess various data types, such as integers, strings, dates, etc., that define the nature of the information stored in them.

A **relationship** refers to an association between two or more entities. Relationships illustrate how entities interact within the domain. For instance, a relationship can represent the borrowing of books by a library member, the assignment of projects to employees, or a customer's purchase transaction.

To define entities, attributes, and relationships, consider the functional requirements of the database and the scenario being modeled. Start with the identification of relevant entities based on the case study or business requirements. Let's depict this with an example:

Consider a library database. The primary entities are likely to include *Book*, *Member*, and *Loan*. For each entity, we identify attributes:

- **Book**
  - ISBN (International Standard Book Number)
  - Title
  - Author
  - Publisher
  - $\text{Year of Publication}$

- **Member**
  - MemberID
  - Name
  - Address
  - Phone Number
  - Membership Date
- **Loan**
  - LoanID
  - BorrowDate
  - ReturnDate

Once entities and their respective attributes are outlined, interactions among these entities can be defined as relationships. In our library example, we can define the following relationships:

- **Borrow** (*Member*, *Book*, *Loan*)

Here, *Borrow* is a relationship between *Member* and *Book*, facilitated by the *Loan* entity, which captures the association details such as borrow and return dates.

For the *Borrow* relationship to be well-defined, we need to establish cardinality constraints, which dictate the number of instances of one entity that can be associated with instances of another entity. Typical cardinalities are one-to-one, one-to-many, and many-to-many. In our library example, the relationship can be many-to-many, as a *Member* can borrow multiple *Books*, and each *Book* can be borrowed by multiple *Members* over time, yet facilitated through individual *Loan* records each time a book is borrowed.

Express these constructs in an ER diagram to visualize the structure:

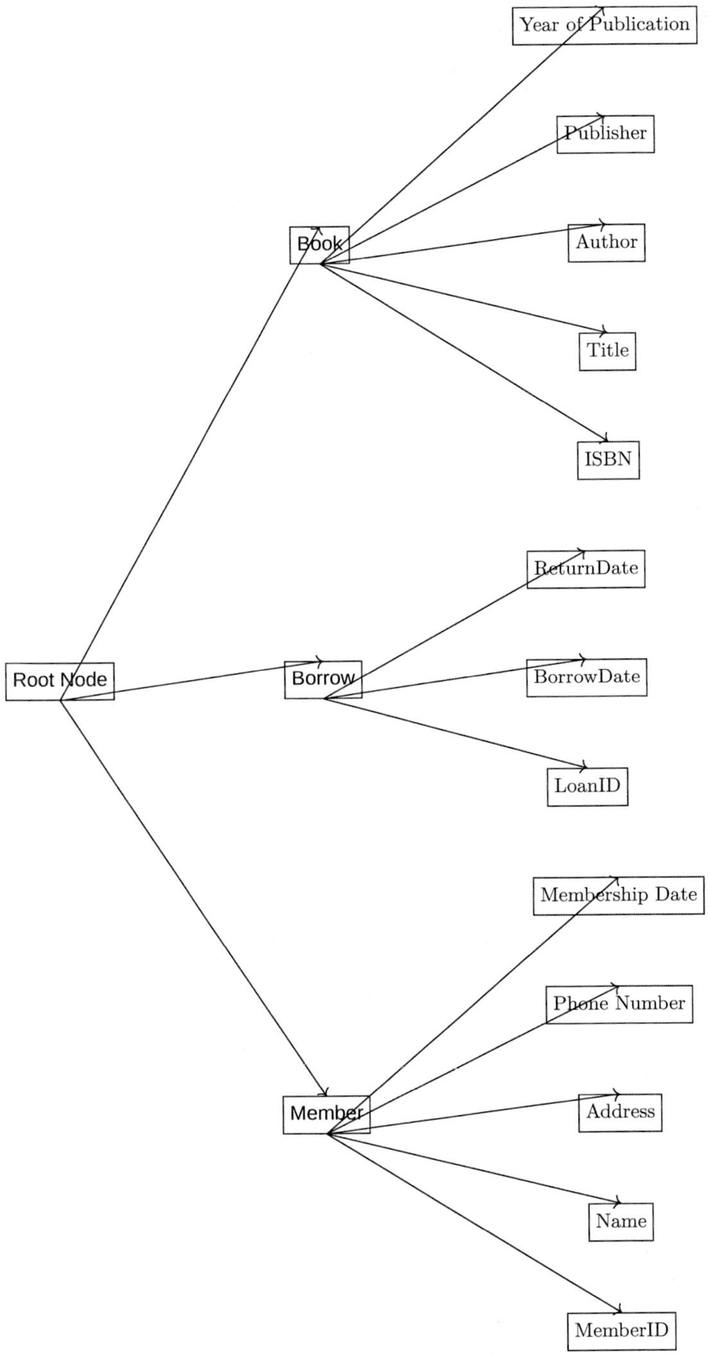
Year of Publication
Publisher
Book
Author
Title
ISBN
ReturnDate
Root Node
Borrow
BorrowDate
LoanID
Membership Date
Phone Number
Member
Address
Name
MemberID

This ER diagram portrays:

- Entities (*Member*, *Book*, *Loan*)
- Attributes (listed within entity nodes)
- Relationships (*Borrow* linking *Member* and *Book* through *Loan*)

Each entity interacts with another via a defined relationship, showcasing the underlying database structure.

To encapsulate data integrity and optimization, entities and relationships should be refined iteratively. Ensure attribute specificity and relevance, accurately define relationships, and apply cardinality constraints effectively to create a robust and efficient database schema. These foundational elements are critical for progressing towards subsequent steps in database normalization and implementation.

4.5 Primary Keys and Foreign Keys

In relational database design, the concepts of primary keys and foreign keys are fundamental. These keys play a critical role in ensuring the integrity and consistency of the data within the database. We explore the definitions, characteristics, and practical applications of these keys.

A **primary key** is a unique identifier for a record in a table. It ensures that each record can be uniquely identified, preventing duplicate records within the table. A primary key must satisfy the following properties:

- **Uniqueness:** Each value of the primary key must be unique across all records in the table.
- **Non-nullability:** A primary key column cannot contain NULL values.
- **Immutability:** Ideally, the value of a primary key should not change over the lifetime of a record.

A primary key can consist of a single column or a combination of multiple columns. When combining multiple columns to form a primary key, it is referred to as a **composite key**. Consider the following SQL syntax for creating a table with a primary key:

```
CREATE TABLE Employees (
    EmployeeID INT PRIMARY KEY,
    LastName VARCHAR(50),
    FirstName VARCHAR(50),
    DateOfBirth DATE
);
```

In the above example, EmployeeID is the primary key for the Employees table, ensuring that each employee has a unique identifier.

A **foreign key** is a field (or a collection of fields) in one table that uniquely identifies a row of another table. The foreign key is defined in a child table, and it references the primary key or a unique key of the parent table. Foreign keys establish and enforce a link between the data in the two tables, providing referential integrity.

A foreign key must satisfy the following properties:

- **Referential Integrity:** Foreign key values must either match primary key values in the referenced table or be NULL.
- **Consistency:** Operations on primary keys (such as updates or deletions) should maintain referential integrity, often managed via cascading actions.

Consider this SQL syntax for creating a table with a foreign key:

```
CREATE TABLE Orders (
    OrderID INT PRIMARY KEY,
    OrderDate DATE,
    CustomerID INT,
    FOREIGN KEY (CustomerID) REFERENCES Customers(CustomerID)
);
```

In this example, the CustomerID field in the Orders table is a foreign key that references the CustomerID primary key in the Customers table.

Let's dive deeper into the functional and structural roles these keys play in database operations:

- **Data Integrity:**
  - Primary keys ensure that each record within a table is unique and identifiable, which is essential for operations like updates and deletions.
  - Foreign keys guarantee that the link between related tables remains consistent, ensuring that an order cannot reference a non-existent customer.

- **Relationship Management:**
  - By establishing foreign keys, we can create complex relationships among tables. Common relationships include one-to-many, many-to-one, and many-to-many.
- **Query Optimization:**
  - Indexed primary keys can significantly speed up query performance. Most databases automatically create an index on primary keys for quick lookups.
  - Foreign key constraints can help the database engine optimize the execution plans for JOIN operations between related tables.
- **Cascading Actions:**
  - Foreign keys can define cascading actions (such as ON DELETE CASCADE), which enforce referential actions to maintain data consistency when a referenced row is deleted or updated.

Here's an example to illustrate these points. Suppose we have two tables: Departments and Employees. The Employees table contains a DepartmentID which is a foreign key referencing the DepartmentID of the Departments table:

```
CREATE TABLE Departments (
    DepartmentID INT PRIMARY KEY,
    DepartmentName VARCHAR(50)
);

CREATE TABLE Employees (
    EmployeeID INT PRIMARY KEY,
    LastName VARCHAR(50),
    FirstName VARCHAR(50),
    DepartmentID INT,
    FOREIGN KEY (DepartmentID) REFERENCES Departments(DepartmentID)
        ON DELETE CASCADE
        ON UPDATE CASCADE
);
```

In this scenario:

- DepartmentID in the Departments table ensures each department is uniquely identifiable.
- DepartmentID in the Employees table maintains referential integrity, ensuring that employees are associated with a valid department.

- The cascading actions ensure that if a department is deleted or its ID is updated, the referenced records in the Employees table are correspondingly deleted or updated, preserving data integrity.

Effective use of primary and foreign keys is essential for designing robust, efficient, and scalable relational databases, ensuring data reliability and facilitating operations across interrelated data entities.

4.6 First Normal Form (1NF)

First Normal Form (1NF) is the foundation of database normalization. Achieving 1NF requires that the table adheres to the following criteria: the table must contain only atomic (indivisible) values, each column must contain values of a single type, and each entry must have a unique identifier, which is typically the primary key.

Atomicity of Values

Atomic values are indivisible, meaning that each column in a table should contain the smallest possible unit of data. Consider the following table, StudentCourses, which does not comply with 1NF:

```
| StudentID | StudentName | Courses |
|-----------|-------------|---------------|
| 1 | John Doe | Math, Science |
| 2 | Jane Smith | English, Arts |
```

The column Courses contains multiple values per row, which violates the atomicity requirement. To correct this, we need to ensure that each column has only one value per row. The normalized version of the table would look like this:

```
| StudentID | StudentName | Course |
|-----------|-------------|----------|
| 1 | John Doe | Math |
| 1 | John Doe | Science |
| 2 | Jane Smith | English |
| 2 | Jane Smith | Arts |
```

Each row now contains a single, indivisible value in the Course column.

Single Type Columns

Each column must contain values of a single data type to ensure consistency and avoid anomalies. Consider the faulty table:

```
| ProductID | ProductInfo |
|-----------|---------------------|
```

```
| 101 | {name: "Pencil", price: 1.00} |
| 102 | {name: "Notebook", price: 2.50} |
```

The ProductInfo column contains a composite value, mixing names and prices. To comply with 1NF, this information must be separated into distinct columns:

```
| ProductID | ProductName | Price |
|-----------|-------------|-------|
| 101 | Pencil | 1.00 |
| 102 | Notebook | 2.50 |
```

Each column is now restricted to a single type: ProductName holds string values, and Price holds numerical values.

Unique Identification of Rows

Ensuring that each row can be uniquely identified requires the presence of a primary key. Without a primary key, it becomes difficult to distinguish between identical rows. In the following table, introducing a primary key resolves this issue:

```
| OrderID | CustomerName | OrderDate |
|----------|--------------|-----------|
| 1 | Alice Brown | 2023-01-22|
| 2 | Bob Green | 2023-02-13|
| 1 | Alice Brown | 2023-01-22|
```

The OrderID column serves as the primary key, ensuring unique identification for each row. If duplicates exist, further steps like introducing composite keys or adding unique constraints might be necessary.

Example of Fixing a Non-1NF Table

Consider the following non-1NF table:

```
| TransactionID | CustomerName | Purchases |
|---------------|--------------|-----------------|
| 001 | Sarah Black | Book, Pen |
| 002 | Jim White | Laptop, Mouse |
```

The Purchases column contains non-atomic values. To normalize this table into 1NF:

```
| TransactionID | CustomerName | Purchase |
|---------------|--------------|----------|
| 001 | Sarah Black | Book |
| 001 | Sarah Black | Pen |
| 002 | Jim White | Laptop |
| 002 | Jim White | Mouse |
```

Now, the Purchases column contains atomic values, adhering to the principles of 1NF.

By ensuring atomicity, single data types in columns, and unique row identification through primary keys, the table is normalized to First Normal Form. This foundational step lays the groundwork for higher levels of normalization, promoting data integrity and avoiding redundancy.

4.7 Second Normal Form (2NF)

For a table to be in the Second Normal Form (2NF), it must first satisfy all the requirements of the First Normal Form (1NF). This means that the table must have a primary key, and all the entries in the table must be atomic. Once 1NF is guaranteed, a table can be evaluated for 2NF, which primarily addresses the concept of eliminating partial dependency.

A partial dependency in the context of database normalization occurs when a non-key attribute is functionally dependent on a part of a composite primary key rather than the whole composite key. To eliminate partial dependencies, every non-prime attribute (an attribute that is not part of any candidate key) should be fully dependent on the entire primary key.

Consider a table with the following schema representing students enrolled in courses:

```
CREATE TABLE Enrollments (
    student_id INT,
    course_code VARCHAR(10),
    student_name VARCHAR(100),
    course_name VARCHAR(100),
    PRIMARY KEY (student_id, course_code)
);
```

In this example, student_id and course_code together form the composite primary key. To determine if this table is in 2NF, we inspect the dependencies of the non-prime attributes:

1. student_name depends only on student_id. 2. course_name depends only on course_code.

Since both student_name and course_name depend on parts of the composite key rather than the whole key, the current table structure has partial dependencies and thus is not in 2NF.

To bring the table into 2NF, we can decompose it into two separate tables, eliminating the partial dependencies. Here is a suitable decomposition:

Enrollments(student_id, course_code)
Students(student_id, student_name)
Courses(course_code, course_name)

For the SQL implementation:

```
CREATE TABLE Enrollments (
    student_id INT,
    course_code VARCHAR(10),
    PRIMARY KEY (student_id, course_code)
);

CREATE TABLE Students (
    student_id INT PRIMARY KEY,
    student_name VARCHAR(100)
);

CREATE TABLE Courses (
    course_code VARCHAR(10) PRIMARY KEY,
    course_name VARCHAR(100)
);
```

This decomposition ensures that all non-prime attributes are fully functionally dependent on the entirety of the candidate key. In the Enrollments table, the composite key remains: student_idcourse_code. The Students table has student_id as the primary key, and student_name depends solely on the entire primary key. Similarly, course_code is the primary key for the Courses table, and course_name depends solely on this key.

Upon successful decomposition into 2NF, the elimination of partial dependencies not only fosters data integrity and reduces redundancy but also simplifies the maintenance process. Updates, deletions, and insertions are now isolated to specific tables, mitigating anomalies.

Revisiting the data stored in this newly structured database:

```
-- Populating the Students table
INSERT INTO Students (student_id, student_name) VALUES
(1, 'Alice'),
(2, 'Bob');

-- Populating the Courses table
INSERT INTO Courses (course_code, course_name) VALUES
('CS101', 'Introduction to Computer Science'),
('MA101', 'Calculus I');

-- Populating the Enrollments table
INSERT INTO Enrollments (student_id, course_code) VALUES
(1, 'CS101'),
(2, 'MA101');
```

The separation ensures atomic transactions within their respective tables, contributing to the overall efficiency and scalability of database operations. Each table focuses on a particular aspect of the data, promoting better insights and facilitating complex querying without redundant or inconsistent data.

Additionally, optimizing data manipulation through this normalization fosters effective indexing, enhancing query performance. Well-defined relationships between tables using foreign keys optimize join operations and minimize unnecessary data duplication.

Elevating the database design to 2NF is a critical milestone towards a fully normalized database, ensuring that entities are correctly and efficiently structured. The abstraction and modularity introduced at this stage lay the groundwork for further normalization processes, guiding towards Third Normal Form (3NF) and beyond.

4.8 Third Normal Form (3NF)

The Third Normal Form (3NF) builds upon the foundation laid by the Second Normal Form (2NF). To recall, a relation is in 2NF if it is in the First Normal Form (1NF) and all non-key attributes are fully functionally dependent on the primary key. However, 2NF does not solve the problem of transitive dependencies, where non-key attributes depend on other non-key attributes rather than directly on the primary key.

A relation is in 3NF if it satisfies two conditions:

- It is in 2NF.
- There are no transitive dependencies. In other words, for any non-trivial functional dependency $X \to Y$, either X is a superkey, or Y is a prime attribute (i.e., it appears in a candidate key).

To better understand this, consider a table containing the following attributes: student ID, student name, course ID, and course instructor. If the course instructor is functionally dependent on the course ID, and the course ID is functionally dependent on the student ID, then a transitive dependency exists (student ID $\to$ course ID $\to$ course instructor). To achieve 3NF, these dependencies need to be eliminated through decomposition.

Example:

Consider the following relation:

StudentID	CourseID	InstructorName
S1	C1	Prof. Miller
S2	C2	Prof. Clark
S3	C1	Prof. Miller
S4	C3	Prof. Davis

In this table, the attribute InstructorName depends on the CourseID, which in turn depends on StudentID. The transitive dependency means changing the InstructorName for a specific course will lead to inconsistent data if not all rows are updated correctly.

To transition this table into 3NF, it is necessary to decompose it into two separate tables:

StudentID	CourseID
S1	C1
S2	C2
S3	C1
S4	C3

CourseID	InstructorName
C1	Prof. Miller
C2	Prof. Clark
C3	Prof. Davis

The decomposition eliminates the transitive dependency, as InstructorName is now directly associated with CourseID rather than StudentID. This normalization ensures that the database schema adheres to the 3NF, resulting in reduced redundancy and minimized update anomalies.

Transitional Example Using SQL:

To solidify understanding, consider the steps to decompose the given table into two 3NF compliant tables using SQL:

First, create the original table:

```
CREATE TABLE StudentCourses (
    StudentID CHAR(10) NOT NULL,
    CourseID CHAR(10) NOT NULL,
    InstructorName VARCHAR(50),
    PRIMARY KEY (StudentID, CourseID)
);
```

Insert sample data:

```
INSERT INTO StudentCourses (StudentID, CourseID, InstructorName) VALUES
('S1', 'C1', 'Prof. Miller'),
('S2', 'C2', 'Prof. Clark'),
('S3', 'C1', 'Prof. Miller'),
('S4', 'C3', 'Prof. Davis');
```

Now, decompose the table into two separate tables:

```
CREATE TABLE CourseInstructors (
    CourseID CHAR(10) PRIMARY KEY,
    InstructorName VARCHAR(50)
);

CREATE TABLE StudentEnrollments (
    StudentID CHAR(10) NOT NULL,
    CourseID CHAR(10) NOT NULL,
    PRIMARY KEY (StudentID, CourseID),
    FOREIGN KEY (CourseID) REFERENCES CourseInstructors(CourseID)
);
```

Move the data into the new tables:

```
INSERT INTO CourseInstructors (CourseID, InstructorName) VALUES
('C1', 'Prof. Miller'),
('C2', 'Prof. Clark'),
('C3', 'Prof. Davis');

INSERT INTO StudentEnrollments (StudentID, CourseID) VALUES
('S1', 'C1'),
('S2', 'C2'),
('S3', 'C1'),
('S4', 'C3');
```

The execution of these SQL commands results in the following contents for each table:

```
StudentEnrollments table:
+-----------+----------+
| StudentID | CourseID |
+-----------+----------+
| S1        | C1       |
| S2        | C2       |
| S3        | C1       |
| S4        | C3       |
+-----------+----------+

CourseInstructors table:
+----------+----------------+
| CourseID | InstructorName |
+----------+----------------+
| C1       | Prof. Miller   |
| C2       | Prof. Clark    |
| C3       | Prof. Davis    |
+----------+----------------+
```

The resulting tables conform to the requirements of 3NF. The CourseInstructors table encapsulates the CourseID and InstructorName, ensuring direct dependency between these two attributes. The StudentEnrollments table maintains the relationship between StudentID and CourseID, with CourseID serving as a foreign key referencing the CourseInstructors table. This restructuring removes redundant data and isolates dependencies efficiently, thus maintaining data integrity and facilitating smoother data manipulation and querying.

4.9 Boyce-Codd Normal Form (BCNF)

Boyce-Codd Normal Form (BCNF) is a refinement of the Third Normal Form (3NF). A relation is in BCNF if it is in 3NF and every determinant is a candidate key. Here, a determinant is an attribute – or a set of attributes – on which some other attribute is fully functionally dependent. This normalization form addresses the anomalies that 3NF does not resolve, particularly those arising from functional dependencies that involve overlapping candidate keys.

To illustrate BCNF, consider the concept of candidate keys. In any given relation, a candidate key is a minimal superkey, meaning it is a minimal set of attributes that can uniquely identify a tuple in that relation. The critical requirement of BCNF is that every determinant must be a candidate key. If any non-candidate key attribute can determine another attribute, then the table cannot be in BCNF.

Consider the following example relation:

```
CREATE TABLE ExampleRelation (
    A INT,
    B INT,
    C INT,
    PRIMARY KEY (A)
);
```

Assume the functional dependencies for this relation are as follows: 1. $A \rightarrow B$ 2. $B \rightarrow C$

Since $A \rightarrow B$ makes A a potential candidate key, we need to examine whether B is a candidate key. Here, $B \rightarrow C$ indicates that B can determine C. As B is not a candidate key yet determines another attribute, this relation does not satisfy the BCNF condition.

To normalize this relation into BCNF, we can decompose it into two relations where all determinants are candidate keys:

```
CREATE TABLE ExampleRelation1 (
    A INT,
    B INT,
    PRIMARY KEY (A)
```

```
);

CREATE TABLE ExampleRelation2 (
    B INT,
    C INT,
    PRIMARY KEY (B),
    FOREIGN KEY (B) REFERENCES ExampleRelation1(B)
);
```

In the above tables, A uniquely decides B, and B uniquely decides C. Both tables now satisfy the BCNF criteria because each determinant is a candidate key.

The importance of BCNF is emphasized in its ability to handle certain types of redundancy not addressed by 3NF. For instance, consider the following relation:

```
CREATE TABLE StudentCourse (
    StudentID INT,
    CourseID INT,
    InstructorID INT,
    PRIMARY KEY (StudentID, CourseID)
);
```

If the functional dependencies are: 1. $(StudentID, CourseID) \rightarrow InstructorID$ 2. $InstructorID \rightarrow CourseID$

The composite key $(StudentID, CourseID)$ serves as the primary key but $InstructorID \rightarrow CourseID$ reveals a dependency that $InstructorID$ should determine $CourseID$. Thus, without decomposing, some redundancy is inevitable, leading to potential anomalies. To adhere to BCNF, one must decompose the relation as follows:

```
CREATE TABLE StudentInstructor (
    StudentID INT,
    InstructorID INT,
    PRIMARY KEY (StudentID, InstructorID)
);

CREATE TABLE InstructorCourse (
    InstructorID INT,
    CourseID INT,
    PRIMARY KEY (InstructorID, CourseID)
);
```

This decomposition ensures that each table conforms to BCNF as $InstructorID \rightarrow CourseID$ is eliminated by separating out the dependencies correctly.

To operationalize the concepts of BCNF in practice, it is essential to:

- Identify all candidate keys of the relation.
- Determine all functional dependencies within the relation.
- Ensure that each functional dependency's left-hand side is a candidate key.
- Decompose the relation appropriately if any functional dependency violates the BCNF condition.

Normalization to BCNF is crucial in database design to ensure the elimination of redundancies and to mitigate update, insertion, and deletion anomalies. Subsequent stages in the chapter will build upon these principles to explore denormalization strategies and performance considerations, balancing theoretical purity with practical efficiency in real-world applications.

4.10 Denormalization and Performance Considerations

Denormalization is the process of introducing redundancy into a database to improve read performance. It involves deliberately violating normalization rules to optimize query responses at the expense of increased storage and potential anomalies during data modification operations. Denormalization can be employed selectively to address performance bottlenecks identified through comprehensive analysis of database workload and query patterns.

Advantages of Denormalization

1. *Improved Query Performance:* One of the primary motivations for denormalization is to enhance query performance. By reducing the number of joins needed to retrieve data from multiple tables, denormalization can expedite data retrieval operations. This is particularly beneficial for read-heavy applications where fast access to data is a priority.

2. *Simplified Query Logic:* Denormalized structures often lead to simpler and more straightforward query designs. This simplification can make both the writing and debugging of queries easier, which is advantageous for developers and database administrators.

3. *Reduced I/O Operations:* Fewer joins and simpler queries typically result in reduced disk I/O operations, which can significantly lower

query response times. This reduction in I/O is especially important for large databases where disk access times can be a limiting factor in performance.

Disadvantages of Denormalization

1. *Increased Storage Requirements:* Denormalized databases require more storage space due to the redundancy introduced. The extent of this increase depends on the amount of denormalization and the volume of data being stored.

2. *Data Anomalies:* Redundancy can lead to data anomalies, including update, insert, and delete anomalies. Maintaining data consistency becomes more challenging as the same data may exist in multiple locations and updating it in one place requires corresponding updates elsewhere.

3. *Increased Complexity of Data Modification:* While read operations may be faster, data modification operations (insert, update, delete) can become more complex due to the need to ensure consistency across redundant data representations.

Practical Considerations for Denormalization

When considering denormalization, it is crucial to identify specific use cases and query patterns that would benefit most from this approach. The process typically involves analyzing slow queries, identifying their bottlenecks, and assessing whether denormalization would alleviate these issues.

Consider a database designed to support a high-traffic e-commerce application where the primary performance concerns revolve around the speed of retrieving product details and processing user transactions. Suppose the current normalized design involves multiple joins across tables such as Products, Categories, Users, and Transactions. The join operations, particularly for complex analytical queries or reporting, may lead to performance degradation.

Denormalization may involve the following specific actions:

- **Aggregating Frequently Accessed Data**: For instance, creating a summary table to store aggregated sales data to improve the performance of sales reports.
- **Precomputing Joins**: Combining tables that are frequently joined, such as merging Products and Categories into a single table that can be quickly queried by both product and category

attributes.

- **Introducing Redundant Columns**: Adding columns like CategoryName directly into the Products table to eliminate the need for joins when filtering products by category name.

An example demonstrating denormalization can be illustrated with SQL commands:

```
-- Original normalized structure
CREATE TABLE Products (
    ProductID INT PRIMARY KEY,
    ProductName VARCHAR(255),
    CategoryID INT,
    Price DECIMAL(10, 2),
    FOREIGN KEY (CategoryID) REFERENCES Categories(CategoryID)
);

CREATE TABLE Categories (
    CategoryID INT PRIMARY KEY,
    CategoryName VARCHAR(255)
);

-- Example query to retrieve product and category name
SELECT p.ProductName, c.CategoryName, p.Price
FROM Products p
JOIN Categories c ON p.CategoryID = c.CategoryID;

-- Denormalized structure
CREATE TABLE Products_Denormalized (
    ProductID INT PRIMARY KEY,
    ProductName VARCHAR(255),
    CategoryID INT,
    CategoryName VARCHAR(255),
    Price DECIMAL(10, 2)
);

-- Populating the denormalized table
INSERT INTO Products_Denormalized (ProductID, ProductName, CategoryID,
    CategoryName, Price)
SELECT p.ProductID, p.ProductName, p.CategoryID, c.CategoryName, p.Price
FROM Products p
JOIN Categories c ON p.CategoryID = c.CategoryID;

-- Query against denormalized table
SELECT ProductName, CategoryName, Price
FROM Products_Denormalized;
```

This example highlights how denormalization simplifies query logic and reduces the computational cost associated with joins. However, it also introduces potential complexities in maintaining data consistency. For instance, whenever a category name changes in the Categories table, the corresponding entries in the Products_Denormalized table must also be updated to reflect this change.

Implementing denormalization should always be accompanied by measures to handle data consistency. Techniques such as triggers, stored procedures, or application-level logic can be employed to ensure that redundant data remains synchronized.

Balancing Normalization and Denormalization

The decision to denormalize should not be taken lightly but rather as a calculated trade-off based on a detailed understanding of the application's performance requirements and data access patterns. Performance testing, monitoring, and profiling are essential activities to empirically assess the impact of denormalization on database operations. By striking an appropriate balance between normalization and denormalization, it is possible to achieve a design that provides both performance efficiency and data integrity.

4.11 Designing for Scalability

Scalability is a critical aspect of modern database design, ensuring that a database can handle increasing loads and expand in capacity as demands grow. This section provides a comprehensive exploration of strategies and principles for designing databases capable of scaling efficiently and effectively.

Scalability is typically categorized into vertical and horizontal types. Vertical scalability, or scaling up, involves enhancing the capacity of existing hardware or adding resources such as CPU, memory, or storage. Horizontal scalability, or scaling out, entails distributing the database load across multiple servers or instances.

Database designers must consider both types of scalability to ensure optimal performance and resource utilization.

Indexing: Proper indexing is a fundamental strategy in achieving scalable database performance. Indexes enable faster retrieval of records by creating a data structure that allows quick searching, sorting, and filtering. Choosing the right columns for indexing is crucial. Frequently queried columns, primary keys, and foreign keys are typical candidates for indexing. Consider the following SQL command to create an index:

```
CREATE INDEX idx_customer_name ON customers (last_name, first_name);
```

This command creates an index on the last_name and first_name columns of the customers table, optimizing query operations involving these columns.

Partitioning: Partitioning divides a large table into smaller, more manageable pieces, distributing the workload and improving query performance. Common partitioning strategies include range partitioning, list partitioning, hash partitioning, and composite partitioning. Range partitioning involves dividing data based on a range of values, such as dates. The following SQL command demonstrates range partitioning:

```
CREATE TABLE orders (
    order_id INT,
    order_date DATE,
    customer_id INT,
    ...
) PARTITION BY RANGE (order_date) (
    PARTITION p0 VALUES LESS THAN (TO_DATE('2022-01-01', 'YYYY-MM-DD'
        )),
    PARTITION p1 VALUES LESS THAN (TO_DATE('2023-01-01', 'YYYY-MM-DD'
        ))
);
```

This command partitions the orders table based on the order_date column, with each partition containing orders within specific date ranges.

Replication: Replication involves copying and maintaining database objects across multiple database servers. It enhances availability, load balancing, and fault tolerance. Synchronous replication ensures that all copies are immediately consistent, while asynchronous replication allows a slight delay between copies. Below is an example of setting up replication using PostgreSQL:

```
# On the primary server:
wal_level = replica
max_wal_senders = 3
wal_keep_segments = 64

# On the replica server:
standby_mode = 'on'
primary_conninfo = 'host=primary_server_address port=5432 user=replication
    password=yourpassword'
restore_command = 'cp /var/lib/postgresql/wal_archive/%f %p'
```

This configuration outlines the primary and replica server settings necessary for replication in PostgreSQL.

Sharding: Sharding is a specific form of horizontal partitioning where data is distributed across multiple database instances. Each instance, or shard, contains a subset of the data, often determined by a shard key. For example, user data can be sharded based on geographical regions to enhance localized query performance. Below is a conceptual approach to sharding:

```
User data:
- Shard 1: Users in North America
```

```
- Shard 2: Users in Europe
- Shard 3: Users in Asia

Shard key: region
```

Caching: Caching stores frequently accessed data in memory for quicker access, reducing the load on the database. Common caching strategies include in-memory databases (e.g., Redis, Memcached) and caching layers integrated into application servers. Implementing an effective caching mechanism can significantly enhance performance, especially for read-heavy applications.

In Python, caching with Redis can be demonstrated as follows:

```
import redis

r = redis.Redis(host='localhost', port=6379, db=0)

# Set a value in cache
r.set('user:1000', 'John Doe')

# Get a value from cache
user = r.get('user:1000')
print(user)
```

```
b'John Doe'
```

Load Balancing: Load balancing distributes incoming database requests across multiple servers to prevent any single server from being overwhelmed. Techniques include using round-robin DNS, proxy servers, or dedicated hardware load balancers. Ensuring effective load balancing mitigates bottlenecks and enhances overall system reliability.

Optimization and Monitoring: Continuous monitoring and optimization are integral to maintaining scalability. Identifying performance bottlenecks, analyzing query execution plans, and refining inefficient queries are essential activities. Tools such as EXPLAIN in SQL can provide insights into query performance:

```
EXPLAIN SELECT * FROM customers WHERE last_name = 'Smith';
```

This command displays the execution plan for the specified query, highlighting potential areas for optimization.

Asynchronous Processing: Offloading resource-intensive tasks to background processes can liberate system resources and enhance responsiveness. Tasks such as report generation, batch processing, and data transformations can be executed asynchronously using job schedulers or message queues (e.g., RabbitMQ, Apache Kafka).

By leveraging these principles and strategies, designing databases for scalability becomes a systematic approach to ensuring performance, reliability, and capacity to accommodate future growth.

4.12 Case Studies in Database Design

In this section, we explore practical applications of the principles and techniques discussed in the preceding chapters through detailed case studies. These examples are drawn from real-world scenarios to illustrate various aspects of database design, normalization, and performance considerations.

Case Study 1: Library Management System

- **Scenario:** A library system needs a database to manage books, members, borrowing activities, and staff.
- **Entities and Relationships:**
  - **Entities:**
    - Book: Attributes include BookID (Primary Key), Title, AuthorID, and PublisherID.
    - Member: Attributes include MemberID (Primary Key), Name, and ContactInfo.
    - Borrow: Attributes include BorrowID (Primary Key), BookID (Foreign Key), MemberID (Foreign Key), and BorrowDate.
    - Staff: Attributes include StaffID (Primary Key), Name, and Role.
    - Author: Attributes include AuthorID (Primary Key), Name.
    - Publisher: Attributes include PublisherID (Primary Key), Name.
  - **Relationships:**
    - Book to Author: One-to-Many (One author can write multiple books)
    - Book to Publisher: One-to-Many (One publisher can publish multiple books)
    - Member to Borrow: One-to-Many (One member can borrow multiple books)

* Book to Borrow: One-to-Many (One book can be borrowed multiple times but only once at a time)

- **Normalization Process:**

  1NF: Ensure each table has a primary key and atomic attributes.
  2NF: Remove partial dependencies.
  3NF: Remove transitive dependencies.
  BCNF: Ensure that every determinant is a candidate key.

```
CREATE TABLE Author (
    AuthorID INT PRIMARY KEY,
    Name VARCHAR(100)
);

CREATE TABLE Publisher (
    PublisherID INT PRIMARY KEY,
    Name VARCHAR(100)
);

CREATE TABLE Book (
    BookID INT PRIMARY KEY,
    Title VARCHAR(100),
    AuthorID INT,
    PublisherID INT,
    FOREIGN KEY (AuthorID) REFERENCES Author(AuthorID),
    FOREIGN KEY (PublisherID) REFERENCES Publisher(PublisherID)
);

CREATE TABLE Member (
    MemberID INT PRIMARY KEY,
    Name VARCHAR(100),
    ContactInfo VARCHAR(100)
);

CREATE TABLE Borrow (
    BorrowID INT PRIMARY KEY,
    BookID INT,
    MemberID INT,
    BorrowDate DATE,
    FOREIGN KEY (BookID) REFERENCES Book(BookID),
    FOREIGN KEY (MemberID) REFERENCES Member(MemberID)
);

CREATE TABLE Staff (
    StaffID INT PRIMARY KEY,
    Name VARCHAR(100),
    Role VARCHAR(50)
);
```

Case Study 2: E-commerce Platform

- **Scenario:** An e-commerce platform needs a robust database to manage products, customers, orders, and inventory.
- **Entities and Relationships:**
  - **Entities:**

    * Product: Attributes include ProductID (Primary Key), Name, Description, and Price.
    * Customer: Attributes include CustomerID (Primary Key), Name, and Email.
    * Order: Attributes include OrderID (Primary Key), CustomerID (Foreign Key), and OrderDate.
    * OrderDetail: Attributes include OrderDetailID (Primary Key), OrderID (Foreign Key), ProductID (Foreign Key), and Quantity.
    * Inventory: Attributes include InventoryID (Primary Key), ProductID (Foreign Key), and StockLevel.

  - **Relationships:**
    * Product to OrderDetail: One-to-Many (One product can appear in multiple order details)
    * Customer to Order: One-to-Many (One customer can place multiple orders)
    * Order to OrderDetail: One-to-Many (One order can have multiple order details)
    * Product to Inventory: One-to-One (One product is tracked in one inventory record)

- **Normalization Process:**

  1NF: Ensure each table has a primary key and atomic attributes.
  2NF: Remove partial dependencies.
  3NF: Remove transitive dependencies.
  BCNF: Ensure that every determinant is a candidate key.

```
CREATE TABLE Product (
    ProductID INT PRIMARY KEY,
    Name VARCHAR(100),
    Description TEXT,
    Price DECIMAL
);

CREATE TABLE Customer (
    CustomerID INT PRIMARY KEY,
    Name VARCHAR(100),
    Email VARCHAR(100)
);

CREATE TABLE Order (
    OrderID INT PRIMARY KEY,
    CustomerID INT,
    OrderDate DATE,
    FOREIGN KEY (CustomerID) REFERENCES Customer(CustomerID)
);

CREATE TABLE OrderDetail (
    OrderDetailID INT PRIMARY KEY,
    OrderID INT,
```

```
    ProductID INT,
    Quantity INT,
    FOREIGN KEY (OrderID) REFERENCES Order(OrderID),
    FOREIGN KEY (ProductID) REFERENCES Product(ProductID)
);

CREATE TABLE Inventory (
    InventoryID INT PRIMARY KEY,
    ProductID INT,
    StockLevel INT,
    FOREIGN KEY (ProductID) REFERENCES Product(ProductID)
);
```

Case Study 3: University Enrollment System

- **Scenario:** The university requires a database to keep track of students, courses, enrollment, and faculty.
- **Entities and Relationships:**
  - **Entities:**
    * Student: Attributes include StudentID (Primary Key), Name, and Major.
    * Course: Attributes include CourseID (Primary Key), Title, and Credits.
    * Enrollment: Attributes include EnrollmentID (Primary Key), StudentID (Foreign Key), CourseID (Foreign Key), and EnrollmentDate.
    * Faculty: Attributes include FacultyID (Primary Key), Name, and Department.
  - **Relationships:**
    * Course to Enrollment: One-to-Many (One course can have multiple enrollments)
    * Student to Enrollment: One-to-Many (One student can enroll in multiple courses)
- **Normalization Process:**

  1NF: Ensure each table has a primary key and atomic attributes.
  2NF: Remove partial dependencies.
  3NF: Remove transitive dependencies.
  BCNF: Ensure that every determinant is a candidate key.

```
CREATE TABLE Student (
    StudentID INT PRIMARY KEY,
    Name VARCHAR(100),
    Major VARCHAR(100)
);
```

```
CREATE TABLE Course (
    CourseID INT PRIMARY KEY,
    Title VARCHAR(100),
    Credits INT
);

CREATE TABLE Enrollment (
    EnrollmentID INT PRIMARY KEY,
    StudentID INT,
    CourseID INT,
    EnrollmentDate DATE,
    FOREIGN KEY (StudentID) REFERENCES Student(StudentID),
    FOREIGN KEY (CourseID) REFERENCES Course(CourseID)
);

CREATE TABLE Faculty (
    FacultyID INT PRIMARY KEY,
    Name VARCHAR(100),
    Department VARCHAR(100)
);
```

These case studies demonstrate the application of database design principles to create efficient, normalized databases capable of supporting various types of applications. The provided SQL scripts illustrate the structure and constraints required to maintain data integrity and optimize performance.

Chapter 5

Working with Multiple Tables: Joins and Subqueries

This chapter examines techniques for working with multiple tables, focusing on various types of joins, including INNER, LEFT, RIGHT, FULL OUTER, CROSS, and self joins. It offers an introduction to subqueries and their applications within SELECT statements as well as WHERE and HAVING clauses. The chapter also addresses correlated subqueries and provides insights into performance considerations when using joins and subqueries.

5.1 Introduction to Joins

When working with relational databases, a fundamental operation is the ability to combine records from two or more tables based on related columns. This operation is known as a **join**. In SQL (Structured Query Language), joins are used to retrieve data from multiple tables and are essential for performing complex queries that mirror real-world data relationships.

To comprehend joins, it is important to first understand the concept of table relationships. In a well-designed relational database, tables are often related through foreign keys. A foreign key is a column (or a group of columns) in one table that uniquely identifies a row in another table. This relational structure allows us to perform joins by matching the foreign key(s) in one table with the primary key(s) in another.

There are several types of joins in SQL, each serving a different purpose depending on the desired outcome. The primary types of joins are:

- **INNER JOIN**: Retrieves records that have matching values in both tables.
- **LEFT JOIN** (or LEFT OUTER JOIN): Retrieves all records from the left table and the matched records from the right table. If there is no match, the result is NULL on the side of the right table.
- **RIGHT JOIN** (or RIGHT OUTER JOIN): Retrieves all records from the right table and the matched records from the left table. If there is no match, the result is NULL on the side of the left table.
- **FULL OUTER JOIN**: Retrieves records when there is a match in either left or right table. Records with no match in one of the tables will contain NULL values for columns from that table.
- **CROSS JOIN**: Returns the Cartesian product of the two tables. Every row in the first table is combined with every row in the second table.
- **SELF JOIN**: A join where a table is joined with itself.

To illustrate the use of joins, let us consider two tables: Employees and Departments. The Employees table may contain the following columns: EmployeeID, FirstName, LastName, DepartmentID, and HireDate. The Departments table may include DepartmentID and DepartmentName. The DepartmentID column in the Employees table is a foreign key that references the DepartmentID column in the Departments table.

```
CREATE TABLE Employees (
    EmployeeID INT PRIMARY KEY,
    FirstName VARCHAR(50),
    LastName VARCHAR(50),
    DepartmentID INT,
    HireDate DATE,
    FOREIGN KEY (DepartmentID) REFERENCES Departments(DepartmentID)
);

CREATE TABLE Departments (
    DepartmentID INT PRIMARY KEY,
    DepartmentName VARCHAR(50)
);
```

An **INNER JOIN** can be used to retrieve the list of employees along with their department names:

```
SELECT Employees.EmployeeID, Employees.FirstName, Employees.LastName,
       Departments.DepartmentName
FROM Employees
INNER JOIN Departments
ON Employees.DepartmentID = Departments.DepartmentID;
```

In this query, we are selecting columns from both Employees and Departments tables. The ON clause specifies the condition for the join, which in this case is the matching DepartmentID in both tables. The result will include only those employees who have a corresponding department in the Departments table.

For illustrative purposes, consider the following example data in the tables:

```
Employees:
-------------
EmployeeID | FirstName | LastName | DepartmentID | HireDate
1          | John      | Doe      | 1            | 2020-01-15
2          | Jane      | Smith    | 2            | 2019-03-22
3          | Bob       | Brown    | NULL         | 2021-07-30

Departments:
--------------
DepartmentID | DepartmentName
1            | HR
2            | IT
3            | Finance
```

Executing the INNER JOIN query would yield:

```
EmployeeID | FirstName | LastName | DepartmentName
1          | John      | Doe      | HR
2          | Jane      | Smith    | IT
```

Notice how Bob Brown does not appear in the result set since he does not have a corresponding DepartmentID.

Understanding the basic mechanics of joins will build a foundation for exploring more advanced SQL queries and data retrieval techniques. As we progress through this chapter, we will delve deeper into each type of join, demonstrating their use cases and subtleties with comprehensive examples.

5.2 INNER JOIN

The INNER JOIN is a fundamental and widely used type of join in SQL. It combines rows from two or more tables based on a related column between them. The result of an INNER JOIN only includes rows where the join condition is true for both tables involved, thereby excluding rows that do not meet the join criteria.

An INNER JOIN is specified in an SQL query using the INNER JOIN keyword followed by the ON clause that defines the condition for the join. The basic syntax is as follows:

```
SELECT column_list
FROM table1
INNER JOIN table2
ON table1.column_name = table2.column_name;
```

In this syntax, column_list specifies the columns to be retrieved, table1 and table2 are the tables to be joined, and the ON clause defines the relationship between the columns in these tables.

Example of INNER JOIN

Consider two tables, Customers and Orders, structured as follows:

Customers table:

```
+-------------+----------+
| CustomerID  | Name     |
+-------------+----------+
| 1           | Alice    |
| 2           | Bob      |
| 3           | Charlie  |
+-------------+----------+
```

Orders table:

```
+---------+-------------+--------+
| OrderID | CustomerID  | Amount |
+---------+-------------+--------+
| 101     | 1           | 50.00  |
| 102     | 2           | 150.00 |
| 103     | 2           | 200.00 |
| 104     | 4           | 100.00 |
+---------+-------------+--------+
```

To list all customers who have placed orders and their corresponding order amounts, an INNER JOIN can be used:

```
SELECT Customers.Name, Orders.Amount
FROM Customers
INNER JOIN Orders
ON Customers.CustomerID = Orders.CustomerID;
```

The result of this query will be:

Name	Amount
Alice	50.00
Bob	150.00
Bob	200.00

The query returns rows where there is a match between Customers.CustomerID and Orders.CustomerID. Note that Charlie, who has no corresponding orders, is not included in the result.

Using Aliases with INNER JOIN

To make queries cleaner and more readable, table aliases can be employed. This allows for shorter query syntax, especially when dealing with complex joins:

```
SELECT C.Name, O.Amount
FROM Customers AS C
INNER JOIN Orders AS O
ON C.CustomerID = O.CustomerID;
```

The result is the same as the previous example but uses aliases C for Customers and O for Orders.

Joining Multiple Tables

INNER JOIN can also be used to combine more than two tables. For instance, consider three tables Customers, Orders, and Products:

Products table:

ProductID	Price
1	10.00
2	15.00
3	20.00

Assuming the Orders table has an additional ProductID column:

OrderID	CustomerID	Amount	ProductID
101	1	50.00	1
102	2	150.00	2
103	2	200.00	3
104	4	100.00	2

To retrieve the customer names along with their order amounts and product prices, a nested INNER JOIN can be applied:

```
SELECT C.Name, O.Amount, P.Price
FROM Customers AS C
INNER JOIN Orders AS O
ON C.CustomerID = O.CustomerID
INNER JOIN Products AS P
ON O.ProductID = P.ProductID;
```

The result will be:

```
+-------+--------+-------+
| Name  | Amount | Price |
+-------+--------+-------+
| Alice |  50.00 | 10.00 |
| Bob   | 150.00 | 15.00 |
| Bob   | 200.00 | 20.00 |
+-------+--------+-------+
```

This query joins the Customers, Orders, and Products tables, using CustomerID and ProductID as the connecting points.

Handling Duplicate Column Names in INNER JOIN

When columns in the joined tables have the same names, it is essential to differentiate them using the table name or alias. For instance, if both Customers and Orders have a column named ID, the query should clearly specify the table they belong to:

```
SELECT Customers.Name, Orders.ID AS OrderID, Orders.Amount
FROM Customers
INNER JOIN Orders
ON Customers.ID = Orders.CustomerID;
```

In cases where column names are not adequately distinguished, ambiguity errors will result. Proper column aliasing ensures clarity and prevents errors by explicitly differentiating columns from each table.

Filtering Results in INNER JOIN

Filters can be added to an INNER JOIN to narrow down the results. For example, to list customers who have placed orders with an amount greater than 100:

```
SELECT Customers.Name, Orders.Amount
FROM Customers
INNER JOIN Orders
ON Customers.CustomerID = Orders.CustomerID
WHERE Orders.Amount > 100;
```

This query will return:

```
+--------+---------+
| Name   | Amount |
+--------+---------+
| Bob    | 150.00 |
| Bob    | 200.00 |
+--------+---------+
```

Applying filters to the INNER JOIN not only combines the relevant rows but also refines the data by the conditions specified in the WHERE clause. This practice is beneficial when working with large datasets, ensuring that only pertinent information is retrieved for analysis.

5.3 LEFT JOIN

The LEFT JOIN operation, synonymous with LEFT OUTER JOIN, is employed to include all records from the left table (the first table mentioned in the query), together with the matched records from the right table (the second table mentioned). If there are no matches, the result is still a row in the result set with NULL values in columns from the right table.

Consider two illustrative tables: employees and departments. The employees table keeps records of employee details, while the departments table holds information about various departments within the company.

```
CREATE TABLE employees (
    employee_id INT PRIMARY KEY,
    employee_name VARCHAR(100),
    department_id INT
);

CREATE TABLE departments (
    department_id INT PRIMARY KEY,
    department_name VARCHAR(100)
);
```

Suppose we want to retrieve a list of all employees along with the department name they belong to. Here, a LEFT JOIN ensures that even employees who are not assigned to any department are included in the result set.

```
SELECT e.employee_id, e.employee_name, d.department_name
FROM employees e
LEFT JOIN departments d ON e.department_id = d.department_id;
```

To understand the result, consider the following sample data:

```
INSERT INTO employees (employee_id, employee_name, department_id)
VALUES
(1, 'John Doe', 10),
```

```
(2, 'Jane Roe', 20),
(3, 'Alex Smith', NULL);

INSERT INTO departments (department_id, department_name)
VALUES
(10, 'HR'),
(20, 'Finance');
```

Executing the LEFT JOIN query provided yields the following result:

```
employee_id | employee_name | department_name
------------+---------------+-----------------
          1 | John Doe      | HR
          2 | Jane Roe      | Finance
          3 | Alex Smith    | NULL
```

In this result:

- John Doe from employee ID 1 is matched with the HR department. - Jane Roe from employee ID 2 is matched with the Finance department. - Alex Smith from employee ID 3 has no matching department, thus the department name is NULL.

This guarantees that no employee record is omitted from the result set, irrespective of whether there is a corresponding department.

To further explore the application of LEFT JOIN, consider a scenario where it is necessary to list all employees and their respective managers. Suppose our database schema includes an employees table with a self-referencing foreign key to represent manager-employee relationships:

```
CREATE TABLE employees (
    employee_id INT PRIMARY KEY,
    employee_name VARCHAR(100),
    manager_id INT
);
```

Sample data is inserted as follows:

```
INSERT INTO employees (employee_id, employee_name, manager_id)
VALUES
(1, 'John Doe', NULL),
(2, 'Jane Roe', 1),
(3, 'Alex Smith', 1),
(4, 'Emily Davis', 2);
```

The task is to generate a list of employees along with their manager's name:

```
SELECT e.employee_name AS employee, m.employee_name AS manager
FROM employees e
LEFT JOIN employees m ON e.manager_id = m.employee_id;
```

This self LEFT JOIN yields the following result:

```
employee    | manager
------------+-----------
John Doe    | NULL
Jane Roe    | John Doe
Alex Smith  | John Doe
Emily Davis | Jane Roe
```

In this instance:

- John Doe has no manager, producing a NULL value in the manager column. - Jane Roe and Alex Smith both report to John Doe. - Emily Davis reports to Jane Roe.

Performance considerations when using LEFT JOIN involve aspects such as indexing and the volume of data. Indexing the join keys can significantly enhance query performance. For example, creating an index on department_id in both employees and departments table optimizes the efficiency of the join operation.

```
CREATE INDEX idx_dept_id ON employees(department_id);
CREATE INDEX idx_dept_id ON departments(department_id);
```

Proper indexing reduces the computational load during the join operation, especially with large datasets. Moreover, query optimizers in SQL engines can use indexes to expedite data retrieval, resulting in faster query execution times. Nonetheless, one must balance the use of indexes, as excessive indexing can impact insert, update, and delete operations.

In complex queries involving multiple LEFT JOINs, careful attention should be paid to the database design and the logical structure of queries to minimize redundancy and unnecessary computational overhead.

5.4 RIGHT JOIN

The RIGHT JOIN returns all records from the right table (Table B), and the matched records from the left table (Table A). The result is NULL from the left side when there is no match. Conceptually, it is the opposite of the LEFT JOIN. If there is no criterion for join or there are no matches, the results will display NULL values for all columns from Table A that do not find corresponding matches in Table B.

To illustrate this further, consider two tables, Employees and Departments. The Employees table contains employee details, whereas the

Departments table contains department details.

```
CREATE TABLE Employees (
    EmployeeID INT PRIMARY KEY,
    Name VARCHAR(100),
    DepartmentID INT
);

INSERT INTO Employees (EmployeeID, Name, DepartmentID) VALUES
(1, 'Alice', 1),
(2, 'Bob', 2),
(3, 'Charlie', 3),
(4, 'David', NULL);
```

```
CREATE TABLE Departments (
    DepartmentID INT PRIMARY KEY,
    DepartmentName VARCHAR(100)
);

INSERT INTO Departments (DepartmentID, DepartmentName) VALUES
(1, 'HR'),
(2, 'Engineering'),
(3, 'Marketing'),
(4, 'Sales');
```

Given these datasets, performing a RIGHT JOIN between Employees and Departments involves matching records primarily based on DepartmentID.

```
SELECT Employees.EmployeeID, Employees.Name, Departments.DepartmentID,
       Departments.DepartmentName
FROM Employees
RIGHT JOIN Departments
ON Employees.DepartmentID = Departments.DepartmentID;
```

The expected result set from executing this RIGHT JOIN query is as follows:

```
EmployeeID  Name     DepartmentID  DepartmentName
----------------------------------------------
1           Alice        1          HR
2           Bob          2          Engineering
3           Charlie      3          Marketing
NULL          NULL          4          Sales
```

In this result set:

- Employee Alice is matched with the HR department.
- Employee Bob is matched with the Engineering department.
- Employee Charlie is matched with the Marketing department.
- The Sales department from the Departments table does not have any corresponding employee in the Employees table, resulting in NULL values for EmployeeID and Name.

This example demonstrates the RIGHT JOIN functionality, ensuring visibility of all records from the right table and filling unmatched records from the left table with NULL values.

It is important to understand that the conditional logic and result structuring remain consistent with the concept of full inclusion from the referenced (right) table. The RIGHT JOIN serves practical purposes in scenarios where the primary focus of data retrieval is on ensuring complete data from the right-hand side, with supplementary matches from the left-hand data set. This retains completeness for analysis or reporting requirements where the right table's data is of primary consideration.

In practice, it is often observed that RIGHT JOIN usage is less prevalent compared to LEFT JOIN due to the ease of logical structuring from a left-to-right data perspective. However, understanding both joins' behaviours can enhance flexibility in SQL querying and aid in selecting the appropriate join type to satisfy specific requirements.

Execution of RIGHT JOIN may also involve considerations of indexing and query performance, particularly in large datasets where NULL results propagation may affect query optimizations and necessitate careful indexing strategies on key columns to ensure efficient data retrieval. As with any join operation, thorough testing and analysis are recommended to validate performance characteristics relevant to the specific database environment and workload patterns.

5.5 FULL OUTER JOIN

The FULL OUTER JOIN is an essential type of join operation in SQL that enables the combination of data from two tables while ensuring that no data is lost from either table. This join type returns all records from both the left and right tables, with NULL values in place where no match is found in the opposing table.

To understand the behavior of a FULL OUTER JOIN, consider two tables: employees and departments. The employees table contains information about employees, including their names and department IDs, while the departments table contains department details, such as department IDs and department names.

```
CREATE TABLE employees (
    emp_id INT PRIMARY KEY,
    emp_name VARCHAR(100),
    dept_id INT
);
```

```
CREATE TABLE departments (
    dept_id INT PRIMARY KEY,
    dept_name VARCHAR(100)
);

INSERT INTO employees VALUES
(1, 'Alice', 1),
(2, 'Bob', 2),
(3, 'Charlie', NULL),
(4, 'David', 4);

INSERT INTO departments VALUES
(1, 'Human Resources'),
(2, 'Finance'),
(3, 'Marketing'),
(5, 'IT');
```

The employees table contains four employees, with department IDs provided for Alice and Bob, while Charlie does not have an assigned department, and David is linked to a non-existent department (ID 4). The departments table lists four departments but does not include an ID 4 department, having instead a department with ID 5.

Performing a FULL OUTER JOIN on these tables can be accomplished using the following SQL query:

```
SELECT
    employees.emp_id,
    employees.emp_name,
    employees.dept_id AS emp_dept_id,
    departments.dept_id AS dept_dept_id,
    departments.dept_name
FROM
    employees
FULL OUTER JOIN
    departments
ON
    employees.dept_id = departments.dept_id;
```

The result of the above query is as follows:

```
emp_id | emp_name | emp_dept_id | dept_dept_id |      dept_name
--------+----------+-------------+--------------+--------------------
      1 | Alice    |           1 |            1 | Human Resources
      2 | Bob      |           2 |            2 | Finance
      3 | Charlie  |        NULL |         NULL | NULL
      4 | David    |           4 |         NULL | NULL
   NULL | NULL     |        NULL |            3 | Marketing
   NULL | NULL     |        NULL |            5 | IT
```

This result contains all employees and departments, including those that do not have a matching record in the other table. Key points illustrated by this output include:

- Alice and Bob have their department details fully matched.

- Charlie appears with NULL in the department columns due to the absence of any department assignment.
- David shows with department ID 4, but with NULL in the department details as there is no corresponding department with ID 4.
- Departments like Marketing (ID 3) and IT (ID 5) appear with NULL in the employee columns as there are no employees linked to those departments.

A FULL OUTER JOIN can be visualized as a union of the results from a LEFT JOIN and a RIGHT JOIN operation. This ensures all data from both tables are retained, filling unmatched columns with NULLs, which is particularly useful for generating comprehensive reports and datasets where completeness of records is critical.

When using FULL OUTER JOIN, performance considerations should be kept in mind, particularly with large datasets. The join operation can be computationally expensive due to the need to combine all rows from both tables and process the resultant dataset with null values padding unmatched columns. Indexing strategies and query optimization techniques should be carefully considered to mitigate potential performance bottlenecks.

Additionally, different SQL database systems might implement FULL OUTER JOIN with varying syntax or optimizations, so reviewing database-specific documentation and conducting performance benchmarks may yield practical insights for achieving efficient query execution.

5.6 CROSS JOIN

A CROSS JOIN is a type of join operation that returns the Cartesian product of the two tables involved in the join. Unlike other joins, which combine rows based on related columns, the CROSS JOIN pairs each row from the first table with every row from the second table. This results in a combination of every row in the first table with every row in the second table, which can quickly lead to a large number of result rows.

To understand the CROSS JOIN operation, consider two tables, TableA and TableB:

```
CREATE TABLE TableA (
    id INT,
    value VARCHAR(50)
);

INSERT INTO TableA (id, value) VALUES
(1, 'A1'),
(2, 'A2');
```

```
CREATE TABLE TableB (
    id INT,
    description VARCHAR(50)
);

INSERT INTO TableB (id, description) VALUES
(1, 'Description1'),
(2, 'Description2'),
(3, 'Description3');
```

Executing a CROSS JOIN on these tables will generate a result set that includes every combination of rows from TableA and TableB. The SQL syntax for a CROSS JOIN is straightforward:

```
SELECT TableA.id AS TableA_id, TableA.value, TableB.id AS TableB_id, TableB.
    description
FROM TableA
CROSS JOIN TableB;
```

The output of this CROSS JOIN query will be:

```
TableA_id value TableB_id description
----------------------------------------
1         A1    1         Description1
1         A1    2         Description2
1         A1    3         Description3
2         A2    1         Description1
2         A2    2         Description2
2         A2    3         Description3
```

In this result, each row from TableA is paired with every row from TableB, yielding a total of 6 rows (2 rows from TableA $\times$ 3 rows from TableB).

It is important to be cautious when using CROSS JOIN, especially with large tables, as the result set size grows exponentially. For example, if TableA has 1000 rows and TableB has 1000 rows, the result would consist of $1000 \times 1000 = 1,000,000$ rows. This can lead to significant performance issues and resource consumption.

In practice, CROSS JOINs are useful in specific scenarios, such as generating all possible combinations of elements, performing combinatorial analyses, or creating test data sets for various conditions.

Additionally, the CROSS JOIN can be implicitly created using a comma separator between tables in the FROM clause. For example:

```
SELECT TableA.id AS TableA_id, TableA.value, TableB.id AS TableB_id, TableB.
    description
FROM TableA, TableB;
```

This syntax is equivalent to the explicit CROSS JOIN and will produce the same Cartesian product result. However, using the explicit CROSS JOIN syntax is generally preferred for readability and clarity.

Understanding the implications of CROSS JOIN ensures that it is used appropriately, thereby avoiding unnecessary computational overhead and ensuring efficient query execution. When used judiciously, CROSS JOIN can be a powerful tool in SQL, providing the ability to construct complex datasets and relationships between table rows.

5.7 Self Joins

A self join is a type of join in which a table is joined with itself. This technique is frequently used when you need to compare rows within the same table or to find relationships within a single table. To distinguish the table from itself, it is necessary to use table aliases.

Consider the following example table named 'Employees':

```
CREATE TABLE Employees (
    EmployeeID INT PRIMARY KEY,
    FirstName VARCHAR(50),
    LastName VARCHAR(50),
    ManagerID INT
);
```

The 'Employees' table includes an 'EmployeeID', 'FirstName', 'LastName', and 'ManagerID', which is a reference to the 'EmployeeID' of the manager. To retrieve the manager's name along with each employee, a self join is employed. Here is how it can be done:

```
SELECT e1.EmployeeID, e1.FirstName AS EmployeeFirstName, e1.LastName AS
     EmployeeLastName,
     e2.FirstName AS ManagerFirstName, e2.LastName AS ManagerLastName
FROM Employees e1
LEFT JOIN Employees e2 ON e1.ManagerID = e2.EmployeeID;
```

In this query, the 'Employees' table is joined to itself using aliases 'e1' and 'e2'. The 'LEFT JOIN' ensures that employees who do not have a manager (i.e., 'ManagerID' is 'NULL') are still included in the results with their own details displayed and 'NULL' values for the manager's details.

Consider the following data in the ‘Employees‘ table:

EmployeeID	FirstName	LastName	ManagerID
1	John	Doe	NULL
2	Jane	Smith	1
3	Bob	Johnson	1
4	Alice	Lee	2

The result of the self join will be:

```
EmployeeID | EmployeeFirstName | EmployeeLastName | ManagerFirstName | ManagerLastName
---------------------------------------------------------------------------------
1          | John              | Doe              | NULL             | NULL
2          | Jane              | Smith            | John             | Doe
3          | Bob               | Johnson          | John             | Doe
4          | Alice             | Lee              | Jane             | Smith
```

This technique can be extended to many scenarios, such as identifying hierarchical relationships within the same table or finding matches within rows sharing some criteria.

When working with complex conditions, the ‘AND‘ and ‘OR‘ operators can be used to refine the joins further. Here is a more intricate example demonstrating employees working in the same department, using a theoretical ‘DepartmentID‘ field:

```
CREATE TABLE Employees (
    EmployeeID INT PRIMARY KEY,
    FirstName VARCHAR(50),
    LastName VARCHAR(50),
    ManagerID INT,
    DepartmentID INT
);

SELECT e1.FirstName AS EmployeeFirstName, e1.LastName AS EmployeeLastName,
       e2.FirstName AS ColleagueFirstName, e2.LastName AS ColleagueLastName
FROM Employees e1
JOIN Employees e2
  ON e1.DepartmentID = e2.DepartmentID AND e1.EmployeeID <> e2.EmployeeID;
```

This query finds all pairs of employees who work in the same department without matching an employee to themselves. The condition ‘e1.EmployeeID <> e2.EmployeeID‘ ensures that employees are only matched to their colleagues, not themselves.

```
EmployeeFirstName | EmployeeLastName | ColleagueFirstName | ColleagueLastName
------------------------------------------------------------------------
John              | Doe              | Jane               | Smith
John              | Doe              | Bob                | Johnson
Jane              | Smith            | John               | Doe
Jane              | Smith            | Bob                | Johnson
Bob               | Johnson          | John               | Doe
Bob               | Johnson          | Jane               | Smith
```

Self joins are particularly useful for generalized transitive relationships, such as identifying connections or paths within hierarchical data structures. For example, to find all levels of management for a given employee, recursive techniques or iterative self joins can be utilized.

Performance considerations for self joins involve careful indexing and query optimization. Since the table is accessed multiple times, ensuring that the joining columns are indexed will significantly improve query performance. Additionally, understanding the cardinality and selectivity of the data can further optimize the query execution plan, avoiding full table scans where possible.

This method provides powerful capabilities for analyzing and querying hierarchical and self-referential data structures within a SQL database efficiently.

5.8 Introduction to Subqueries

In SQL, subqueries, also known as inner queries or nested queries, are essential tools for extracting and manipulating data that satisfy specific criteria. A subquery is a query embedded within another query. Typically, it is enclosed in parentheses and can be found in various clauses, including SELECT, FROM, WHERE, and HAVING.

Subqueries enable complex queries to be broken down into manageable parts. By constructing a query in layers, subqueries can make otherwise intricate tasks more readable and maintainable. Their versatility allows them to be used in different contexts, enhancing SQL's expressive capability.

To understand subqueries thoroughly, one must first recognize the types of subqueries and their applications.

Types of Subqueries

Subqueries can be classified based on their output and how they are used within a larger query. The main types include:

- **Scalar Subqueries**: These return a single value. They can be used wherever a single value is expected, such as in comparisons in the WHERE clause or in expressions in the SELECT list.
- **Row Subqueries**: These return a single row of values. They are typically used in comparisons where multiple columns are evaluated.

- **Table or Multiple-Row Subqueries**: These return multiple rows, which can be used by IN, EXISTS, and in other contexts where a full set of values is required.

Scalar Subqueries Example

Scalar subqueries are quite common and useful. Consider a scenario where you want to find employees whose salary is above the average salary in the company. The subquery calculates the average salary, and the outer query selects employees with a salary higher than this average.

```
SELECT employee_id, first_name, last_name, salary
FROM employees
WHERE salary > (SELECT AVG(salary) FROM employees);
```

The embedded subquery (SELECT AVG(salary) FROM employees) computes the average salary. The outer query then retrieves the details of employees whose salaries exceed that average.

Row Subqueries Example

Row subqueries are used when you need to compare a set of columns from one row. For example, to find employees in the same department as a given employee (e.g., employee with ID 101), you might use a row subquery.

```
SELECT employee_id, first_name, last_name
FROM employees
WHERE (department_id, job_id) =
    (SELECT department_id, job_id FROM employees WHERE employee_id = 101)
        ;
```

In this case, the subquery (SELECT department_id, job_id FROM employees WHERE employee_id = 101) returns the department ID and job ID of employee 101. The outer query then finds all employees who belong to the same department and hold the same job.

Table Subqueries Example

Table subqueries are used extensively with the IN and EXISTS operators. For instance, you might want to find departments that have more than a certain number of employees. Such a query involves counting employees in a subquery and using that result in the outer query.

```
SELECT department_name
FROM departments
WHERE department_id IN
    (SELECT department_id
     FROM employees
     GROUP BY department_id
```

```
    HAVING COUNT(*) > 5);
```

Here, the subquery (SELECT department_id FROM employees GROUP BY department_id HAVING COUNT(*) > 5) lists department IDs with more than five employees. The outer query then retrieves the names of those departments.

Subqueries in Data Manipulation

Subqueries are not limited to SELECT statements. They can also be used in INSERT, UPDATE, and DELETE statements. For example, you might insert data into a table where the data is fetched through a subquery.

```
INSERT INTO high_earners (employee_id, first_name, last_name, salary)
SELECT employee_id, first_name, last_name, salary
FROM employees
WHERE salary > (SELECT AVG(salary) FROM employees);
```

In this case, employees earning above the average salary are inserted into the high_earners table.

Similarly, subqueries can update or delete records based on complex criteria derived from other tables or aggregated results.

Considerations for Using Subqueries

While subqueries are powerful, they can have performance implications. Optimizing subqueries by ensuring they are appropriately indexed and minimizing their execution cost is crucial. In some scenarios, rewriting subqueries as joins or using window functions can lead to more efficient execution plans.

Subqueries are instrumental in constructing expressive and performant SQL queries required for comprehensive data analysis and manipulation tasks.

5.9 Using Subqueries in SELECT Statements

Subqueries, also known as inner queries or nested queries, are essential components in SQL for performing complex queries that require results from other queries. In the context of a SELECT statement, subqueries can be instrumental in filtering, transforming, and aggregating data.

Fundamentals of Subqueries in SELECT

A subquery within a SELECT statement is executed first and its results are then used by the main or outer query. The fundamental syntax of a subquery is as follows:

```
SELECT column1, ...
FROM table1
WHERE column_name OPERATOR (SELECT column_name
                            FROM table2
                            WHERE condition);
```

In this notation, the subquery is encapsulated within parentheses and is executed to provide a value or set of values for the outer query's conditions.

Scalar Subqueries in SELECT

Scalar subqueries return a single value and can be integrated directly into the select clause to compute or retrieve specific data elements. Consider the database schema involving two tables, employees and departments:

```
employees table:
| employee_id | name   | department_id | salary |
|-------------|--------|---------------|--------|
| 1           | John   | 10            | 70000  |
| 2           | Jane   | 20            | 80000  |
| 3           | Alice  | 10            | 60000  |
| 4           | Bob    | 30            | 85000  |
| 5           | Carol  | 10            | 95000  |

departments table:
| department_id | department_name |
|---------------|-----------------|
| 10            | HR              |
| 20            | Finance         |
| 30            | IT              |
```

The following example demonstrates how a scalar subquery is used to include the department name in the SELECT results without an explicit join:

```
SELECT employee_id, name, salary,
       (SELECT department_name
        FROM departments
        WHERE departments.department_id = employees.department_id)
        AS department
FROM employees;
```

Column Subqueries in SELECT

A column subquery returns a single column of values that can be treated as a list or array. For example, to find employees who earn more than the average salary in their respective departments:

```
SELECT name, salary
FROM employees
WHERE salary > (SELECT AVG(salary)
                FROM employees AS e
                WHERE e.department_id = employees.department_id);
```

Here, the subquery calculates the average salary per department, and the main query fetches employees whose salaries are above the computed values.

Row Subqueries in SELECT

Row subqueries return a single row of data with one or multiple columns. This can be particularly useful for comparisons involving multiple fields. Here's an example where a row subquery is used to identify the employee with the highest salary in each department:

```
SELECT department_id, employee_id, name, salary
FROM employees
WHERE (department_id, salary) IN
    (SELECT department_id, MAX(salary)
     FROM employees
     GROUP BY department_id);
```

The subquery groups employees by department and finds the maximum salary for each. The outer query then matches these results to find respective employees.

Table Subqueries in SELECT

Table subqueries return a table as a result set, which can often be used in place of a table expression or for generating derived tables. The following example illustrates how a subquery can be utilized to create a temporary table:

```
SELECT avg_salary.department_id, avg_salary.average_salary, e.employee_id, e.
      name, e.salary
FROM (
    SELECT department_id, AVG(salary) AS average_salary
    FROM employees
    GROUP BY department_id
) AS avg_salary
JOIN employees e ON e.department_id = avg_salary.department_id;
```

In this example, the subquery computes the average salary per department and the main query utilizes this temporary table to list each employee along with the department's average salary.

Using Subqueries with IN Operator

The IN operator is used to filter records based on a list of values provided by a subquery. Here's how to select employees belonging to departments with specific criteria:

```
SELECT name, department_id
FROM employees
WHERE department_id IN (SELECT department_id
                        FROM departments
                        WHERE department_name LIKE '%Finance%');
```

The inner query retrieves department IDs with names containing 'Finance', passed to the outer query which fetches matching employee records.

Performance Considerations

While subqueries are a powerful feature, they can sometimes lead to performance bottlenecks, especially with large datasets. Database engines might not optimize subqueries as efficiently as joins. Therefore, when performance concerns arise, consider alternative strategies such as restructuring queries to use joins or employing indexed views.

Overall, understanding subqueries in SELECT statements enables writing flexible and powerful SQL queries, allowing for sophisticated data manipulation and retrieval that can address a wide range of application needs.

5.10 Using Subqueries in WHERE and HAVING Clauses

Subqueries are extremely versatile and can be used in various parts of an SQL statement, including the WHERE and HAVING clauses. Using subqueries in these clauses allows for more complex and flexible queries by enabling conditional operations that rely on the results of other queries. The subquery results can be used to filter records or to define conditions that must be met for the records to be included in the final result set. This section provides a detailed exploration of how subqueries can be utilized effectively in the WHERE and HAVING clauses.

Using Subqueries in WHERE Clauses

In the WHERE clause, subqueries serve as a criterion to filter results based on a comparison with values returned by the subquery. An essential characteristic of subqueries in WHERE clauses is that they often use comparison operators such as =, <, >, IN, and EXISTS. Consider the following SQL tables:

```
CREATE TABLE employees (
    emp_id INT,
    name VARCHAR(100),
    department_id INT,
    salary DECIMAL(10, 2)
);

CREATE TABLE departments (
    department_id INT,
    department_name VARCHAR(100)
);
```

Suppose we need to find employees who work in the 'Sales' department. This can be achieved by using a subquery within the WHERE clause:

```
SELECT emp_id, name
FROM employees
WHERE department_id = (SELECT department_id
                       FROM departments
                       WHERE department_name = 'Sales');
```

In this query, the subquery retrieves the department_id of the 'Sales' department, and the main query uses this value to filter employees.

Using the IN Operator in WHERE Clauses

The IN operator allows for checking whether a value matches any value in a list or subquery. For example, to find employees who work in either the 'Sales' or 'HR' departments, the query would be:

```
SELECT emp_id, name
FROM employees
WHERE department_id IN (SELECT department_id
                        FROM departments
                        WHERE department_name IN ('Sales', 'HR'));
```

Here, the subquery returns multiple department IDs, and the main query checks if the employees' department IDs are in this list.

Using the EXISTS Operator in WHERE Clauses

The EXISTS operator tests for the existence of rows in a subquery result set. It returns TRUE if the subquery returns any rows. For example, to find employees who belong to any department, we write:

```
SELECT emp_id, name
FROM employees E
WHERE EXISTS (SELECT 1
              FROM departments D
              WHERE E.department_id = D.department_id);
```

In this case, the subquery checks if there is at least one matching department for each employee. The SELECT 1 in the subquery is sufficient because EXISTS only needs to check for existence, not specific values.

Using Subqueries in HAVING Clauses

The HAVING clause is used to filter results after an aggregation operation has been performed. Subqueries in the HAVING clause allow for filtering groups based on the results of another query. Consider the following extension of the employees and departments tables:

```
CREATE TABLE sales (
    sale_id INT,
    emp_id INT,
    amount DECIMAL(10, 2),
    sale_date DATE
);
```

To find department IDs where the total sales exceed the average total sales per department, we can use the HAVING clause with a subquery:

```
SELECT department_id, SUM(amount) AS total_sales
FROM sales
GROUP BY department_id
HAVING SUM(amount) > (SELECT AVG(total_sales)
                      FROM (SELECT department_id, SUM(amount) AS total_sales
                            FROM sales
                            GROUP BY department_id) AS department_sales);
```

In this query, the subquery calculates the average total sales per department. The HAVING clause then filters for departments whose total sales exceed this average.

Combining Multiple Subqueries

Often, multiple subqueries can be combined to form more complex queries. For example, to find employees whose total sales exceed the average total sales per employee across all departments:

```
SELECT emp_id, SUM(amount) AS total_sales
FROM sales
GROUP BY emp_id
HAVING SUM(amount) > (SELECT AVG(total_sales)
                      FROM (SELECT emp_id, SUM(amount) AS total_sales
                            FROM sales
                            GROUP BY emp_id) AS employee_sales);
```

The internal subquery computes the total sales per employee, and the parent subquery calculates the average of these total sales. The HAVING clause filters employees whose total sales exceed this average.

Conclusion with Application

Utilizing subqueries within the WHERE and HAVING clauses enhances the flexibility and power of SQL queries. By carefully crafting subqueries, one can achieve intricate filtering and grouping conditions, which are otherwise difficult to implement.

5.11 Correlated Subqueries

A correlated subquery, unlike a standalone subquery, depends on the outer query for its values. It operates row-by-row, referencing columns from the outer query within its inner WHERE clause. This relationship implies that for each row processed by the outer query, the subquery is executed, making correlated subqueries inherently different from non-correlated subqueries which are executed only once and remain independent of the outer query.

To illustrate this, consider the following table structures:

```
CREATE TABLE employees (
    id INT PRIMARY KEY,
    name VARCHAR(100),
    department_id INT
);

CREATE TABLE departments (
    id INT PRIMARY KEY,
    department_name VARCHAR(100)
);
```

Suppose we aim to retrieve the names of employees along with their department names. A correlated subquery can be used as follows:

```
SELECT
    e.name,
    (SELECT d.department_name
     FROM departments d
     WHERE d.id = e.department_id) AS department_name
FROM
    employees e;
```

In this query, the subquery (SELECT d.department_name FROM departments d WHERE d.id = e.department_id) is correlated to the outer query by referring to e.department_id. For each row processed by the outer query (representing an employee), the subquery fetches the corresponding department name.

This correlation ensures that each execution of the inner query uses values from the current row of the outer table, thus binding the subquery to each row of the outer query.

Performance Implications

A pivotal aspect of correlated subqueries is their performance impact. Given that the subquery executes once for each row processed by the outer query, the computational cost can be significant, particularly for large datasets. Optimizing these queries often involves indexing and sometimes rethinking the approach using joins, which generally perform better due to set-based operations rather than row-by-row processing.

Example: Identifying Maximum Salaries by Department

Consider another example where we need to determine the maximum salary within each department:

```
CREATE TABLE salaries (
    employee_id INT,
    salary DECIMAL(15, 2),
    department_id INT
);
```

We aim to list all employees who have the highest salary in their respective departments. This query employs a correlated subquery to achieve the desired result:

```
SELECT
    s.employee_id,
    s.salary,
    s.department_id
FROM
    salaries s
WHERE
    s.salary = (SELECT MAX(salary)
                FROM salaries sub_s
                WHERE sub_s.department_id = s.department_id);
```

Here, the subquery (SELECT MAX(salary) FROM salaries sub_s WHERE sub_s.department_id = s.department_id) is correlated with the outer query through sub_s.department_id = s.department_id. For each row in the salaries table, the subquery finds the maximum salary for the respective department, ensuring that only employees with the highest salary per department are returned.

Use Cases

Correlated subqueries are particularly useful when:

- The requirement involves comparing each row against an aggregated result from the same table.
- Data entries need conditioning based on related hierarchical data.

- The use case necessitates filtering results on a per-row basis involving parent-child relationships within the data.

Alternative Approaches

Given their potential performance overhead, alternative methods are sometimes preferable. For example, using joins combined with GROUP BY clauses can often reproduce the same results more efficiently. Rewriting the above maximum salary query using a join:

```
SELECT
    s1.employee_id,
    s1.salary,
    s1.department_id
FROM
    salaries s1
JOIN
    (SELECT department_id, MAX(salary) AS max_salary
     FROM salaries
     GROUP BY department_id) AS s2
ON
    s1.department_id = s2.department_id AND s1.salary = s2.max_salary;
```

This join operation typically performs better because database engines are usually optimized for set-based operations. The benefits are particularly noticeable on larger datasets.

Integrating a thoughtful approach to choosing between correlated subqueries and joins can lead to significant efficiency improvements. Proficiency in using correlated subqueries involves not only understanding their construction but also recognizing scenarios where alternative solutions might provide better performance.

5.12 Performance Considerations with Joins and Subqueries

When working with multiple tables in SQL, efficiency and performance become paramount, especially as the size of the data grows. Understanding the underlying mechanics of joins and subqueries enables the optimization of complex queries to ensure that they run efficiently.

Indexes: One of the most critical factors influencing query performance is the presence and design of indexes. Indexes are structures that improve the speed of data retrieval operations at the cost of additional storage space and potential overhead on write operations. For joins, indexes on the columns involved in the join conditions can significantly reduce the time complexity. Consider a join operation between two tables A and B on column id:

```
SELECT A.id, A.name, B.salary
FROM A
JOIN B ON A.id = B.id;
```

Creating indexes on A.id and B.id can facilitate quicker lookups during the join process:

```
CREATE INDEX idx_A_id ON A(id);
CREATE INDEX idx_B_id ON B(id);
```

Execution Plans: SQL databases utilize execution plans to determine the most efficient way to execute a query. Analyzing these plans, which can be generated using EXPLAIN or EXPLAIN ANALYZE statements in databases like PostgreSQL or MySQL, provides insights into how a query is executed and which parts of it might be causing performance bottlenecks.

```
EXPLAIN ANALYZE
SELECT A.id, A.name, B.salary
FROM A
JOIN B ON A.id = B.id;
```

The output of this command will detail the steps the database engine takes to execute the query, highlighting areas for potential optimization.

```
Hash Join  (cost=35.50..70.54 rows=1000 width=50) (actual time=0.050..0.092 rows=5 loops=1)
  Hash Cond: (A.id = B.id)
  ->  Seq Scan on A  (cost=0.00..18.00 rows=1000 width=25) (actual time=0.010..0.040 rows=5 loops=1)
  ->  Hash  (cost=18.00..18.00 rows=1000 width=25) (actual time=0.020..0.020 rows=5 loops=1)
        Buckets: 1024  Batches: 1  Memory Usage: 10kB
        ->  Seq Scan on B  (cost=0.00..18.00 rows=1000 width=25) (actual time=0.010..0.010 rows=5 loops=1)
```

Join Types and Performance: Different join types have varying performance characteristics.

- **INNER JOIN:** Usually efficient when appropriate indexes are in place. - **LEFT/RIGHT JOIN:** Can be more expensive than INNER JOIN due to needing to include rows with no matches. - **FULL OUTER JOIN:** Typically the most resource-intensive due to the necessity of combining the entire contents of both tables. - **CROSS JOIN:** Generally avoided with large tables due to its Cartesian product result, which significantly increases the amount of processed data.

Subqueries vs. Joins: Subqueries can sometimes be less performant than joins. This often happens when the subquery executes independently for each row of the outer query.

```
SELECT A.name, (SELECT MAX(B.salary) FROM B WHERE B.department_id = A.
    department_id) AS max_salary
```

```
FROM A;
```

In some cases, rewriting subqueries as joins can lead to performance improvements by allowing the database's optimizer to find more efficient execution paths.

```
SELECT A.name, MAX(B.salary) AS max_salary
FROM A
JOIN B ON A.department_id = B.department_id
GROUP BY A.name;
```

Correlated Subqueries: These are subqueries that reference columns from the outer query and can be particularly challenging from a performance perspective. They are executed once for each row processed by the outer query. Hence, they should be used judiciously.

Optimizing Large Joins: For very large datasets, considering physical database design changes such as partitioning can aid performance. Data partitioning involves splitting large tables into smaller, more manageable pieces.

Caching and Materialized Views: Materialized views store the results of a query and can be refreshed periodically. They are helpful for complex joins or subqueries that are computationally expensive but queried frequently.

```
CREATE MATERIALIZED VIEW mv_example AS
SELECT A.id, A.name, B.salary
FROM A
JOIN B ON A.id = B.id;
```

Efficient database querying involves a blend of proper index usage, analyzing and interpreting execution plans, choosing appropriate join types, and intelligently using subqueries. By understanding and applying these principles, performance can be optimized, leading to quicker and more efficient data retrieval.

Chapter 6

Database Transactions and Concurrency

This chapter explores the core concepts of database transactions and concurrency. It explains ACID properties and transaction control commands such as COMMIT, ROLLBACK, and SAVEPOINT. The chapter covers isolation levels and serializability, along with different locking mechanisms and deadlock resolution strategies. Both optimistic and pessimistic concurrency control methods are discussed, including handling long-running transactions and best practices for transaction management, supported by practical case studies.

6.1 Introduction to Database Transactions

A fundamental aspect of any reliable database system is managing transactions. Transactions provide a way to execute a sequence of operations on a database in an atomic, consistent, isolated, and durable manner. These properties, collectively known as ACID properties, ensure that database systems can handle errors and maintain data integrity reliably.

A transaction typically involves a group of SQL statements that perform a single unit of work. For example, consider a banking system where funds are transferred from one account to another. The process involves debiting one account and crediting another. If either of these operations fails, it could result in an inconsistent state. This is where the concept of a transaction becomes vital; it ensures that either both operations are executed successfully, or none are executed at all, thereby maintaining the integrity of the data.

The syntax for initiating a transaction varies slightly across different SQL databases, but the principle remains consistent. In most SQL databases, a transaction begins implicitly with the execution of the first SQL statement and ends when a COMMIT or ROLLBACK command is issued. Below is an example illustrating how to manage a transaction in SQL.

```
BEGIN TRANSACTION;

UPDATE accounts
SET balance = balance - 100
WHERE account_id = 'A123';

UPDATE accounts
SET balance = balance + 100
WHERE account_id = 'B456';

COMMIT;
```

In this example, the transaction ensures that both updates are treated as a single unit. If any error occurs during the execution of these updates, a ROLLBACK can be issued to undo the changes and revert the database to its previous consistent state.

ROLLBACK;

To elaborate, when a transaction begins, the database takes a snapshot of the current state. Any changes made during the transaction are initially recorded in a temporary area. If the transaction is committed, these changes are then permanently written to the database. Conversely, if a ROLLBACK is issued, all changes made during the transaction are discarded, and the database state is reverted to the snapshot taken at the beginning of the transaction.

```
Starting transaction...
Updating account A123: new balance = initial balance - 100
Updating account B456: new balance = initial balance + 100
Transaction committed successfully.
```

The ability to manage transactions effectively is crucial for ensuring data integrity and consistency, especially in multi-user environments where concurrent access to data is common. Transactions help in preventing data anomalies such as dirty reads, non-repeatable reads, and phantom reads, which can occur when multiple transactions are executed concurrently in an uncoordinated manner.

Transactional control helps in adhering to business rules such as *all-or-nothing* operations, making sure that even in the case of system failures, the system can recover to a known consistent state. For this reason, databases provide mechanisms to control the behavior of transactions, allowing developers to fine-tune isolation levels and concurrency control strategies according to the specific requirements of their applications.

As we delve deeper into this chapter, we will explore various aspects of transaction management, beginning with the detailed examination of ACID properties, isolation levels, and practical implementations of transaction control commands. Understanding transactions at this fundamental level sets the stage for grasping more complex topics such as serializability, locking mechanisms, and concurrency control, ensuring the maintenance of data integrity and consistency across diverse scenarios.

6.2 ACID Properties

The ACID properties are fundamentally critical for ensuring reliable and consistent transactions within a database system. ACID is an acronym representing Atomicity, Consistency, Isolation, and Durability. Each of these properties addresses different aspects of a transaction's integrity and reliability, providing a framework that guarantees robust transaction management.

Atomicity ensures that a series of database operations within a transaction are either all completed successfully, or none are applied. This all-or-nothing principle is vital for maintaining the integrity of data, especially in scenarios where system failures might occur. For example, in a financial application when transferring funds from one account to another, atomicity guarantees that both the debit from one account and the credit to the other account are fully executed, or neither is, thereby avoiding scenarios where funds might disappear or be duplicated.

To implement atomicity, databases use a mechanism called logs, often referred to as write-ahead logs (WAL). These logs keep a record of all modifications that are about to be performed. If the transaction cannot be completed, the log is used to roll back the changes, ensuring that partial updates do not occur. Below is an example to demonstrate the concept of write-ahead logging in a simplified form:

```
BEGIN;

UPDATE accounts
SET balance = balance - 100
WHERE account_id = 'A001';

INSERT INTO transaction_log (account_id, amount, transaction_date)
VALUES ('A001', -100, NOW());

UPDATE accounts
SET balance = balance + 100
WHERE account_id = 'A002';

INSERT INTO transaction_log (account_id, amount, transaction_date)
VALUES ('A002', 100, NOW());

COMMIT;
```

In this SQL transaction, the steps involved in transferring funds between two accounts are logged before the transaction is committed, thereby ensuring that incomplete transactions can be aborted safely.

Consistency ensures that a database transitions from one valid state to another valid state after a transaction. This means that any data written to the database must be valid according to all defined rules, including constraints, triggers, cascades, and any combination of predefined database conditions. Consistency guarantees that database invariants are preserved.

A consistency check can involve various database components:

- Ensuring data types match expected formats.
- Maintaining unique constraints such as primary keys.
- Validating foreign key constraints.
- Ensuring that any application-defined rules are enforced.

For example, in a relational database maintaining an 'orders' and 'customers' table, a consistency rule could ensure that every order references an existing customer.

```
-- Ensure that all orders reference a valid customer
ALTER TABLE orders
ADD CONSTRAINT fk_customer
FOREIGN KEY (customer_id)
REFERENCES customers(customer_id);
```

Isolation refers to the ability of a transaction to operate independently from other transactions. Isolation ensures that concurrently executing transactions do not interfere with each other. This is essential for maintaining data integrity in a multi-user environment where transactions may run simultaneously.

Isolation levels define the degree to which the operations in one transaction are isolated from those in other transactions. The SQL standard specifies four levels of isolation, each providing a different balance between performance and consistency: Read Uncommitted, Read Committed, Repeatable Read, and Serializable.

An example of setting the isolation level in SQL is shown below:

```
-- Set isolation level to Repeatable Read
SET TRANSACTION ISOLATION LEVEL REPEATABLE READ;
```

This ensures that other transactions cannot modify the data read by the current transaction until it is complete, thus avoiding phenomena like non-repeatable reads and phantom reads.

Durability guarantees that once a transaction has been committed, it will remain so, even in the event of a system failure such as a crash or power loss. After a transaction is confirmed, its effects are permanent and stored in non-volatile memory.

Durability is often achieved through the use of transaction logs and database backups. The database system ensures that changes made by a transaction are written to disk before confirming the transaction's success:

```
COMMIT;
-- Ensures the transaction is written to disk
```

Even if a subsequent system crash occurs, recovery mechanisms will use these logs to restore the database to a consistent state.

The ACID properties form the foundation of reliable transaction processing in database systems. These properties ensure that transactions are executed in a safe, consistent, and isolated manner, providing a robust mechanism for handling complex operations and maintaining data integrity. By understanding and applying these principles, database systems can prevent data corruption and provide a dependable environment for critical applications.

6.3 Transaction Control Commands: COMMIT, ROLLBACK, SAVEPOINT

In database systems, transaction control commands are essential for ensuring the integrity and consistency of data. These commands allow the database to maintain ACID properties, enabling applications to handle data modifications effectively. The three primary transaction control commands are COMMIT, ROLLBACK, and SAVEPOINT.

COMMIT:

The COMMIT command is used to permanently save all changes made during the current transaction to the database. Once a COMMIT is issued, the transaction is considered complete, and all modifications are made durable. This action ensures that the database moves from one consistent state to another.

```
BEGIN TRANSACTION;
INSERT INTO employees (id, name, position) VALUES (1, 'Alice', 'Manager');
UPDATE inventory SET stock = stock - 1 WHERE product_id = 10;
COMMIT;
```

In this example, the changes made by the INSERT and UPDATE statements are confirmed and made permanent in the database when the COMMIT command is executed.

ROLLBACK:

The ROLLBACK command undoes all changes made in the current transaction. This command is invoked to abort a transaction and revert the database to its state at the beginning of the transaction. ROLLBACK is crucial for error handling and maintaining database consistency in the event of a failure or unexpected behavior during transaction execution.

```
BEGIN TRANSACTION;
UPDATE accounts SET balance = balance - 100 WHERE account_id = 123;
UPDATE accounts SET balance = balance + 100 WHERE account_id = 456;

-- Suppose an error occurs here
ROLLBACK;
```

In this case, if an error occurs after the second UPDATE statement, issuing the ROLLBACK command will undo both updates, ensuring the database returns to its initial state before the transaction began.

SAVEPOINT:

The SAVEPOINT command allows for partial rollback within a transaction by setting a savepoint, or a marker, within the transaction. If a partial error occurs, the transaction can be rolled back to the nearest savepoint without affecting preceding operations. This command is particularly useful for complex transactions that may involve conditional logic.

```
BEGIN TRANSACTION;
DELETE FROM orders WHERE order_date < '2022-01-01';
SAVEPOINT before_update;
UPDATE customers SET status = 'inactive' WHERE last_order_date < '2021-01-01';

-- Error occurs
ROLLBACK TO before_update;

INSERT INTO audit_log (action, timestamp) VALUES ('update_rollback', NOW());
COMMIT;
```

Here, after deleting orders and setting a savepoint, an update operation occurs. If an error happens during the update, the transaction can roll back to the before_update savepoint and proceed with subsequent operations. The final INSERT into the audit_log table and the COMMIT command ensure that only the intended changes are saved.

The interplay of these commands allows for robust transaction management, ensuring data consistency and reliability. A deeper understanding of these commands provides the foundation for efficient and effective database operations.

6.4 Isolation Levels and Read Phenomena

Isolation levels are a fundamental concept in database transactions, determining how transaction integrity is visible to other transactions and system components. The SQL standard specifies four isolation levels: Read Uncommitted, Read Committed, Repeatable Read, and Serializable. Each level offers a tradeoff between data consistency and system performance, addressing specific read phenomena that may disrupt transaction outcomes.

The SQL standard defines several undesirable read phenomena: dirty reads, non-repeatable reads, and phantom reads. Understanding these read phenomena is essential to grasp the implications of each isolation level.

Read Uncommitted: This is the lowest isolation level, offering minimal protection against read anomalies. Transactions operating at this level can read uncommitted changes made by other transactions, leading to dirty reads. A dirty read happens when a transaction reads data that is written by another transaction that has not yet been committed. This phenomenon compromises data consistency as demonstrated below:

```
-- Transaction A starts
UPDATE accounts SET balance = balance - 100 WHERE account_id = 1;
-- Transaction B starts and reads the same row
SELECT balance FROM accounts WHERE account_id = 1;
-- Transaction A rolls back
ROLLBACK;
-- Transaction B reads a dirty value which does not exist anymore
```

Read Committed: At this isolation level, a transaction can read only committed data, effectively preventing dirty reads. However, it does not guard against non-repeatable reads, which occur when a transaction reads the same row twice and sees different data each time due to another transaction's commits.

```
-- Transaction A starts and commits a change
UPDATE accounts SET balance = balance - 100 WHERE account_id = 1;
COMMIT;
-- Transaction B starts and reads the balance
SELECT balance FROM accounts WHERE account_id = 1;
-- Transaction A performs another update and commits
UPDATE accounts SET balance = balance - 50 WHERE account_id = 1;
COMMIT;
-- Transaction B reads the balance again, getting a different value
SELECT balance FROM accounts WHERE account_id = 1;
-- Results in non-repeatable read
```

Repeatable Read: This isolation level ensures that if a transaction reads a row, it will read the same value if it reads that row again. It prevents both dirty reads and non-repeatable reads; however, it does not protect against phantom reads, which happen when a transaction re-executes a query returning a set of rows that satisfy a condition and finds that the set of rows satisfying the condition has changed due to another recently committed transaction.

```
-- Transaction A starts
SELECT * FROM accounts WHERE balance > 100;
-- Transaction B inserts a new row with balance > 100 and commits
INSERT INTO accounts (account_id, balance) VALUES (3, 150);
COMMIT;
-- Transaction A executes the same query again
SELECT * FROM accounts WHERE balance > 100;
-- Transaction A reads a different result due to the newly inserted row
-- Results in a phantom read
```

Serializable: This is the highest isolation level, where transactions are executed in such a way that the results are the same as if the transactions had been executed serially, one after the other. It prevents dirty reads, non-repeatable reads, and phantom reads. However, achieving serializable transactions can dramatically reduce concurrency and system performance because it often requires locking the entire set of rows a transaction might access.

```
-- Transaction A starts
SELECT * FROM accounts WHERE balance > 100;
-- Transaction B attempts to insert a new row which would affect Transaction A's
    query
INSERT INTO accounts (account_id, balance) VALUES (3, 150);
-- Transaction B is blocked until Transaction A completes
COMMIT;
```

These isolation levels are implemented using a variety of mechanisms, such as locking, multiversion concurrency control (MVCC), and others. Achieving a balance between performance and consistency requirements is crucial in transaction management. The chosen isolation level should align with the business requirements and the nature of the database system's workload to ensure efficient and reliable transaction processing.

6.5 Serializability

Serializability is a fundamental concept in the realm of database transactions, serving as a core criterion for ensuring the correctness of concurrent transactions. It ensures that the execution of a set of transactions preserves the consistency of the database, equivalent to some sequential order of those transactions.

Serializability defines the conditions under which the interleaving of operations from concurrent transactions produces a consistent state as though the transactions had been executed serially, one after the other. The emphasis on correctness makes serializability crucial in multi-user database systems, where concurrent transaction execution is common.

Consider the importance of serializability through an example. Suppose we have two transactions T_1 and T_2:

- T_1: Read(X); X = X + 100; Write(X)
- T_2: Read(X); X = X * 2; Write(X)

Without serializability, the concurrent execution of these transactions could lead to inconsistent states. The interleaved execution of T_1 and

T_2 should produce a result equivalent to either T_1 followed by T_2 or T_2 followed by T_1.

Conflict Serializability: This form of serializability addresses conflicts that arise between transactions. It is based on the idea that certain operations conflict if their execution order can affect the outcome. Conflicting operations include:

- **Read-Write Conflict:** When one transaction reads a data item and another writes to the same item.
- **Write-Write Conflict:** When two transactions write to the same data item.
- **Write-Read Conflict:** When one transaction writes to a data item and another reads the same item.

The transactions are conflict serializable if they can be reordered based on these conflicts so that their execution order retains consistency.

Consider an example where conflicts arise:

```
T1: Read(A)
    A = A + 10
    Write(A)
T2: Read(A)
    A = A * 2
    Write(A)
```

If T_2 reads A before T_1 writes A, the final state differs from the reverse order. Conflict serializability helps to guarantee that conflicts are controlled to maintain consistency.

View Serializability: This is a more generalized form of serializability, considering both reads and writes. Two schedules (interleaved sequences of operations) are view serializable if they result in the same final state and:

- Transactions read the same initial values.
- The write operations produce the same final set of values.
- Each transaction reads the same values in both schedules.

Consider the following schedules:

```
S1:
T1: Read(A), Write(A)
T2: Read(A), Write(A)

S2:
T1: Read(A)
T2: Read(A), Write(A)
T1: Write(A)
```

Both schedules are view serializable if they result in the same final database state and produce the same reads and writes.

Testing for Serializability: To ensure that a schedule is serializable, it is often represented as a precedence graph (or serialization graph), where:

- Nodes represent individual transactions.
- Directed edges indicate dependencies due to conflicts.

A cycle in this graph indicates non-serializable schedules. Let's build a precedence graph for conflict detection:

```
T1: Read(A); A = A + 10; Write(A); Read(B); B = B - 5; Write(B)
T2: Read(A); A = A * 2; Write(A); Read(B); B = B + 20; Write(B)
```

The graph would have nodes T_1 and T_2. Arcs indicate T_2 reading A and B before T_1 writes A and B, generating cycles if dependencies create conflicts.

Serializability, thus rooted in ensuring correctness through equivalence to sequential execution, is indispensable for database transaction management to guarantee integrity and consistent outcomes. Adhering to these principles allows database systems to manage concurrency without compromising reliability. The upcoming sections delve into locking mechanisms and other control methods to manage concurrent executions while maintaining serializability.

6.6 Locking Mechanisms

Locking mechanisms are a crucial component in managing concurrent access to a database. They ensure data integrity and consistency by controlling how multiple transactions can access the same data concurrently. Various types of locks exist, each with distinct characteristics and use cases. In this section, we delve into different locking mechanisms, their functionalities, and their application in database systems.

A lock can be seen as a flag or signal that controls access to a database resource. When a transaction locks a piece of data, other transactions must wait until the lock is released before they can access the data. The most common types of locks are binary locks, shared locks, and exclusive locks.

Binary Locks: A binary lock can be in one of two states: locked or unlocked. This type of lock is straightforward; it allows or disallows access to a data item.

```
LOCK(item)
  if item is already locked then
    wait until item is unlocked
  lock item
END LOCK

UNLOCK(item)
  unlock item
END UNLOCK
```

In the context of multi-user database systems, binary locks are not versatile enough to prevent conflicts effectively since they do not distinguish between read and write operations.

Shared and Exclusive Locks: Shared (read) and exclusive (write) locks address this limitation. Multiple transactions can hold a shared lock on the same data item simultaneously, allowing them to read the item without conflicting. However, an exclusive lock ensures exclusivity for both read and write operations, ensuring no other transaction can access the item until the exclusive lock is released.

- **Shared Lock (S):** Allows multiple transactions to read a data item.
- **Exclusive Lock (X):** Allows only one transaction to read and write a data item.

```
LOCK_S(item)
  if item is not locked with X-lock then
```

```
    grant shared (S) lock on item
  else
    wait until X-lock is released
END LOCK_S

LOCK_X(item)
  if item is not locked with any lock then
    grant exclusive (X) lock on item
  else
    wait until all locks are released
END LOCK_X

UNLOCK(item)
  release lock on item
END UNLOCK
```

Lock Granularity: Lock granularity refers to the size of the data item being locked, which can affect both performance and the level of concurrency. Common granularities include:

- **Field-Level Locks:** Locks individual fields within a record.
- **Record-Level Locks:** Locks entire records.
- **Page-Level Locks:** Locks data pages, typically blocks of records.
- **Table-Level Locks:** Locks entire tables.
- **Database-Level Locks:** Locks the entire database.

Choosing the appropriate lock granularity often involves a trade-off between concurrency and overhead. Fine-grained locks (e.g., field-level) offer higher concurrency but are complex to manage, whereas coarse-grained locks (e.g., table-level) are simpler but limit concurrency.

Two-Phase Locking Protocol: The two-phase locking protocol (2PL) is a concurrency control mechanism that ensures serializability. The protocol divides the execution of a transaction into two phases:

- **Growing Phase:** The transaction can acquire locks but cannot release any locks.
- **Shrinking Phase:** The transaction can release locks but cannot acquire any new locks.

A transaction that follows the 2PL protocol ensures that once it releases its first lock, it will not request any more locks, effectively preventing conflicts.

```
BEGIN TRANSACTION
  // Growing phase
  LOCK_X(item1)
  LOCK_S(item2)
  // Perform operations
  UPDATE item1 SET ...
  SELECT * FROM item2 WHERE ...
  // Shrinking phase
  UNLOCK(item2)
  UNLOCK(item1)
COMMIT TRANSACTION
```

Deadlocks: A deadlock occurs when two or more transactions block each other by holding locks that the other transactions need. Resolving deadlocks typically requires one transaction to relinquish its locks, allowing others to proceed.

Common deadlock detection and resolution strategies include:

- **Wait-Die Scheme:** Older transactions wait for younger transactions to release locks. If a younger transaction requests a lock held by an older transaction, it is aborted.

- **Wound-Wait Scheme:** Older transactions preempt younger transactions, forcing younger transactions to abort if they request a lock held by an older transaction.

- **Timeouts:** Transactions are aborted if they wait longer than a specified time for a lock, assuming a deadlock has occurred.

Each technique helps manage concurrent access, ensuring database integrity and availability in multi-user environments. Understanding and implementing appropriate locking mechanisms is critical for effective transaction management and achieving optimal performance in database systems.

6.7 Deadlocks and Deadlock Resolution

In multi-user database systems, deadlocks are a common challenge that must be addressed to ensure smooth and efficient operations. A deadlock occurs when two or more transactions are waiting for resources held by each other, creating a cycle of dependencies that prevents any of the transactions from proceeding. Understanding and resolving deadlocks is crucial for maintaining database integrity and performance.

A deadlock can be described using the wait-for graph, where transactions are represented as nodes and edges indicate waiting for resources. A cycle in this graph indicates a deadlock. For instance, consider two transactions T_1 and T_2:

- T_1 locks resource A and waits for resource B.
- T_2 locks resource B and waits for resource A.

In this situation, both transactions are in a circular wait, resulting in a deadlock.

The following code snippet demonstrates a simple scenario in which a deadlock can occur:

```
-- Transaction T1
START TRANSACTION;
UPDATE accounts SET balance = balance - 100 WHERE
    account_id = 1;
-- Transaction T1 is waiting for the lock on account_id = 2

-- Transaction T2
START TRANSACTION;
UPDATE accounts SET balance = balance - 200 WHERE
    account_id = 2;
-- Transaction T2 is waiting for the lock on account_id = 1
```

The deadlock-free condition can be ensured if at least one of the following conditions is violated:

- Mutual Exclusion: At least one resource must be held in a non-shareable mode.

- Hold and Wait: A transaction holding one resource can request additional resources.
- No Preemption: Resources cannot be forcibly taken from holding transactions.
- Circular Wait: There exists a set of transactions such that each transaction is waiting for a resource held by the next transaction in the set.

Deadlock detection and resolution can be approached through multiple strategies:

Deadlock Prevention: This approach ensures that at least one of the necessary conditions for deadlocks cannot occur. Techniques for prevention include:

- **Wait-Die Scheme:** Older transactions are allowed to wait for younger ones, but younger transactions are aborted and restarted if they request resources held by older transactions.
- **Wound-Wait Scheme:** Older transactions preempt resources from younger transactions by forcing younger transactions to abort and restart.

Deadlock Detection: This method involves periodic checks of the wait-for graph to find cycles. Once a cycle is detected, one or more transactions within the cycle are chosen as deadlock victims and are aborted to break the cycle. An example of deadlock detection can be demonstrated with the following pseudo-code:

```
def detect_deadlock(wait_for_graph):
    visited = set()
    stack = set()

    def visit(node):
        if node in stack:
            return True # Cycle (deadlock) detected
        if node in visited:
            return False
        stack.add(node)
        visited.add(node)
        for neighbor in wait_for_graph[node]:
            if visit(neighbor):
```

```
                return True
        stack.remove(node)
        return False

    for node in wait_for_graph:
        if visit(node):
            return True
    return False
```

This code checks for cycles in the wait-for graph and returns True if a deadlock is detected.

Deadlock Resolution: Once detected, deadlocks must be resolved by aborting one or more of the involved transactions. The criteria for choosing which transaction to abort often include:

- **Transaction Priority:** Abort the transaction with the lowest priority.
- **Transaction Age:** Abort the younger transaction to minimize the loss of work.
- **Resource Utilization:** Abort the transaction that holds fewer resources.
- **Restart Cost:** Abort the transaction with the lower cost of recovery and restart.

The following SQL code demonstrates how to handle deadlock by catching SQL exceptions:

```
DECLARE CONTINUE HANDLER FOR SQLEXCEPTION
BEGIN
  ROLLBACK;
  -- Logic to handle the deadlock, e.g., log and restart the transaction
END;

START TRANSACTION;
UPDATE accounts SET balance = balance - 100 WHERE
    account_id = 1;
UPDATE accounts SET balance = balance + 100 WHERE
    account_id = 2;
COMMIT;
```

When a deadlock occurs, the transaction is rolled back, and appropriate recovery steps are executed.

By understanding the causes and strategies for managing deadlocks, database administrators can effectively handle these issues and ensure the stability and performance of database systems.

6.8 Optimistic vs. Pessimistic Concurrency Control

Concurrency control methodologies in database systems aim to manage simultaneous operations without conflicting. Two predominant strategies emerge: optimistic concurrency control (OCC) and pessimistic concurrency control (PCC). Understanding both paradigms and their application contexts is crucial for robust transaction management.

Optimistic concurrency control operates under the assumption that conflicts between concurrent transactions are rare. Thus, transactions are allowed to execute without restrictions, with conflict detection deferred until the commit phase. This approach is advantageous in environments where contention is minimal, enhancing performance by reducing the overhead associated with locking.

The OCC mechanism typically involves three phases: read, validation, and write. In the read phase, a transaction reads values from the database into its local workspace, making changes without influencing the actual database. During the validation phase, the system checks if the transaction's read set conflicts with other concurrently committed transactions. If no conflicts are detected, the transaction proceeds to the write phase, applying its changes to the database.

Consider the following pseudocode illustrating an OCC mechanism:

```
BEGIN TRANSACTION
  /* Read Phase */
  SELECT * FROM inventory WHERE item_id = 101 INTO
      localData;

  /* Modification in local workspace */
  localData.quantity = localData.quantity - 1;

  /* Validation Phase */
  IF (No conflicts detected) THEN
```

```
    /* Write Phase */
    UPDATE inventory SET quantity = localData.quantity WHERE
        item_id = 101;
    COMMIT;
  ELSE
    ROLLBACK;
END TRANSACTION;
```

In this scenario, the transaction reads the quantity of a specific item_id into localData. After modifying localData, it validates for conflicts before applying the changes to the inventory.

PCC, in contrast, assumes that conflicts between concurrent transactions are common and thus actively inhibits conflict occurrences by employing locks. Transactions acquire locks on the data they wish to manipulate, ensuring that no other transactions can access locked data until the locks are released. This approach guarantees data integrity at the cost of potential performance bottlenecks due to lock contention and deadlocks.

PCC typically uses several types of locks, such as shared (S) locks for reading and exclusive (X) locks for writing. A transaction with a shared lock can coexist with other transactions holding shared locks on the same data, but no transaction can acquire an exclusive lock on that data until all shared locks are released. Conversely, an exclusive lock blocks both shared and exclusive locks from other transactions.

The following pseudocode exemplifies a PCC mechanism:

```
BEGIN TRANSACTION
  /* Locking Phase */
  LOCK TABLE inventory IN EXCLUSIVE MODE;

  /* Read and Write Phase */
  SELECT quantity FROM inventory WHERE item_id = 101;
  UPDATE inventory SET quantity = quantity - 1 WHERE item_id
      = 101;

  /* Commit Phase */
  COMMIT;
  /* Release Lock */
END TRANSACTION;
```

Here, the transaction locks the inventory table in exclusive mode before reading and updating the quantity. This prevents other transactions from accessing the table concurrently, mitigating conflicts.

In comparing OCC and PCC, the choice of method hinges on system workload characteristics and performance requirements. OCC is more suitable for read-heavy environments with low contention, as it optimizes throughput by avoiding locks unless necessary. However, OCC faces challenges with high contention, where the overhead of validation failures and transaction retries can surpass the costs of locking.

PCC, on the other hand, guarantees conflict prevention through locking, making it ideal for write-heavy workloads with significant data manipulation and higher contention. While PCC ensures transactional integrity, it can lead to reduced concurrency and potential deadlocks, requiring deadlock detection and resolution mechanisms.

The outputs of these mechanisms can be observed through example scenarios. Consider two transactions, T1 and T2, operating on the same data record:

```
T1: BEGIN;
   SELECT quantity FROM inventory WHERE item_id = 101;
   UPDATE inventory SET quantity = quantity - 1 WHERE item_id = 101;
   COMMIT;

T2: BEGIN;
   SELECT quantity FROM inventory WHERE item_id = 101;
   UPDATE inventory SET quantity = quantity - 1 WHERE item_id = 101;
   COMMIT;
```

Under OCC, both transactions might proceed to the validation phase, where one may be rolled back if a conflict is detected at commit time. Under PCC, T2 would be blocked by T1's lock until T1 completes, eliminating the conflict by serializing access.

Optimally deploying OCC or PCC is pivotal for ensuring database performance, integrity, and concurrency. Mastery over these methodologies enables database practitioners to tailor solutions befitting specific use cases, adapting to dynamic workload patterns and performance exigencies.

6.9 Two-Phase Commit

The Two-Phase Commit (2PC) protocol is a distributed algorithm that ensures all participating nodes in a distributed database either commit or abort a transaction uniformly. This protocol is essential in achieving atomicity in distributed systems, preventing scenarios where some nodes commit while others do not, thereby maintaining consistent and reliable datasets across multiple locations.

The 2PC protocol operates through two sequential phases: the prepare phase and the commit phase. Each phase involves specific roles and responsibilities that participants in the transaction must adhere to.

Prepare Phase:

1. *Transaction Initiation:* The process begins with the coordinator (often a distributed transaction manager) requesting a transaction. 2. *Vote Request:* The coordinator sends a VOTE_REQUEST message to all participating nodes (participants).

```
COORDINATOR:
    send VOTE_REQUEST to all participants
```

3. *Vote Response:* Each participant processes the VOTE_REQUEST and responds with either a VOTE_COMMIT (indicating the ability to commit the transaction) or a VOTE_ABORT (indicating inability to commit).

```
PARTICIPANT:
    if transaction can be committed then
        send VOTE_COMMIT to coordinator
    else
        send VOTE_ABORT to coordinator
```

4. *Local Decision Logging:* Participants log their decision locally to ensure no information is lost in case of a failure.

Commit Phase:

1. *Global Decision:* The coordinator collects all votes. If all participants sent VOTE_COMMIT, the global decision is to commit. If any participant sent VOTE_ABORT, the global decision is to abort.

```
COORDINATOR:
    if all votes are VOTE_COMMIT then
        decision = COMMIT
    else
        decision = ABORT
```

2. *Decision Broadcast:* The coordinator broadcasts the decision (COMMIT or ABORT) to all participants.

```
COORDINATOR:
    send DECISION to all participants
```

3. *Commit/Abort Actions:* Upon receiving the decision, participants commit or abort the transaction as directed.

```
PARTICIPANT:
    if decision == COMMIT then
        commit transaction
    else
        abort transaction
```

4. *Acknowledgments:* Each participant acknowledges the coordinator after completing the commit/abort action.

```
PARTICIPANT:
    send ACK to coordinator
```

5. *Finalization:* The coordinator, having received acknowledgments from all participants, finalizes the transaction.

The two-phases of the 2PC protocol ensure that all nodes agree on a uniform transaction outcome, thus preserving the ACID properties, specifically atomicity and durability, in distributed transactions.

Failure Handling:

In distributed systems, nodes or the network can fail at any time, requiring robust failure handling mechanisms within the 2PC protocol:

- *Coordinator Failure During Prepare Phase:* If the coordinator fails before broadcasting VOTE_REQUEST, no participant will have received the decision. The transaction effectively becomes aborted as participants have not altered their state.

- *Coordinator Failure During Commit Phase:* If the coordinator fails after sending the VOTE_REQUEST but before reaching a decision, the participants, upon timeout waiting for a decision, can manage this through a protocol restart. The decision can be reconstructed either by electing a new coordinator or by utilizing heuristics.

- *Participant Failure During Prepare Phase:* If a participant fails to respond to a VOTE_REQUEST, the coordinator treats non-response as VOTE_ABORT.

- *Participant Failure During Commit Phase:* After receiving a global decision, if a participant fails before acknowledging, it will check the log upon recovery and complete the necessary commit or abort based on the recorded transaction state.

Practical Implementation Example:

Consider a bank's distributed transaction system involving two databases: one for accounts and another for loans. Assume a transaction transfers funds from a customer's savings account (in database A) to a loan account (in database B).

```
COORDINATOR:
    send VOTE_REQUEST to both Database A and Database B

DATABASE A:
    if funds are available then
        log VOTE_COMMIT
        send VOTE_COMMIT to coordinator
    else
        log VOTE_ABORT
        send VOTE_ABORT to coordinator

DATABASE B:
    prepare to receive funds
    log VOTE_COMMIT
    send VOTE_COMMIT to coordinator
```

If the coordinator receives VOTE_COMMIT from both databases, it sends COMMIT messages to both:

```
COORDINATOR:
    send COMMIT to Database A and Database B

DATABASE A:
    deduct funds from savings account
    log COMMIT
    send ACK to coordinator

DATABASE B:
    add funds to loan account
    log COMMIT
    send ACK to coordinator
```

This example ensures that funds are either transferred successfully or the transaction is aborted without partial completion, maintaining consistency across both databases. During the whole process, local logs guarantee that any node can recover its precise state, preserving the atomicity and durability properties of the transaction.

6.10 Handling Long-Running Transactions

Long-running transactions (LRTs) pose unique challenges in database management due to their extensive duration and the potential for conflicts with other concurrent transactions. Proper handling of LRTs is essential to maintaining performance and ensuring data integrity.

1. Definition and Characteristics

Long-running transactions are transactions that span extended periods, ranging from minutes to hours or even days. These transactions typically involve complex operations, large datasets, or workflows requiring user input at various stages. Their extended duration exposes them to higher risks of conflicts, deadlocks, and resource contention compared to short-lived transactions.

2. Challenges Associated with Long-Running Transactions

- **Concurrency Control:** LRTs can lock resources for substantial periods, increasing the likelihood of conflicts with other transactions. Managing concurrency effectively in such scenarios becomes critical.
- **Resource Contention:** Prolonged holding of database locks and other resources by LRTs may lead to contention, adversely affecting the performance of other transactions.
- **Deadlocks:** The lengthy duration of LRTs increases the probability of deadlocks, requiring robust deadlock detection and resolution mechanisms.
- **Failure Recovery:** In the event of a system failure, recovering LRTs can be more complex than recovering short transactions due to their size and complexity.
- **State Management:** Keeping track of intermediate states and partial progress is essential, especially when transactions may involve human interaction or multiple systems.

3. Strategies for Managing Long-Running Transactions

a. Process Orchestration:

One approach to managing LRTs is to break them into smaller sub-transactions or tasks that can be independently committed. This strategy, often referred to as sagas or process orchestration, involves:

- **Division into Sub-transactions:** The LRT is decomposed into a series of smaller, manageable sub-transactions. Each sub-transaction is designed to achieve a specific part of the overall work.
- **Compensation Mechanisms:** Each sub-transaction has an associated compensating transaction that can undo its effects, ensuring that partial failures can be effectively managed.
- **Orchestration Logic:** An orchestration engine coordinates the execution of sub-transactions, handling retries, compensations, and any user interventions required.

Example in Pseudocode:

```
transaction_status := SUCCESS
for sub_transaction in long_running_transaction:
    result := execute(sub_transaction)
    if result == FAILURE:
        compensation_needed = True
        break
if compensation_needed:
    for executed_transaction in
         reverse_executed_sub_transactions:
        compensate(executed_transaction)
    transaction_status := FAILURE
return transaction_status
```

b. Optimistic Concurrency Control:

Optimistic concurrency control (OCC) is a technique used to handle LRTs by allowing transactions to execute without locking resources. Conflicts are checked only at the time of commit:

- **Execution without Locks:** Transactions proceed without acquiring locks, reducing contention.

- **Validation Phase:** Upon completion, the transaction's read and write sets are validated. If no conflicts are detected with other committed transactions, the transaction is allowed to commit.
- **Retry Mechanism:** In case of a conflict, the transaction is rolled back and retried, ensuring eventual consistency.

Example:

```
START TRANSACTION
...
-- Operations without locks
...
VALIDATE TRANSACTION
if validation_successful:
    COMMIT
else:
    ROLLBACK
    Retry transaction
```

c. Savepoints and Partial Commits:

Savepoints allow a transaction to set intermediate points of progress within its execution, enabling partial rollbacks without affecting the entire transaction. This is particularly useful in LRTs where certain segments of work are independent:

- **Creating Savepoints:** Savepoints mark specific points within a transaction where the state can be saved.
- **Rolling Back to Savepoints:** If an error occurs, the transaction can be rolled back to the last savepoint, preserving the work done before that point.
- **Reducing Rollback Overhead:** By limiting rollbacks to the nearest savepoint, the overhead associated with handling errors is minimized.

Example in SQL:

```
BEGIN TRANSACTION;
...
SAVEPOINT sp1;
...
```

```
-- Some operations
...
if (error_condition):
    ROLLBACK TO sp1;
else:
    ...
COMMIT;
```

d. State Persistence:

Persisting the state of a transaction periodically helps to recover from failures without restarting from the beginning. This technique involves:

- **Periodic State Saving:** The transaction state is persistently saved at regular intervals or specific milestones.
- **Recovery Procedures:** Upon a failure, the transaction can resume from the last saved state rather than restarting.
- **Reducing Redundant Work:** Helps avoid re-execution of already completed steps, reducing redundancy.

4. Example Scenario: A Complex E-Commerce Transaction

Consider an e-commerce platform's complex transaction involving a series of actions: inventory check, payment processing, order confirmation, and shipment initiation. Each action may require interactions with different services and user inputs.

```
BEGIN TRANSACTION;

-- Check inventory
SAVEPOINT check_inventory;
SELECT * FROM inventory WHERE product_id = 101;
if (inventory_available):
    UPDATE inventory SET quantity = quantity - 1 WHERE
        product_id = 101;
else:
    ROLLBACK TO check_inventory;
    -- handle error

-- Process payment
SAVEPOINT process_payment;
CALL processPayment(user_id, amount);
```

```
if (payment_successful):
    UPDATE orders SET status = 'Paid' WHERE order_id =
        202;
else:
    ROLLBACK TO process_payment;
    -- handle error

-- Confirm order
SAVEPOINT confirm_order;
UPDATE orders SET status = 'Confirmed' WHERE order_id =
    202;
if (order_confirmed):
    ...
else:
    ROLLBACK TO confirm_order;
    -- handle error

-- Initiate shipment
SAVEPOINT initiate_shipment;
CALL initiateShipment(order_id = 202);
if (shipment_initiated):
    UPDATE orders SET status = 'Shipped' WHERE order_id
        = 202;
else:
    ROLLBACK TO initiate_shipment;
    -- handle error

COMMIT;
```

This example demonstrates the use of savepoints to manage error handling and partial rollbacks within a long-running transaction. By structuring the transaction with intermediate savepoints, the system maintains progress and ensures that failures can be addressed without restarting the entire process.

Adopting these strategies for handling long-running transactions ensures that databases can efficiently manage complex operations, minimize conflicts, and maintain data integrity even under challenging conditions.

6.11 Best Practices for Transaction Management

Effective transaction management is critical for ensuring consistency, reliability, and performance in a database environment. Employing best practices for transaction management minimizes the risk of data anomalies, resource contention, and performance bottlenecks. The following subsections elaborate on various techniques and considerations that can help in achieving optimal transaction management.

1. Minimize Transaction Duration

Shortening the length of transactions reduces the likelihood of locking conflicts and deadlocks. This is particularly relevant in systems with high levels of concurrency. Decompose long transactions into smaller, manageable units that address specific tasks:

```
-- Example of a long transaction
BEGIN TRANSACTION;
    UPDATE accounts SET balance = balance - 500 WHERE
        account_id = 1;
    UPDATE accounts SET balance = balance + 500 WHERE
        account_id = 2;
    -- Additional complex operations...
COMMIT;

-- Decomposed short transactions
BEGIN TRANSACTION;
    UPDATE accounts SET balance = balance - 500 WHERE
        account_id = 1;
COMMIT;

BEGIN TRANSACTION;
    UPDATE accounts SET balance = balance + 500 WHERE
        account_id = 2;
COMMIT;
```

2. Use Appropriate Isolation Levels

Selecting the correct isolation level is fundamental to balancing data consistency and system performance. Isolation levels such as READ COMMITTED, REPEATABLE READ, and SERIALIZABLE offer various trade-offs between consistency and concurrency. Choose the level appropriate for the application's consistency requirements:

- READ COMMITTED minimizes locking overhead but may allow non-repeatable read phenomena.
- REPEATABLE READ prevents non-repeatable reads but may lead to more frequent locks.
- SERIALIZABLE provides the highest level of consistency but restricts concurrency significantly.

```
-- Setting isolation level to READ COMMITTED
SET TRANSACTION ISOLATION LEVEL READ COMMITTED;
```

3. Avoid Unnecessary Locking

Excessive and inappropriate locking strategies can severely hamper performance. When possible, employ row-level or finer-grained locks instead of table-level locks to enhance concurrency:

- Opt for optimistic concurrency control when conflicts are rare.
- Use locking hints judiciously to prevent escalation to higher-level locks.

```
-- Example of row-level locking
BEGIN TRANSACTION;
SELECT * FROM orders WHERE order_id = 1001 FOR UPDATE;
UPDATE orders SET status = 'processed' WHERE order_id = 1001;
COMMIT;
```

4. Implement Robust Deadlock Detection and Resolution

Detecting and resolving deadlocks efficiently is essential to maintaining system stability. Use database management system (DBMS) features like deadlock detection algorithms and timeout settings to automate resolution. Ensure that the application logic catches exceptions and handles deadlocks gracefully:

```
-- Pseudocode for deadlock detection
TRY
    BEGIN TRANSACTION;
    -- Operations prone to deadlock
    COMMIT;
```

```
CATCH deadlock_exception
    ROLLBACK;
    -- Handle deadlock resolution
END TRY;
```

5. Utilize Savepoints for Partial Rollbacks

Savepoints allow rollback of specific parts of a transaction without undoing the entire transaction. This can be particularly useful in complex transactions involving multiple update operations. Establish savepoints at critical junctures to maintain finer control over transaction integrity:

```
BEGIN TRANSACTION;
    SAVEPOINT before_update;
    UPDATE inventory SET quantity = quantity - 10 WHERE
        product_id = 50;
    -- Complex operation prone to failure
    -- Rollback to savepoint upon failure
    ROLLBACK TO before_update;
    -- Continue with other operations
COMMIT;
```

6. Monitor and Optimize Transaction Performance

Constant monitoring of transaction performance metrics, such as response times and throughput, assists in identifying bottlenecks. Leverage database profiling tools and performance tuning techniques to optimize transaction execution:

- Index critical columns involved in transactions to speed up query performance.
- Use query optimization techniques to reduce execution time.
- Regularly review and refactor transaction logic to remove inefficiencies.

7. Maintain Consistent Backup and Recovery Strategies

Solid backup and recovery procedures ensure data integrity and availability. Regularly scheduled backups and well-tested recovery plans minimize downtime and data loss in the event of failures:

```
-- Example of a backup schedule
BACKUP DATABASE mydatabase TO DISK = 'C:\backups\
    mydatabase.bak';
```

8. Enforce Application-Level Transaction Management

While DBMS features provide robust transaction management capabilities, application-level logic should also enforce business rules and consistency requirements. Ensure that the application properly initiates, commits, and rolls back transactions based on logic:

```
# Example in Python
import psycopg2

conn = psycopg2.connect("dbname=test user=postgres")
cur = conn.cursor()

try:
    cur.execute("BEGIN;")
    cur.execute("UPDATE accounts SET balance = balance - 100
        WHERE account_id = 1;")
    cur.execute("UPDATE accounts SET balance = balance + 100
        WHERE account_id = 2;")
    conn.commit()
except Exception as e:
    conn.rollback()
    print("Transaction failed:", e)
finally:
    cur.close()
    conn.close()
```

Applying these best practices consistently leads to enhanced transaction management, ensuring that database systems perform efficiently and reliably under various workloads and conditions. Ensuring thorough understanding and thoughtful application of these principles is essential for both novice and experienced database administrators and developers.

6.12 Case Studies in Transaction Management

To illustrate the practical application of the concepts discussed in this chapter, we will examine several case studies that demonstrate effective transaction management strategies in diverse scenarios. The selected case studies highlight challenges and solutions related to ACID properties, concurrency control, deadlock resolution, and other critical aspects of transaction management.

Case Study 1: Online Retail System

An online retail company operates a global e-commerce platform where users can purchase various products. The system must handle a high volume of concurrent transactions, including order processing, payment handling, and inventory management. Ensuring consistency and isolation while maintaining high performance is crucial.

Problem: Multiple users often attempt to purchase the same limited-quantity items simultaneously, leading to potential overselling or data inconsistencies.

Solution: The system employs a combination of locking mechanisms and isolation levels to handle these scenarios. Specifically, the Repeatable Read isolation level is utilized to ensure that once a transaction reads a set of data, no other transaction can modify this data until the first transaction completes. Additionally, row-level locking is applied to protect specific inventory entries.

```
-- Example SQL for handling inventory updates with row-level locking
START TRANSACTION;

SELECT quantity FROM inventory WHERE product_id = '12345'
    FOR UPDATE;

IF (quantity > 0) THEN
  UPDATE inventory SET quantity = quantity - 1 WHERE
      product_id = '12345';
  -- Process payment and complete order
  COMMIT;
ELSE
  ROLLBACK;
  -- Notify user item is out of stock
ENDIF;
```

To prevent long-term locks and potential deadlocks, transactions are designed to be as short and efficient as possible, focusing on critical sections that require isolation.

Case Study 2: Banking System

A multinational bank manages millions of accounts and processes numerous financial transactions daily. Ensuring the atomicity and durability of transactions is vital to prevent data inconsistencies and financial loss.

Problem: Concurrent transactions involving the same accounts, such as simultaneous deposits and withdrawals, can lead to issues like lost updates or temporary inconsistencies.

Solution: The bank uses the Serializable isolation level for transactions involving critical account updates, ensuring complete isolation. Additionally, the two-phase commit protocol is implemented for distributed transactions to guarantee atomicity across different branches.

```
-- Example SQL for transferring funds between accounts using
    Serializable isolation level
SET TRANSACTION ISOLATION LEVEL SERIALIZABLE;
START TRANSACTION;

UPDATE accounts SET balance = balance - 500 WHERE
    account_id = 'A123';
UPDATE accounts SET balance = balance + 500 WHERE
    account_id = 'B456';

COMMIT;
```

By using the Serializable isolation level, the system ensures that transactions are executed as if they occurred sequentially, preventing any concurrent transaction interference.

Case Study 3: Manufacturing Company

A manufacturing company uses a database to manage its supply chain, including raw material orders, production schedules, and shipping logistics. The system must handle long-running transactions that span several hours or even days.

Problem: Long-running transactions can lock resources for extended periods, causing deadlocks or blocking other transactions, significantly impacting system performance.

Solution: The company utilizes optimistic concurrency control to handle long-running transactions. Periodic validation checks are performed to ensure consistency without holding locks for the entire duration of a transaction.

```
-- Pseudocode for optimistic concurrency control
START TRANSACTION;

READ current_state FROM supplies WHERE order_id = '789';

-- Perform necessary operations (e.g., schedule production)

VALIDATE new_state WHERE order_id = '789';

IF (new_state == current_state) THEN
  -- Commit the transaction if the state is consistent
  COMMIT;
ELSE
  -- Rollback if the state has changed
  ROLLBACK;
  -- Retry or handle conflict
ENDIF;
```

Optimistic concurrency control reduces the likelihood of deadlocks by avoiding long-term locks, allowing the system to scale and perform efficiently even with long-running tasks.

Case Study 4: Social Media Platform

A social media platform with millions of users processes interactions like posting, commenting, and reacting in real-time. Ensuring the responsiveness and correctness of these interactions is essential.

Problem: The platform must serve user interactions rapidly while maintaining data integrity and avoiding phenomena like dirty reads or non-repeatable reads.

Solution: The platform implements a combination of Snapshot Isolation and Multi-Version Concurrency Control (MVCC) to address these challenges. This allows users to read consistent snapshots of data without interfering with concurrent updates.

```
-- Example SQL using Snapshot Isolation
SET TRANSACTION ISOLATION LEVEL SNAPSHOT;
START TRANSACTION;

-- Read current state of user post
SELECT * FROM posts WHERE post_id = '987';

-- Perform interactions like adding a comment
```

```
INSERT INTO comments (post_id, user_id, comment) VALUES ('
    987', 'user123', 'Nice post!');

COMMIT;
```

Snapshot Isolation ensures that transactions see a consistent view of the database, eliminating issues like dirty reads or non-repeatable reads, thus maintaining both performance and data integrity.

Each of these case studies demonstrates how different strategies and mechanisms can be applied to manage transactions effectively in various environments. By understanding these practical applications, one can better appreciate the importance of thorough and well-considered transaction management in database systems.

Chapter 7

Indexing and Query Optimization

This chapter focuses on the principles and practices of indexing and query optimization. It details various types of indexes such as B-Tree, Hash, and Bitmap, and provides instructions on creating and dropping indexes. Indexing strategies and their applications in queries are discussed. The chapter also covers understanding execution plans using tools like EXPLAIN and EXPLAIN ANALYZE, optimizing SELECT, INSERT, UPDATE, and DELETE queries, data partitioning, and the role of database statistics in cost-based optimization. Practical case studies in query optimization are included.

7.1 Introduction to Indexes

Indexes in databases serve as a powerful mechanism to enhance query performance, enabling efficient data retrieval. By maintaining an auxiliary data structure that holds pointers to the actual data, indexes significantly reduce the amount of data that the database needs to scan to fulfill a query. Understanding the underpinnings of indexes is crucial for designing efficient databases and optimizing queries.

An index is essentially a data structure that improves the speed of data retrieval operations on a table at the cost of additional storage space and increased maintenance time during data insertions, updates, and deletions. The primary purpose of an index is to reduce the number of disk I/O operations required to locate data. This is particularly beneficial for large datasets where full table scans can be prohibitively time-consuming.

```
CREATE INDEX index_name ON table_name(column_name);
```

The above SQL command creates an index named index_name on the specified column_name of table_name. The creation of an index involves sorting the indexed column's data and constructing a search tree to allow for rapid data access.

Indexes can be classified into several types: B-Tree, Hash, and Bitmap, among others. Each type has unique characteristics and is suited for different use cases. B-Tree indexes, for instance, are widely used due to their balanced structure, allowing logarithmic-time queries. Hash indexes are useful for exact-match lookups but are not suitable for range queries. Bitmap indexes, on the other hand, are efficient for columns with a limited number of distinct values and are often used in data warehousing applications.

Consider the following execution plan generated for a query without an index:

```
EXPLAIN ANALYZE SELECT * FROM table_name WHERE
    column_name = 'value';
```

```
Seq Scan on table_name (cost=0.00..431.00 rows=250 width=12) (actual time=0.012..15.175 rows=1 loops=1)
  Filter: (column_name = 'value')
  Rows Removed by Filter: 999
Planning time: 0.151 ms
Execution time: 15.204 ms
```

The execution plan above shows a sequential scan (Seq Scan) being performed, where the database examines every row of table_name to find the matching column_name = 'value'. This approach is inefficient for large tables.

Now, let us consider the execution plan after creating an index on column_name:

```
EXPLAIN ANALYZE SELECT * FROM table_name WHERE
    column_name = 'value';
```

```
Index Scan using index_name on table_name (cost=0.29..8.42 rows=5 width=12) (actual time=0.021..0.042 rows=1 loops=1)
  Index Cond: (column_name = 'value')
Planning time: 0.205 ms
Execution time: 0.064 ms
```

In this case, the execution plan indicates that an index scan (Index Scan) is utilized, significantly reducing the query execution time from 15.204 ms to 0.064 ms. This efficiency gain underscores the importance of proper index utilization.

The advantages of indexes, however, come with trade-offs. Indexes consume additional disk space and memory, and they can impact the performance of data modification operations. Each insert, update, or delete operation on a table with indexes necessitates corresponding modifications to the indexes. Hence, it is vital to judiciously select columns to index, focusing on those frequently involved in query predicates and join conditions.

Indices are especially beneficial in the contexts of primary keys and unique constraints, where they enforce uniqueness and expedite lookup operations. Furthermore, indexes support various database features, such as clustered indexes, which determine the physical ordering of data in a table, and covering indexes, where the index contains all the columns required by a query, negating the need to access the table data.

Understanding and implementing indexes are fundamental steps in the journey to mastering SQL and database design, providing the tools to optimize query performance and maintain efficient data access patterns in diverse application scenarios.

7.2 Types of Indexes: B-Tree, Hash, Bitmap

Indexes play a crucial role in enhancing database performance by reducing the amount of data that needs to be scanned to locate rows that meet certain criteria. This section examines three primary types of indexes: B-Tree, Hash, and Bitmap. Each has different use cases based on the nature of the data and the types of queries being executed.

B-Tree Indexes

B-Tree indexes (Balanced Tree indexes) are the most common type of index, particularly well-suited for a wide variety of querying needs. They are particularly effective for range queries, as they maintain their sorted order. A B-Tree is a self-balancing tree data structure that ensures all leaf nodes are at the same depth, thereby keeping the tree balanced.

The structure of a B-Tree index allows for rapid traversal and retrieval operations. When an index is created on a column, the database constructs a B-Tree where leaf nodes contain pointers to the actual data in the table. The process of finding a record involves traversing the tree from the root to the leaf. This traversal time is logarithmic, making B-Tree indexes efficient even for large datasets.

```
CREATE INDEX idx_customer_name ON customers (
    customer_name);
```

Typical operations such as equality searches, range queries, and sorting operations see significant performance improvements when B-Tree indexes are utilized. For example, the following SELECT query would benefit from the previously created B-Tree index if the table includes numerous entries:

```
SELECT * FROM customers WHERE customer_name BETWEEN '
    A' AND 'M';
```

Hash Indexes

Hash indexes are designed for equality searches. They use a hash function to convert a search key into a unique identifier, which is then used to locate the corresponding entry in the table.

Unlike B-Tree indexes, hash indexes do not maintain any order among the indexed values, making them highly inefficient for range queries but highly efficient for exact matches. This characteristic stems from the nature of hash functions, which provide a direct mapping of keys to specific locations in the index based on the hash value.

```
CREATE INDEX idx_customer_id ON customers USING HASH (
    customer_id);
```

A query such as the following would leverage the hash index effectively:

```
SELECT * FROM customers WHERE customer_id = 12345;
```

Bitmap Indexes

Bitmap indexes are particularly useful in environments where the columns contain a limited number of distinct values, such as categorical data. Instead of storing a full pointer to each data row, a bitmap index uses a series of bits (bit array) to represent the presence or absence of a value.

Each bit in the bitmap corresponds to a row in the table, with the bit set to 1 if the row contains the value of interest and 0 otherwise.

This format makes bitmap indexes space-efficient, especially for low-cardinality columns, and ideal for combining multiple indexes quickly. The AND, OR, and NOT operations on the bitmaps allow rapid filtering of rows based on multiple conditions.

```
CREATE BITMAP INDEX idx_gender ON employees (gender);
```

Suppose we need to extract data about employees who are female (gender = 'F'):

```
SELECT * FROM employees WHERE gender = 'F';
```

Utilizing the bitmap index can significantly reduce the I/O operations required to satisfy such queries.

Each type of index has unique advantages and is suited to specific workloads. Careful selection and application of indexes can result in considerable performance gains, underscoring the importance of understanding the nuances and appropriate use cases for B-Tree, Hash, and Bitmap indexes.

7.3 Creating and Dropping Indexes

Creating and dropping indexes are fundamental operations in database management systems (DBMSs) that allow for significant optimization during data retrieval. Proper utilization of these operations can lead to enhanced performance and efficiency of queries.

To create an index, the CREATE INDEX statement is employed. This statement specifies the index name, the table on which the index is to be created, and the columns to be indexed. Depending on the DBMS being used, the syntax may vary slightly, but the following example is representative of a common SQL variant:

```
CREATE INDEX idx_customer_lastname
ON customers (lastname);
```

In this example, an index named idx_customer_lastname is created on the lastname column of the customers table. The chosen column is critical as it determines the efficiency of indexed searches. Careful consideration should be given to selecting columns that are frequently used in query conditions.

Composite indexes involve multiple columns and can be created using a similar syntax. Composite indexes are particularly useful when queries commonly filter or sort based on the combination of the indexed columns. The SQL statement below demonstrates the creation of a composite index:

```
CREATE INDEX idx_order_customer_date
ON orders (customer_id, order_date);
```

The newly created index idx_order_customer_date will enhance query performance for operations involving both the customer_id and order_date columns in the orders table. When deciding the order of columns in a composite index, remember that the DBMS will use the index for queries that match the prefix of the index columns.

Unique indexes enforce uniqueness on the indexed columns, ensuring that no duplicate values exist. They are often utilized on primary key columns. The creation of a unique index is achieved with the following SQL syntax:

```
CREATE UNIQUE INDEX idx_unique_email
ON users (email);
```

Here, idx_unique_email ensures that all entries in the email column of the users table are distinct, preventing the insertion of duplicate email addresses.

Dropping an index removes it from the database schema. This operation can be necessary when an index is no longer required, perhaps due to changes in query patterns or the database schema. The statement to drop an index is straightforward:

```
DROP INDEX idx_customer_lastname;
```

Executing the above command will delete idx_customer_lastname from the database. It's important to understand that dropping an index can affect query performance, as the optimization benefits provided by the index will be lost.

Some DBMSs offer additional options for managing indexes, such as specifying the storage settings or including a partial index, which only indexes a subset of rows meeting a certain condition. For example, in PostgreSQL, a partial index can be created as shown:

```
CREATE INDEX idx_active_customers
```

```
ON customers (lastname)
WHERE active = true;
```

This index idx_active_customers will only include rows where the active column is true, which can be beneficial for optimizing queries that frequently access active customers.

Understanding the underlying physical structure of different index types (such as B-Tree, Hash, Bitmap) is also crucial as it influences how each index type can be employed efficiently. For instance, B-Tree indexes are suitable for range queries, while Hash indexes provide fast lookups but do not support range queries.

Indexes are indispensable for database performance tuning. However, they should be used judiciously as they come with some overhead, especially regarding write operations such as INSERT, UPDATE, and DELETE, because each index must be maintained in conjunction with the base table.

Proper index management involves regular monitoring and analysis using performance tools and metrics to ensure that indexes continue to provide the expected performance benefits, and to identify opportunities for improvement or required adjustments. Balancing index creation to optimize read operations while minimizing the impact on write operations is key to proficient database management.

- Index creation and dropping commands

```
CREATE INDEX idx_customer_lastname ON customers (lastname);
DROP INDEX idx_customer_lastname;
```

7.4 Indexing Strategies

Effective indexing strategies are critical for optimizing database performance. These strategies involve the thoughtful selection and combination of indexes to ensure that query execution is both efficient and accurate. Adopting the appropriate indexing strategies reduces access time and improves query performance significantly. Here, we delve into several impactful indexing strategies.

Composite Indexes: A composite index is an index on multiple columns of a table. Such indexes are highly effective when queries filter or sort by multiple columns simultaneously. For instance, consider a table with columns first_name and last_name. A composite index on both columns can optimize queries that search by both fields:

```
CREATE INDEX idx_name ON employees(first_name, last_name);
```

Such an index benefits queries like:

```
SELECT * FROM employees WHERE first_name = 'John' AND
    last_name = 'Doe';
```

while also assisting with queries that involve just the first indexed column. However, it does not help much with queries only on last_name, emphasizing the need to design composite indexes thoughtfully.

Covering Indexes: A covering index is a special type of composite index where all the columns needed by the query are included in the index. This means the database can retrieve query results directly from the index, bypassing the table entirely. Consider the following query:

```
SELECT first_name, last_name FROM employees WHERE
    department_id = 10;
```

A covering index can be created as:

```
CREATE INDEX idx_cover ON employees(department_id,
    first_name, last_name);
```

In this setup, since the index contains all columns required by the query, it significantly reduces I/O operations.

Clustered vs. Non-Clustered Indexing: Understanding the distinction between clustered and non-clustered indexes is vital. A clustered index sorts and stores the data rows of the table based on the key values. Each table can have only one clustered index because the data rows themselves are stored in the order of the clustered index. This is particularly effective for range queries:

```
CREATE CLUSTERED INDEX idx_cluster ON employees(
    employee_id);
```

Conversely, non-clustered indexes store pointers to the data rows. These indexes are more widely used as they allow multiple indexes per table, catering to varied search conditions and performance improvements:

```
CREATE INDEX idx_noncluster ON employees(last_name);
```

The choice between clustered and non-clustered indexing depends on the nature of queries and the need for sequential access.

Indexing Selective Columns: Indexes work best on columns with high selectivity, meaning a high ratio of distinct values compared to the total number of rows. For example, indexing a gender column with a limited number of unique values (e.g., "M" and "F") is generally ineffective. Instead, columns like email or social_security_number with unique or highly variable data are better choices for indexing:

```
CREATE INDEX idx_email ON employees(email);
```

This strategy ensures the index's utility in significantly narrowing down the search space.

Partial Indexes: Partial indexes are designed to index only a subset of the rows in a table, based on a conditional expression. This reduces the index size and improves performance for queries that focus on that specific subset. For instance, to index only active employees:

```
CREATE INDEX idx_active ON employees(status) WHERE status
    = 'Active';
```

Such an index optimizes queries that filter by the active status, saving on both storage and maintenance costs.

Index Maintenance and Rebuilding: Over time, indexes might become fragmented, leading to suboptimal performance. Regularly rebuilding indexes can mitigate this issue. Fragmentation occurs due to frequent updates, inserts, and deletes. To rebuild an index in MySQL:

```
ALTER TABLE employees REBUILD INDEX idx_name;
```

Similarly, SQL Server provides a command to reorganize indexes:

```
ALTER INDEX idx_name ON employees REORGANIZE;
```

This operation defragments the index, improving its performance and ensuring that queries maintain optimal speed.

Indexing strategies should also consider the underlying infrastructure, such as the storage engine (e.g., InnoDB or MyISAM in MySQL) and the expected workload. For example, read-intensive applications might benefit more from extensive indexing compared to write-intensive scenarios where indexes can slow down frequent writes. Continuous monitoring and tuning are essential to ensure that the indexing strategies align with the evolving usage patterns and data characteristics.

7.5 Using Indexes in Queries

Indexes play a critical role in enhancing database query performance by reducing the amount of data the database engine needs to scan. Through effective use of indexes, queries can achieve faster execution times, which is particularly important for large datasets. This section delves into practical application and advantages of using indexes in different types of SQL queries.

When a query is executed, the database engine determines whether it can use available indexes to minimize the amount of data scanned. For example, consider the following query:

```
SELECT * FROM employees WHERE last_name = 'Smith';
```

If the last_name column in the employees table is indexed, the database engine can rapidly locate all records where the last_name is 'Smith'. The index serves as a sorted lookup table, allowing the engine to quickly skip to the relevant entries without scanning the entire table.

Not all queries benefit uniformly from indexes. The database engine uses indexes in a variety of query types, such as:

- **Equality Searches:** These are queries that match a column to a specific value. For example:

  ```
  SELECT * FROM Products WHERE product_id = 1001;
  ```

- **Range Searches:** These queries search for rows where a column's value falls within a specific range. For instance:

  ```
  SELECT * FROM Orders WHERE order_date BETWEEN
      '2023-01-01' AND '2023-12-31';
  ```

- **Prefix Searches:** Involved in matching patterns using operators like LIKE. For example:

  ```
  SELECT * FROM Customers WHERE first_name LIKE '
      Joh%';
  ```

- **Join Operations:** When multiple tables are involved, indexes can improve the performance of join conditions:

```
SELECT Orders.order_id, Customers.customer_name
FROM Orders
JOIN Customers ON Orders.customer_id = Customers.
    customer_id;
```

In addition to these common usages, indexed columns play a critical role in **aggregate functions** and **sorting**. When executing queries involving GROUP BY, ORDER BY, or aggregate functions like COUNT, SUM, indexed columns can significantly expedite query processing. For instance:

```
SELECT department, COUNT(*)
FROM Employees
GROUP BY department;
```

If the department column is indexed, the database engine has a pre-sorted list to directly access different departments, speeding up the grouping process.

Moreover, compound indexes—indexes on multiple columns—enhance multi-column search efficiency. Consider the following compound index and query:

```
CREATE INDEX idx_employee_name ON Employees (last_name,
    first_name);

SELECT * FROM Employees
WHERE last_name = 'Doe' AND first_name = 'John';
```

In the scenario above, leveraging a compound index, the database engine performs a search operation using both last_name and first_name, making the retrieval more efficient than using separate indexes.

Indexes are also crucial for optimizing *non-trivial* queries, including complex filter conditions and subqueries. For example:

```
SELECT * FROM Orders
WHERE customer_id IN (SELECT customer_id
                      FROM PremiumCustomers);
```

In the query above, if the customer_id columns in both Orders and PremiumCustomers tables are indexed, the database engine can efficiently resolve the subquery and the filtering operation.

Indexes bring notable performance improvements, but they come with trade-offs. They increase storage requirements and can slow down the performance of INSERT, UPDATE, and DELETE operations because the indexes themselves must be maintained.

Understanding query plans generated using tools such as EXPLAIN and EXPLAIN ANALYZE can provide insights into how indexes are utilized. For example:

```
EXPLAIN SELECT * FROM employees WHERE last_name = '
    Smith';
```

The output shows whether the index on last_name is used, the cost estimation, and the number of rows scanned:

```
Index Scan using idx_last_name on employees (cost=0.00..50.00 rows=10 width=20)
  Index Cond: (last_name = 'Smith')
```

Efficient use of indexes necessitates understanding the specific workload and query patterns of the database, making it crucial to regularly monitor and fine-tune indexes based on actual usage and performance metrics.

This pragmatic approach ensures that the indexes serve their intended purpose of enhancing query performance without incurring significant maintainability and resource costs.

7.6 Understanding Execution Plans

When a SQL query is submitted to a database system, the query optimizer selects an optimal execution strategy, often referred to as the execution plan. An execution plan delineates the order of operations to access or modify data in the database effectively. Understanding the intricacies of an execution plan enables database administrators and developers to fine-tune queries and enhance overall performance.

Execution plans are typically represented as a tree structure, where each node denotes a fundamental operation such as a table scan, index scan, join, or sort. The optimizer's goal is to generate an execution plan with the minimal cost, which is an estimate of the resources (e.g., CPU, memory, I/O) required to execute the query.

Key Components of an Execution Plan

- **Sequential Scan (Seq Scan)**: This operation indicates that the entire table is scanned row-by-row to locate the requested data. Sequential scans are generally expensive, especially for large tables.
- **Index Scan**: In contrast to sequential scans, index scans utilize indexes to locate data more efficiently. Various subtypes of index scans exist, such as index-only scans, bitmap index scans, and indexed bounded scans.
- **Join Operations**: Joins combine rows from multiple tables. Common join types include nested loop joins, hash joins, and merge joins, each with varying performance implications depending on the context.
- **Sort Operations**: Sorting is often necessary for queries involving ORDER BY clauses, aggregations, or distinct operations. Sorting can be costly, particularly without appropriate indexes.
- **Filter Operations**: Filter operations represent the application of predicates to eliminate rows that do not meet criteria specified in the WHERE clause.

Analyzing an Execution Plan

Analyzing an execution plan provides insights into the efficiency of query execution. The structure and detail of the execution plan can vary between database systems, but the underlying principles remain similar. Tools such as EXPLAIN in PostgreSQL, EXPLAIN PLAN in Oracle, and SHOWPLAN in Microsoft SQL Server are commonly used to obtain execution plans.

For illustration, consider the following SQL query:

```
SELECT name, department
FROM employees
WHERE salary > 70000
ORDER BY department;
```

Using the PostgreSQL EXPLAIN statement:

```
EXPLAIN
SELECT name, department
FROM employees
WHERE salary > 70000
ORDER BY department;
```

The execution plan might resemble the following output:

```
Sort (cost=345.24..360.57 rows=615 width=42)
  Sort Key: department
  -> Seq Scan on employees (cost=0.00..295.71 rows=615 width=42)
       Filter: (salary > 70000)
```

In this example:

- The Seq Scan on employees indicates a sequential scan of the table, which incurs substantial cost due to the necessity to scan the entire table.
- The Filter node specifies filtering rows where salary > 70000.
- The Sort node indicates sorting the resulting rows by the department field.

Strategies for Execution Plan Optimization

- **Index Utilization**: Implementing appropriate indexes can significantly reduce query execution time by facilitating index scans instead of sequential scans.
- **Query Rewriting**: Rewriting queries to leverage indexed columns or more efficient SQL constructs can lead to better execution plans.
- **Join Strategies**: Choosing the appropriate join type based on the size and indexing of the tables involved can optimize performance. Hash joins are efficient for large, unsorted datasets, whereas merge joins are suitable when both datasets are sorted.
- **Statistics Updates**: Ensuring up-to-date statistics about table data distributions aids the query optimizer in making informed decisions, thereby generating more efficient execution plans.
- **Use of EXPLAIN ANALYZE**: Whereas EXPLAIN provides the estimated execution plan, EXPLAIN ANALYZE executes the query and provides the actual execution plan along with execution times, allowing for deeper analysis and identification of discrepancies between estimated and actual performance.

Here is how EXPLAIN ANALYZE can be used:

```
EXPLAIN ANALYZE
SELECT name, department
FROM employees
WHERE salary > 70000
ORDER BY department;
```

The output will detail both the planned and actual performance metrics:

```
Sort (cost=345.24..360.57 rows=615 width=42) (actual time=15.423..15.927 rows=612 loops=1)
  Sort Key: department
  Sort Method: quicksort  Memory: 79kB
  -> Seq Scan on employees (cost=0.00..295.71 rows=615 width=42) (actual time=0.112..13.725 rows=612 loops=1)
       Filter: (salary > 70000)
       Rows Removed by Filter: 3868
Planning time: 0.733 ms
Execution time: 16.123 ms
```

In this enhanced output:

- actual time provides the precise execution time for each node.
- Rows Removed by Filter indicates the number of rows excluded by the filter criteria.
- Execution time showcases the total time for query execution, enabling a direct comparison with the estimated cost.

By carefully examining execution plans and leveraging tools and techniques to refine them, queries can be optimized to execute more efficiently, thereby improving overall database performance.

7.7 EXPLAIN and EXPLAIN ANALYZE

The EXPLAIN and EXPLAIN ANALYZE commands are crucial tools for understanding and optimizing query performance in SQL databases. Both commands provide insights into the execution plans selected by the database management system (DBMS) for a given query. These execution plans reveal how queries are processed, which indexes are used, the join methods employed, and other critical details.

The EXPLAIN command returns a high-level overview of the execution plan, showing each operation that the database will perform to execute the query. In contrast, EXPLAIN ANALYZE extends this by actually running the query and then displaying a detailed, step-by-step execution plan along with runtime statistics. Understanding the output of these commands is essential for diagnosing performance bottlenecks and improving query efficiency.

Consider the following SQL query:

```
SELECT employee_id, first_name, last_name
FROM employees
WHERE department_id = 10;
```

To analyze this query using EXPLAIN, the command would be:

```
EXPLAIN SELECT employee_id, first_name, last_name
FROM employees
WHERE department_id = 10;
```

The EXPLAIN command generates an output similar to:

```
Seq Scan on employees  (cost=0.00..13.25 rows=5 width=34)
  Filter: (department_id = 10)
```

Explanation of the EXPLAIN Output:

- Seq Scan on employees: Indicates that the sequential scan is being used on the employees table.
- cost=0.00..13.25: Represents the estimated startup and total cost of executing the query. The first number is the cost before the operation starts, and the second number is the total cost after the operation completes.
- rows=5: The estimated number of rows that will be retrieved.
- width=34: The average width (in bytes) of the rows returned.
- Filter: (department_id = 10): Indicates the filter applied to the rows.

To gain more detailed insights and runtime statistics, we use EXPLAIN ANALYZE:

```
EXPLAIN ANALYZE SELECT employee_id, first_name, last_name
FROM employees
WHERE department_id = 10;
```

The output of EXPLAIN ANALYZE might look like:

```
Seq Scan on employees  (cost=0.00..13.25 rows=5 width=34) (actual time=0.011..0.012 rows=2 loops=1)
  Filter: (department_id = 10)
  Rows Removed by Filter: 50
Planning Time: 0.126 ms
Execution Time: 0.052 ms
```

Detailed Breakdown of EXPLAIN ANALYZE Output:

- actual time=0.011..0.012: Shows the actual time in milliseconds that the execution took, with the first number being the startup time and the second being the total time taken.
- rows=2: Indicates the actual number of rows returned.
- loops=1: Tells how many times this operation was executed (relevant for nested loops or repeated operations).
- Rows Removed by Filter: 50: Shows how many rows were filtered out by the condition.
- Planning Time: 0.126 ms: The time taken to plan the query.
- Execution Time: 0.052 ms: The total time taken to execute the query.

These pieces of information are pivotal for identifying performance issues. For instance, if an index scan is more appropriate than a sequential scan, the presence of Seq Scan indicates a potential area for optimization by creating an index on department_id.

Indexing the department_id column could potentially change the query plan as follows:

```
CREATE INDEX idx_department_id ON employees(department_id)
    ;

EXPLAIN ANALYZE SELECT employee_id, first_name, last_name
FROM employees
WHERE department_id = 10;
```

The expected output post-index creation might be:

```
Index Scan using idx_department_id on employees  (cost=0.15..8.17 rows=2 width=34) (actual time=0.018..0.019 rows=2 loops=1)
  Index Cond: (department_id = 10)
  Planning Time: 0.142 ms
  Execution Time: 0.033 ms
```

Changes and Improvements:

- Index Scan using idx_department_id: Indicates that the database now uses an index scan instead of a sequential scan.
- The overall cost and execution time are reduced, showcasing the performance benefits of proper indexing.

By continuously using EXPLAIN and EXPLAIN ANALYZE, database developers and administrators can iteratively refine their queries and indexes, ultimately leading to superior performance and resource efficiency.

7.8 Optimizing SELECT Queries

Optimal performance of SELECT queries is crucial for achieving efficiency in database management systems. Various factors and techniques can influence the speed and resource usage of SELECT statements.

Firstly, proper indexing is essential for efficient query execution. When a SELECT query searches for rows meeting specific criteria, appropriate indexes on the columns involved can drastically reduce the number of scanned rows. For instance, consider a table 'employees' with columns id, name, department, and salary. If frequent queries search by department, an index on this column can significantly accelerate query performance.

```
CREATE INDEX idx_department ON employees(department);
```

The database engine will use this index to locate rows corresponding to a specific department more efficiently than scanning the entire table.

Another crucial aspect is the order of conditions in WHERE clauses. Conditions that can use an index should appear earlier in the WHERE clause. The database query optimizer evaluates the WHERE clause from left to right, so placing the most selective conditions first can result in faster query execution.

```
SELECT name, salary FROM employees
WHERE department = 'Engineering' AND salary > 80000;
```

Here, if there is an index on the department column, it is efficiently used to limit the search space before applying the second condition on salary.

Additionally, reducing the number of columns returned by the SELECT statement helps minimize the data processed and transferred. Only select the necessary columns to avoid unnecessary overhead.

```
SELECT name FROM employees WHERE department = '
    Engineering';
```

Choosing appropriate JOIN types and order also impacts performance. For INNER JOINs, ensuring proper indexes on join columns can speed up matching rows from the involved tables. For example, in joining 'employees' with a 'departments' table on a common department_id column:

```
SELECT e.name, d.department_name
FROM employees e
INNER JOIN departments d ON e.department_id = d.id;
```

Adding indexes on employees.department_id and departments.id can enhance the performance of the join operation.

Furthermore, the use of subqueries versus temporary tables can affect query performance. Although subqueries are concise, they may be less efficient. In complex scenarios, using temporary tables to store intermediate results can provide better performance.

```
CREATE TEMPORARY TABLE high_salary_employees AS
SELECT id, name FROM employees WHERE salary > 80000;

SELECT h.name, d.department_name
FROM high_salary_employees h
JOIN departments d ON h.department_id = d.id;
```

This approach prevents repeated subquery evaluation, resulting in more efficient overall execution.

Utilizing database-specific features, such as Common Table Expressions (CTEs), can also optimize queries for better performance and readability. For example:

```
WITH high_earning AS (
    SELECT id, name, department_id FROM employees WHERE
        salary > 80000
)
SELECT e.name, d.department_name
FROM high_earning e
INNER JOIN departments d ON e.department_id = d.id;
```

CTEs allow for clear segmentation of queries into reusable and logically distinct parts.

Moreover, leveraging database configurations like query caching can minimize execution times by storing and reusing the results of expensive or frequently executed queries.

Careful consideration of execution plans is vital in optimizing SELECT queries. Tools like EXPLAIN and EXPLAIN ANALYZE provide insights into how the database engine processes queries. By examining execution plans, developers can identify bottlenecks and adjustments needed for optimization.

Using hints is another technique to direct the query optimizer's behavior. Database-specific hints can inform the optimizer about the preferred execution strategy for a query, potentially leading to more efficient execution paths.

Lastly, adhering to normalized database design principles ensures minimized redundancy and optimal query performance. Normalization facilitates faster indexing, joining, and searching of data, resulting in streamlined SELECT queries.

Always monitor performance and iterate on query design based on profiling results to achieve the best possible outcomes in terms of speed and resource utilization.

7.9 Optimizing INSERT, UPDATE, DELETE Queries

Optimizing INSERT, UPDATE, and DELETE statements in SQL is critical for maintaining the performance and efficiency of database operations, especially as data volumes grow. These Data Manipulation Language (DML) operations often involve changes to the physical storage of data, requiring thoughtful tuning to minimize their impact on the system.

Optimizing INSERT Queries

The INSERT statement adds new rows to a table. Efficiently managing this operation is crucial for performance, particularly in scenarios involving bulk inserts.

1. Minimizing Index Usage

While indexes improve read operations, they can negatively impact insert performance. Each INSERT operation may require additional write operations to update the indexes. To minimize this, consider the number and types of indexes on frequently inserted tables. Balancing read and write performance through selective indexing is essential.

2. Bulk Inserts

For scenarios involving large volumes of data, bulk inserts can be significantly more efficient than individual row inserts. Instead of executing multiple single-row INSERT statements, a single bulk INSERT can reduce overhead. Example:

```
INSERT INTO students (id, name, age) VALUES
(1, 'John Doe', 20),
(2, 'Jane Smith', 21),
(3, 'Emily Johnson', 22);
```

3. Disabling Constraints

Temporarily disabling constraints such as foreign keys and uniqueness constraints during bulk data load can enhance performance. However, ensure constraints are re-enabled post-insertion and validate data integrity manually when constraints are off.

```
ALTER TABLE students NOCHECK CONSTRAINT all;
-- Perform bulk insert
ALTER TABLE students CHECK CONSTRAINT all;
```

4. Utilizing Batching

In high-throughput environments, batching multiple INSERT operations into a single transaction can reduce the overhead associated with commit operations.

```
BEGIN TRANSACTION;
INSERT INTO students (id, name, age) VALUES (4, 'Mike Brown',
    23);
INSERT INTO students (id, name, age) VALUES (5, 'Sara White',
    24);
COMMIT;
```

Optimizing UPDATE Queries

UPDATE operations modify existing data within a table. The performance of these operations can significantly impact the responsiveness of the database.

1. Targeting Specific Rows

Where possible, ensure that UPDATE statements are highly selective. Using indexes to target specific rows reduces the number of rows scanned and modified.

```
UPDATE students
SET age = 25
WHERE id = 5; -- Assuming 'id' is an indexed column
```

2. Minimizing Locking

UPDATE operations can cause significant row-level locking or even escalate to full table locks, particularly in systems with high concurrent access. Ensure that updates are performed efficiently to minimize locking duration. Batch updates within transactions, but keep the transaction scopes as small as possible.

```
BEGIN TRANSACTION;
UPDATE students SET name = 'Michael Brown' WHERE id = 4;
COMMIT;
```

3. Avoiding Unnecessary Updates

Only update columns that have changed. Avoid setting the same value, which can lead to unnecessary write operations and logging overhead.

```
UPDATE students
SET name = 'Sara White'
WHERE id = 5
AND name <> 'Sara White';
```

Optimizing DELETE Queries

The DELETE statement removes rows from a table and can significantly impact performance, especially when removing large volumes of data.

1. Targeted Deletions

Like UPDATE, ensure DELETE statements are as targeted as possible. Use indexed columns in the WHERE clause to quickly locate the rows to be deleted.

```
DELETE FROM students
WHERE id = 5; -- Assuming 'id' is an indexed column
```

2. Batch Deletions

Performing deletions in batches can help manage large delete operations, reducing the likelihood of lock escalation and system resource exhaustion. Batch deletions also make it easier to manage transaction logs.

```
DECLARE @BatchSize INT = 1000;
WHILE 1=1
BEGIN
    DELETE TOP (@BatchSize) FROM students WHERE age > 30;
    IF @@ROWCOUNT = 0 BREAK;
    COMMIT TRANSACTION;
END;
```

3. Archiving Data

For large deletions, consider archiving the data instead. Move data to an archive table instead of deleting it, allowing you to manage data volume without losing potentially valuable historical data.

```
INSERT INTO archive_students (id, name, age)
SELECT id, name, age FROM students WHERE age > 30;

DELETE FROM students WHERE age > 30;
```

Effective optimization of INSERT, UPDATE, and DELETE operations involves careful planning and consideration of indexes, constraints, batching, and transaction control. By applying these strategies, database performance can be significantly enhanced, particularly in write-heavy environments. Continuous monitoring and adjustment of these strategies in response to changing workloads are essential for maintaining optimal performance.

7.10 Partitioning Data

Partitioning is an essential technique in database management that involves dividing a large database table into smaller, more manageable pieces while maintaining the logical integrity of the data. This technique can significantly improve query performance, simplify maintenance, and enhance scalability by allowing more efficient use of database resources and making it easier to perform operations like backups, archiving, and loading new data.

There are several methods of partitioning data, each with unique characteristics and suitable use cases. This section covers the primary types of partitioning: horizontal partitioning, vertical partitioning, and hybrid partitioning.

Horizontal Partitioning (Sharding) involves splitting a table into multiple tables, each containing a subset of the rows. This type of partitioning is particularly beneficial for distributing data across different storage devices or servers. For example, customer data might be partitioned by geographic region, where each region's data is stored in a separate partition.

Consider an example where we horizontally partition a Customers table based on regions:

```
CREATE TABLE Customers_North AS
SELECT * FROM Customers
WHERE region = 'North';

CREATE TABLE Customers_South AS
SELECT * FROM Customers
WHERE region = 'South';
```

With horizontal partitioning, queries that only need to access a specific region's data can be directed to the respective partition, which can improve query performance by reducing the amount of scanned data. Additionally, this facilitates parallel processing since queries can run concurrently on different partitions.

Vertical Partitioning involves dividing a table into multiple tables based on columns rather than rows. This approach is useful when different groups of columns are often accessed together independently of other columns. Vertical partitioning can optimize performance by minimizing the amount of data read and stored. For example, separating frequently accessed columns from less accessed columns can significantly enhance query efficiency.

Here is an example:

```
CREATE TABLE Customers_Info AS
SELECT customer_id, name, contact_details
FROM Customers;

CREATE TABLE Customers_Stats AS
SELECT customer_id, transaction_history, preferences
FROM Customers;
```

Vertical partitioning ensures that queries only read the relevant columns, thereby improving performance. However, one must manage the relationships between the partitions, typically through primary and foreign key constraints.

Hybrid Partitioning combines both horizontal and vertical partitioning techniques. This method is particularly useful in complex databases where a single table is too vast and frequently queried on different criteria. Hybrid partitioning provides a more granular level of data management, enabling fine-tuned optimization of query performance and maintenance operations.

In practical scenarios, databases also implement table partitioning using native support from the database management system (DBMS). Many modern DBMSs offer comprehensive partitioning features, allowing for various partitioning strategies such as RANGE, LIST, and HASH partitioning.

RANGE Partitioning divides a table into partitions based on a range of values in a specific column. This is suitable for time-series data or any dataset where entries are sequential.

```
CREATE TABLE Sales (
  sale_id INT,
  sale_date DATE,
  amount DECIMAL(10, 2)
) PARTITION BY RANGE (sale_date) (
  PARTITION p_2020 VALUES LESS THAN ('2021-01-01'),
  PARTITION p_2021 VALUES LESS THAN ('2022-01-01')
);
```

LIST Partitioning segregates data based on predefined lists of values. This is useful when a limited set of distinct values is known in advance.

```
CREATE TABLE Orders (
  order_id INT,
  order_status VARCHAR(20)
) PARTITION BY LIST (order_status) (
  PARTITION p_pending VALUES IN ('pending', '
      awaiting_payment'),
  PARTITION p_completed VALUES IN ('completed', 'shipped')
);
```

HASH Partitioning distributes rows across a set of partitions based on the result of a hash function applied to a partitioning key. This method is effective for ensuring even distribution of data, which helps in balancing loads.

```
CREATE TABLE Users (
  user_id INT,
  username VARCHAR(50)
) PARTITION BY HASH (user_id) PARTITIONS 4;
```

Each partitioning strategy has its trade-offs and scenarios where it is most effective. Key considerations when choosing a partitioning strategy include the nature of the queries, the patterns of data access, and the operational requirements for data management.

Effective indexing on partitioned tables can further enhance performance. In partitioned tables, indexes may be global (spanning all partitions) or local (separate for each partition). The choice between global and local indexes depends on the type of queries and the specific performance requirements. Local indexes can improve performance for queries targeting specific partitions, while global indexes provide consistency and improved performance for queries that span multiple partitions.

As shown, partitioning is a powerful technique for improving database performance and manageability, particularly in environments with large datasets and complex query patterns. Proper implementation and appropriate use of different partitioning strategies are crucial for leveraging the full potential of this technique in real-world database applications.

7.11 Database Statistics and Cost-Based Optimization

Database statistics are critical metadata that describe the distribution and storage characteristics of data within a database table or index. These statistics are an essential component of the cost-based optimization process used by modern relational database management systems (RDBMS) to determine the most efficient way to execute a query. The cost-based optimizer (CBO) uses statistical information to estimate the cost, in terms of resource usage, of various execution plans and to select the plan with the lowest estimated cost.

Types of Database Statistics

There are several key types of statistics that are generally collected and used by the CBO:

- **Table Statistics:** These include the number of rows, the number of data blocks, and average row length. They provide a high-level overview of the size and structure of the table.
- **Column Statistics:** These include the number of distinct values (NDV), the minimum and maximum values, data distribution (histograms), and the percentage of null values. Column statistics inform the optimizer about the selectivity of filters and joins.
- **Index Statistics:** These include the number of leaf blocks, height of the index (levels), clustering factor, and index key cardinality. Index statistics help the optimizer understand the efficiency of using an index to access data.
- **System Statistics:** These include CPU and IO performance characteristics. System statistics enable the optimizer to factor in system performance when evaluating query costs.

Collecting and Maintaining Statistics

Statistics can become outdated as the data in the database changes. Therefore, it is important to regularly collect and maintain accurate statistics. Most RDBMS provide built-in utilities to gather statistics. For example, in PostgreSQL, the ANALYZE command is used:

```
ANALYZE;
```

This command updates statistics for all tables in the current database. In other systems, such as Oracle, the DBMS_STATS package is commonly used:

```
EXEC DBMS_STATS.GATHER_DATABASE_STATS;
```

Automatic statistics gathering features can be configured to run during off-peak hours, ensuring that the CBO has up-to-date information with minimal impact on database performance.

The Role of Cost-Based Optimization

The CBO evaluates multiple potential execution plans for a given query. Each plan is assigned a cost based on statistical information and system performance metrics. The cost of a plan is typically proportional to the estimated time resources required, such as CPU cycles and disk I/O operations. The plan with the lowest cost is selected for query execution.

To illustrate the differences between cost-based plans, consider the following example in a SQL environment:

```
EXPLAIN ANALYZE
SELECT * FROM employees WHERE department_id = 10;
```

The output of this command provides detailed information on the execution plan chosen by the CBO. A typical output might look like this:

```
Seq Scan on employees  (cost=0.00..35.50 rows=10 width=60) (actual time=0.010..0.012 rows=2 loops=1)
  Filter: (department_id = 10)
  Rows Removed by Filter: 998
  Planning Time: 0.051 ms
  Execution Time: 0.033 ms
```

In this example, the CBO has chosen a sequential scan with a filter condition. The cost estimates (0.00..35.50) and actual execution times (0.010..0.012) provide insights into the efficiency of the plan.

Histograms and Data Skew

One challenge for the CBO is dealing with non-uniform or skewed data distributions. Simply knowing the minimum, maximum, and average values may be insufficient for accurate cost estimation. Histograms provide more granular information by dividing the range of values into buckets and recording the distribution within each bucket.

For example, consider a column salary with a highly skewed distribution. A histogram might reveal that most employees earn between $50,000 and $70,000, with only a few outliers earning significantly more. This information allows the optimizer to make more accurate estimates for queries with conditions on the salary column.

Oracle supports several types of histograms, including:

- **Frequency histograms:** Capture the exact frequency of each distinct value.
- **Top-frequency histograms:** Combine the characteristics of frequency and height-balanced histograms.
- **Height-balanced histograms:** Equal-width histograms that distribute the bucket boundaries as evenly as possible across the column's range.

```
EXEC DBMS_STATS.GATHER_TABLE_STATS('HR', '
    EMPLOYEES', METHOD_OPT => 'FOR ALL COLUMNS
    SIZE AUTO');
```

This code collects histograms automatically for all columns in the EMPLOYEES table of the HR schema.

Optimizer Hints

Sometimes, the CBO may not select the optimal execution plan due to outdated statistics or complex queries. In such cases, optimizer hints can be used to influence the CBO's decisions. Hints are included in SQL queries to guide the optimizer:

```
SELECT /*+ INDEX(employees emp_dept_idx) */ * FROM
    employees WHERE department_id = 10;
```

Here, the INDEX hint directs the optimizer to use the emp_dept_idx index.

Accurate and up-to-date database statistics are fundamental to the effective operation of cost-based optimizers. The ability to collect comprehensive and detailed statistics on tables, columns, and indexes allows the optimizer to make informed decisions regarding query execution plans. This, in turn, enhances the overall performance and efficiency of the database system. Properly managed statistics and judicious use of optimizer hints ensure that databases perform optimally under a wide variety of workloads and query patterns.

7.12 Case Studies in Query Optimization

Case studies provide practical insights into the intricacies of query optimization, elucidating the application of theoretical principles in real-world situations. By dissecting various scenarios, we draw a comprehensive understanding of the methodologies and strategies employed in optimizing database queries.

Case Study 1: Optimizing a SELECT Query in an E-commerce Database

In an e-commerce database, a common requirement is to fetch frequently accessed data, such as product details, user information, and order history, with minimal latency. Consider the following query that retrieves product details along with category information:

```
SELECT p.product_id, p.name, p.price, c.category_name
FROM products p
INNER JOIN categories c ON p.category_id = c.category_id
WHERE p.price > 100 AND c.category_name = 'Electronics';
```

To optimize this query, we must analyze the indexes on the involved tables and the query execution plan.

Step 1: Analyzing Existing Indexes

First, inspect existing indexes on the products and categories tables:

```
SHOW INDEX FROM products;
SHOW INDEX FROM categories;
```

Assume we discover there is an index on category_id in the products table but no composite index involving price or category_name.

Step 2: Creating Composite Indexes

To refine the query performance, create a composite index on category_name and category_id in the categories table, and on price and category_id in the products table:

```
CREATE INDEX idx_category_name_id ON categories (
    category_name, category_id);
CREATE INDEX idx_price_category_id ON products (price,
    category_id);
```

Step 3: Reviewing the Execution Plan

Utilize the EXPLAIN command to review the optimized query execution plan:

```
EXPLAIN SELECT p.product_id, p.name, p.price, c.category_name
FROM products p
INNER JOIN categories c ON p.category_id = c.category_id
WHERE p.price > 100 AND c.category_name = 'Electronics';
```

```
id | select_type | table | type | possible_keys              | key                   | key_len | ref   | rows | Extra
1  | SIMPLE      | c     | ref  | PRIMARY,idx_category...    | idx_category_name_id  | 767     | const | 10   | Using where
1  | SIMPLE      | p     | ref  | idx_price_category_id      | idx_price_category_id | 4       | const | 500  | Using where
```

The revamped execution plan displays the use of multi-column indexes idx_category_name_id and idx_price_category_id, effectively reducing the number of scanned rows and boosting query performance.

Case Study 2: Optimizing UPDATE Queries in a Banking Database

In a banking database, suppose we need to update the interest rate of accounts based on account balance conditions. The initial query looks as follows:

```
UPDATE accounts
SET interest_rate = 5.0
WHERE balance > 10000;
```

The optimization can be approached by creating a filtered index on the balance column targeting high-value accounts.

Step 1: Reviewing Existing Indexes

Check for existing indexes:

```
SHOW INDEX FROM accounts;
```

Let's assume there is an index on account_id but none on balance.

Step 2: Creating a Filtered Index

Create an index specifically for the condition in the WHERE clause:

```
CREATE INDEX idx_balance_high ON accounts (balance) WHERE
    balance > 10000;
```

Step 3: Verifying Optimization with EXPLAIN

Analyze the update query plan using EXPLAIN:

```
EXPLAIN UPDATE accounts
SET interest_rate = 5.0
WHERE balance > 10000;
```

```
id | select_type | table    | type   | possible_keys     | key             | key_len | ref   | rows  | Extra
1  | SIMPLE      | accounts | range  | idx_balance_high  | idx_balance... | 4       | NULL  | 2000  | Using where
```

The EXPLAIN output now shows that the filtered index idx_balance_high is utilized, significantly narrowing down the rows to be scanned and updated.

Case Study 3: Optimizing Complex JOINs in a Social Media Application

Consider a query in a social media application that retrieves user profiles and their posts, filtered by specific conditions:

```
SELECT u.user_id, u.username, p.post_id, p.content
```

```
FROM users u
JOIN posts p ON u.user_id = p.user_id
WHERE u.active = 1 AND p.created_at > '2023-01-01';
```

To optimize this query, ensuring proper indexing and analyzing query execution plans are essential.

Step 1: Inspecting Indexes on Relevant Tables

First, examine the indexes on the users and posts tables:

```
SHOW INDEX FROM users;
SHOW INDEX FROM posts;
```

Suppose we find indexes on user_id in both tables but no comprehensive indexes on active or created_at.

Step 2: Creating Efficient Indexes

Create indexes to cover the filter conditions:

```
CREATE INDEX idx_user_active ON users (active);
CREATE INDEX idx_post_created_at ON posts (created_at);
```

Step 3: Evaluating the Execution Plan

Analyze the modified query execution plan:

```
EXPLAIN SELECT u.user_id, u.username, p.post_id, p.content
FROM users u
JOIN posts p ON u.user_id = p.user_id
WHERE u.active = 1 AND p.created_at > '2023-01-01';
```

```
id | select_type | table | type  | possible_keys         | key                 | key_len | ref   | rows  | Extra
1  | SIMPLE      | u     | ref   | PRIMARY,idx_user..    | idx_user_active     | 1       | const | 1000  | Using where
1  | SIMPLE      | p     | range | idx_post_created..    | idx_post_created_at | 5       | NULL  | 10000 | Using where
```

The execution plan reveals that the newly created indexes idx_user_active and idx_post_created_at are employed, which optimizes the query by reducing the set of rows to be joined and filtered.

In each case study, the optimization process involves analyzing existing indexes, creating targeted indexes based on query conditions, and leveraging the EXPLAIN command to validate the improvements. The strategic application of indexes significantly enhances the performance of SELECT, UPDATE, and JOIN operations in various database scenarios.

Chapter 8

Stored Procedures, Triggers, and Functions

This chapter introduces stored procedures, triggers, and user-defined functions (UDFs). It covers the creation, execution, and management of stored procedures, including handling parameters and errors. The chapter explains how to create and use triggers for auditing and validation purposes. Additionally, it provides detailed instructions on creating scalar and table-valued functions and discusses best practices for implementing and maintaining these database objects.

8.1 Introduction to Stored Procedures

Stored procedures are a fundamental aspect of database management systems (DBMS) that provide an array of benefits in terms of performance, security, and maintainability. A stored procedure is a precompiled collection of one or more SQL statements which are stored within the database. These procedures can be invoked by applications, triggers, or other stored procedures, allowing for the encapsulation of complex business logic within the database layer.

Definition and Advantages

Stored procedures are defined and stored in the database schema. This allows the database engine to parse, compile, and optimize SQL statements once, and reuse these query plans on subsequent executions. This reduces the overhead associated with query parsing and planning, potentially leading to significant performance improvements. Additionally, because stored procedures execute within the database engine, they reduce the need for transmitting large SQL statements over the network, resulting in reduced network traffic.

Another key advantage of stored procedures is enhanced security. They provide a mechanism to control data access and enforce business rules consistently. With stored procedures, database administrators can grant execute permissions to users without giving them direct access to the underlying data tables. This encapsulation ensures that data integrity is maintained and unauthorized data manipulations are prevented.

Syntax and Basic Usage

Creating a stored procedure typically involves the CREATE PROCEDURE statement followed by the procedure's logic enclosed within a BEGIN and END block. Consider the following simple example that creates a stored procedure to insert a new row into a students table:

```
CREATE PROCEDURE InsertStudent
    (@StudentID INT, @FirstName NVARCHAR(50), @LastName
        NVARCHAR(50))
AS
BEGIN
    INSERT INTO Students (StudentID, FirstName, LastName)
    VALUES (@StudentID, @FirstName, @LastName)
END
```

In this example, the stored procedure InsertStudent is defined with three parameters: @StudentID, @FirstName, and @LastName. The procedure inserts these values into the Students table. When called, this procedure requires that the user provides the necessary parameters, ensuring that data is inserted according to predefined rules.

Execution of Stored Procedures

Stored procedures can be executed using the EXEC or EXECUTE statement. The following example illustrates how to call the InsertStudent procedure:

```
EXEC InsertStudent @StudentID = 1, @FirstName = 'John',
    @LastName = 'Doe'
```

Upon execution, the InsertStudent procedure inserts a new row with the specified StudentID, FirstName, and LastName values into the Students table. This encapsulation of SQL logic improves code reuse and consistency, making it easier to manage complex SQL operations within the database.

Conditional Logic and Flow Control

Stored procedures support conditional logic and flow control constructs, such as IF...ELSE, WHILE, and CASE statements, allowing for the implementation of sophisticated business logic. Here is an example of a stored procedure that demonstrates the use of conditional logic to update student details only if the student exists:

```
CREATE PROCEDURE UpdateStudentDetails
    (@StudentID INT, @FirstName NVARCHAR(50), @LastName
        NVARCHAR(50))
AS
BEGIN
    IF EXISTS (SELECT 1 FROM Students WHERE StudentID =
        @StudentID)
    BEGIN
        UPDATE Students
        SET FirstName = @FirstName, LastName = @LastName
        WHERE StudentID = @StudentID
    END
    ELSE
    BEGIN
        PRINT 'Student ID not found.'
    END
END
```

This example includes an IF...ELSE statement to check if a student with a given StudentID exists before attempting to update their details. If the student does not exist, a message indicating the absence of the student ID is displayed. This approach ensures that updates are performed only on valid records, maintaining data integrity.

Benefits for Development and Maintenance

Using stored procedures in application development can significantly simplify coding and maintenance tasks. By encapsulating database operations within stored procedures, developers can avoid writing repetitive code across different parts of an application. This also promotes consistency and reduces the risk of introducing errors.

Stored procedures facilitate easier maintenance and versioning of database logic. Changes can be made in a single location—the procedure definition—rather than updating multiple application codebases. This central management of database logic improves the maintainability of database applications and allows for streamlined updates and patches.

Stored procedures are a powerful tool for encapsulating and managing complex database operations. They provide numerous advantages, including improved performance, enhanced security, and simplified maintenance. Understanding how to create and utilize stored procedures is essential for any database professional seeking to build efficient, secure, and maintainable database applications.

8.2 Creating Stored Procedures

A stored procedure is a set of SQL statements with an assigned name that is stored in the database in compiled form so that it can be shared by a number of programs. The creation of a stored procedure is essential for encapsulating repetitive and complex tasks within the database, thus allowing for efficient execution and maintenance. The following instructions and examples will elucidate each necessary step in creating stored procedures.

The standard SQL statement for creating a stored procedure is the CREATE PROCEDURE statement. It is followed by the procedure name and a set of parentheses that can include input and output parameters. The body of the procedure typically contains a compound statement, which is a block of SQL including multiple statements enclosed by BEGIN and END.

```
CREATE PROCEDURE GetEmployeeInfo
AS
BEGIN
    SELECT EmployeeID, FirstName, LastName, Department
    FROM Employees;
END;
```

This example creates a stored procedure named GetEmployeeInfo, which retrieves employee information from the Employees table. No parameters are passed to this procedure as it executes a simple SELECT query.

Parameters can be added to stored procedures, allowing for dynamic modification of the SQL statements based on input values. Parameters are classified into three types: IN (input), OUT (output), and INOUT (both). This provides robust interaction with the database, enabling more versatile procedures.

```
CREATE PROCEDURE GetEmployeeByID
    @EmployeeID INT
AS
BEGIN
    SELECT EmployeeID, FirstName, LastName, Department
    FROM Employees
    WHERE EmployeeID = @EmployeeID;
END;
```

In this example, GetEmployeeByID takes an input parameter @EmployeeID of type INT. The procedure filters the data from the Employees table to return only the row corresponding to the passed EmployeeID.

A stored procedure can also include output parameters to return values back to the calling program. This feature is crucial when the procedure needs to compute or fetch a single value, such as a count or a sum.

```
CREATE PROCEDURE GetEmployeeDepartment
    @EmployeeID INT,
    @Department NVARCHAR(50) OUTPUT
AS
BEGIN
    SELECT @Department = Department
    FROM Employees
    WHERE EmployeeID = @EmployeeID;
END;
```

Here, GetEmployeeDepartment includes both an input parameter, @EmployeeID, and an output parameter, @Department. The retrieved department name is assigned to the output parameter, which can then be accessed by the calling program.

Using multiple parameters, both input and output, enhances the interactivity and functionality of stored procedures. Conditional logic within the procedure body introduces further complexity and control.

```
CREATE PROCEDURE UpdateEmployeeDepartment
    @EmployeeID INT,
```

```
    @NewDepartment NVARCHAR(50)
AS
BEGIN
    IF EXISTS (SELECT 1 FROM Employees WHERE EmployeeID
        = @EmployeeID)
    BEGIN
        UPDATE Employees
        SET Department = @NewDepartment
        WHERE EmployeeID = @EmployeeID;
    END
    ELSE
    BEGIN
        INSERT INTO Employees (EmployeeID, Department)
        VALUES (@EmployeeID, @NewDepartment);
    END
END;
```

This procedure, UpdateEmployeeDepartment, updates an employee's department if the EmployeeID exists; otherwise, it inserts a new record. This illustrates how conditional statements in SQL, such as IF... ELSE, manage various scenarios.

Error handling within stored procedures is vital for ensuring stability and reliability. Using BEGIN TRY and BEGIN CATCH blocks enables trapping and managing exceptions.

```
CREATE PROCEDURE SafeDeleteEmployee
    @EmployeeID INT
AS
BEGIN
    BEGIN TRY
        DELETE FROM Employees
        WHERE EmployeeID = @EmployeeID;
    END TRY
    BEGIN CATCH
        PRINT 'An error occurred while trying to delete the
            employee.';
        -- Additional error handling code here
    END CATCH
END;
```

This example shows SafeDeleteEmployee where any errors during the deletion process are caught, and an error message is printed. Developers can add more sophisticated error handling mechanisms as needed.

Creating stored procedures involves several critical considerations such as namespacing, security permissions, and performance. Ensuring that stored procedure names are clear and descriptive aids in maintainability. Appropriate security measures, such as granting or denying permissions to specific users, must be enforced to prevent unauthorized access. Performance can be optimized by indexing relevant columns and avoiding unnecessary complexity within stored procedures.

Mastery of creating stored procedures requires understanding both the SQL syntax and the strategic considerations that ensure their effective and secure implementation within a database environment. Properly designed stored procedures can significantly enhance the robustness, efficiency, and security of database applications.

8.3 Executing Stored Procedures

Executing stored procedures is a critical aspect of leveraging the full power of your database management system. Stored procedures encapsulate complex SQL logic within a compiled, reusable object that can be invoked with minimal overhead. This section covers various methodologies to execute stored procedures, handle outputs, and manage execution contexts within both interactive SQL environments and application code.

Basic Execution Syntax

The basic syntax for executing a stored procedure in SQL is straightforward. Assuming a stored procedure named GetEmployeeInfo exists, the simplest invocation can be achieved through the EXEC or EXECUTE statement:

```
EXEC GetEmployeeInfo;
```

Alternatively, you can omit the EXEC keyword, which is implicitly understood by the database:

```
GetEmployeeInfo;
```

Passing Parameters

Stored procedures often accept parameters to perform more dynamic operations. Parameters can be input, output, or both. Consider a stored procedure GetEmployeeById that requires an EmployeeID as an input parameter:

```
EXEC GetEmployeeById @EmployeeID = 12345;
```

For output parameters, the execution syntax captures the returned value through a declared variable. Assume a stored procedure GetEmployeeName that takes EmployeeID as input and returns EmployeeName as output:

```
DECLARE @EmployeeName NVARCHAR(100);
EXEC GetEmployeeName @EmployeeID = 12345, @EmployeeName
    = @EmployeeName OUTPUT;
SELECT @EmployeeName AS EmployeeName;
```

Handling Execution Results

The results from stored procedures can either be single result sets, multiple result sets, or data processed through output parameters and return codes. Most database management systems support structured mechanisms to handle these outputs programmatically.

For single result sets, consider viewing the output directly using a standard SELECT statement:

```
DECLARE @Result TABLE (EmployeeID INT, EmployeeName
    NVARCHAR(100));
INSERT INTO @Result
EXEC GetEmployeeInfo;
SELECT * FROM @Result;
```

When dealing with multiple result sets, ensure your client application or SQL code can iterate through the sets correctly. For instance, in T-SQL, the NEXT RESULT clause can help manage such scenarios.

Return Codes

Stored procedures can return integer status codes to indicate the result of execution. A return code of zero typically signifies successful completion, while a non-zero return indicates various error conditions. Capture the return code using:

```
DECLARE @ReturnCode INT;
EXEC @ReturnCode = GetEmployeeById @EmployeeID = 12345;
IF @ReturnCode <> 0
```

```
BEGIN
    PRINT 'Error: Employee not found.';
END
ELSE
BEGIN
    PRINT 'Success: Employee retrieved.';
END
```

Error Handling During Execution

Proper error handling ensures robustness and predictability. SQL Server provides TRY...CATCH constructs while other databases, such as Oracle, might use EXCEPTION blocks. Here is an example using SQL Server:

```
BEGIN TRY
    EXEC GetEmployeeById @EmployeeID = 12345;
    PRINT 'Success';
END TRY
BEGIN CATCH
    PRINT 'Error: ' + ERROR_MESSAGE();
END CATCH;
```

Executing Stored Procedures in Application Code

Database interactions are often performed within application logic written in languages such as C#, Java, or Python. Using prepared statements or callable statements helps execute stored procedures from applications.

In C# using ADO.NET:

```
using (SqlConnection conn = new SqlConnection("
    your_connection_string"))
{
    SqlCommand cmd = new SqlCommand("GetEmployeeById",
        conn);
    cmd.CommandType = CommandType.StoredProcedure;
    cmd.Parameters.AddWithValue("@EmployeeID", 12345);

    conn.Open();
    SqlDataReader reader = cmd.ExecuteReader();
    while (reader.Read())
    {
```

```
        Console.WriteLine(reader["EmployeeName"].ToString());
    }
}
```

In Java using JDBC:

```
Connection conn = DriverManager.getConnection("
    your_connection_string");
CallableStatement stmt = conn.prepareCall("{call GetEmployeeById
    (?)}");
stmt.setInt(1, 12345);
ResultSet rs = stmt.executeQuery();
while (rs.next())
{
    System.out.println(rs.getString("EmployeeName"));
}
```

In Python using PyODBC:

```
import pyodbc

conn = pyodbc.connect("your_connection_string")
cursor = conn.cursor()
cursor.execute("{CALL GetEmployeeById (?)}", (12345,))
for row in cursor:
    print(row.EmployeeName)
```

Proper management of database connections, command preparation, and result set processing within the application's execution environment is crucial for efficient and secure database interactions. Understanding and applying these principles in executing stored procedures will enhance both the performance and reliability of your database-driven applications.

8.4 Parameters in Stored Procedures

Parameters are integral to the functionality of stored procedures, providing a mechanism to pass data to and retrieve data from the procedure. This facilitates reusability and flexibility, allowing the same procedure to operate on different datasets based on the parameters supplied.

Types of Parameters

SQL Server supports three types of parameters in stored procedures:

- **Input parameters**: These are used to pass values into the stored procedure. They are specified using the IN keyword.
- **Output parameters**: These are used to return values from the stored procedure to the caller. They are defined with the OUT keyword.
- **Input/Output parameters**: These parameters serve a dual purpose, allowing values to be passed in and returned from the stored procedure. They are declared using the INOUT keyword.

Syntax for Declaring Parameters

Parameters in stored procedures are declared within the parentheses following the procedure name. Each parameter declaration consists of the parameter name, the data type, and, optionally, the direction (IN, OUT, or INOUT).

```
CREATE PROCEDURE ProcedureName
    @ParameterName1 DataType [IN | OUT | INOUT],
    @ParameterName2 DataType [IN | OUT | INOUT],
    ...
AS
BEGIN
    -- Procedure body
END;
```

Example of a Stored Procedure with Input Parameters

Consider a procedure that retrieves employee details based on the employee ID. This procedure takes an employee ID as an input parameter, performs a query, and returns the employee's information.

```
CREATE PROCEDURE GetEmployeeDetails
    @EmployeeID INT
AS
BEGIN
    SELECT EmployeeName, Department, Salary
    FROM Employees
    WHERE EmployeeID = @EmployeeID;
END;
```

To execute this procedure, the caller must supply an argument for the @EmployeeID parameter.

```
EXEC GetEmployeeDetails @EmployeeID = 101;
```

The output would be displayed as follows:

```
EmployeeName   | Department | Salary
-------------------------------------
John Doe       | IT         | 70000
```

Example of a Stored Procedure with Output Parameters

In stored procedures with output parameters, values calculated or retrieved within the procedure are assigned to the output parameters, which can then be referenced by the calling application or script.

```
CREATE PROCEDURE GetEmployeeSalary
    @EmployeeID INT,
    @Salary INT OUT
AS
BEGIN
    SELECT @Salary = Salary
    FROM Employees
    WHERE EmployeeID = @EmployeeID;
END;
```

To call this procedure and capture the output parameter, the following syntax is used:

```
DECLARE @Salary INT;

EXEC GetEmployeeSalary @EmployeeID = 101, @Salary = @Salary
    OUTPUT;

PRINT 'Employee Salary: ' + CAST(@Salary AS VARCHAR(10));
```

The output in this case would be:

```
Employee Salary: 70000
```

Example of a Stored Procedure with Input/Output Parameters

A procedure with an input/output parameter can modify the value of the parameter and return the modified value to the caller.

```
CREATE PROCEDURE UpdateAndReturnSalary
    @EmployeeID INT,
```

```
    @Salary INT INOUT
AS
BEGIN
    UPDATE Employees
    SET Salary = @Salary
    WHERE EmployeeID = @EmployeeID;

    SELECT @Salary = Salary
    FROM Employees
    WHERE EmployeeID = @EmployeeID;
END;
```

When invoking this procedure, the following syntax is used to pass and retrieve the parameter:

```
DECLARE @NewSalary INT;

SET @NewSalary = 75000;

EXEC UpdateAndReturnSalary @EmployeeID = 101, @Salary =
    @NewSalary INOUT;

PRINT 'Updated Salary: ' + CAST(@NewSalary AS VARCHAR(10))
    ;
```

The output would be:

```
Updated Salary: 75000
```

Default Values for Parameters

Stored procedures can also define default values for input parameters. If the calling application or script does not provide a value for the parameter, the default value is used.

```
CREATE PROCEDURE GetDepartmentEmployees
    @Department NVARCHAR(50) = 'IT'
AS
BEGIN
    SELECT EmployeeName, EmployeeID
    FROM Employees
    WHERE Department = @Department;
END;
```

In this example, if the procedure is called without specifying a department, it defaults to 'IT'.

```
-- Uses default value 'IT'
EXEC GetDepartmentEmployees;

-- Specifying a department
EXEC GetDepartmentEmployees @Department = 'HR';
```

Outputs might be as follows:

```
EmployeeName   | EmployeeID
----------------------------
John Doe       | 101
Jane Smith     | 102
```

Overall, understanding and effectively utilizing parameters within stored procedures enhances the modularity, reuse, and manageability of database operations.

8.5 Error Handling in Stored Procedures

Error handling is a critical aspect of writing robust and reliable stored procedures. Proper error handling ensures that your stored procedures can gracefully recover from unexpected conditions and provide meaningful feedback to the calling applications or users. Without appropriate error handling, stored procedures may fail silently, leading to data inconsistencies and making troubleshooting difficult.

To handle errors effectively in SQL, we use the TRY...CATCH construct, which is similar to exception handling mechanisms found in many programming languages. This construct allows you to capture and respond to errors within the scope of a stored procedure.

The structure of the TRY...CATCH block is as follows:

```
BEGIN TRY
    -- Statements that may cause an error
END TRY
BEGIN CATCH
    -- Statements to handle the error
END CATCH
```

Within the CATCH block, you can use various system functions to retrieve information about the error that occurred. The most commonly used functions include:

- ERROR_NUMBER(): Returns the error number.
- ERROR_SEVERITY(): Returns the severity of the error.
- ERROR_STATE(): Returns the state number of the error.
- ERROR_PROCEDURE(): Returns the name of the stored procedure or trigger where the error occurred.
- ERROR_LINE(): Returns the line number where the error occurred.
- ERROR_MESSAGE(): Returns the complete text of the error message.

These functions can be used to log error details and to provide feedback to the user. Below is an example of a stored procedure with error handling:

```
CREATE PROCEDURE TransferFunds
    @SourceAccount INT,
    @TargetAccount INT,
    @Amount DECIMAL(10,2)
AS
BEGIN
    BEGIN TRY
        BEGIN TRANSACTION

        -- Deduct the amount from the source account
        UPDATE Accounts
        SET Balance = Balance - @Amount
        WHERE AccountID = @SourceAccount;

        -- Add the amount to the target account
        UPDATE Accounts
        SET Balance = Balance + @Amount
        WHERE AccountID = @TargetAccount;

        COMMIT TRANSACTION
    END TRY
    BEGIN CATCH
        ROLLBACK TRANSACTION
```

```
        -- Retrieve error information
        DECLARE @ErrorMessage NVARCHAR(4000) =
            ERROR_MESSAGE();
        DECLARE @ErrorNumber INT = ERROR_NUMBER();
        DECLARE @ErrorSeverity INT = ERROR_SEVERITY();
        DECLARE @ErrorState INT = ERROR_STATE();
        DECLARE @ErrorLine INT = ERROR_LINE();
        DECLARE @ErrorProcedure NVARCHAR(200) =
            ERROR_PROCEDURE();

        -- Log the error details (for example, in an ErrorLog table)
        INSERT INTO ErrorLog (ErrorMessage, ErrorNumber,
            ErrorSeverity, ErrorState, ErrorLine, ErrorProcedure,
            ErrorDateTime)
        VALUES (@ErrorMessage, @ErrorNumber, @ErrorSeverity,
            @ErrorState, @ErrorLine, @ErrorProcedure, GETDATE
            ());

        -- Re-throw the error
        RAISERROR (@ErrorMessage, @ErrorSeverity, @ErrorState)
            ;
    END CATCH
END;
```

This stored procedure performs a fund transfer between two accounts. It begins a transaction to ensure data consistency. If an error occurs at any point during the transaction, the CATCH block is executed, rolling back the transaction to prevent partial updates. It then logs error details into an ErrorLog table and rethrows the error.

Error handling in stored procedures should also consider the possibility of nested transactions and other complexities. SQL Server provides the XACT_STATE() function, which indicates the state of the current transaction. Using XACT_STATE(), you can determine whether a transaction is still valid or needs to be rolled back:

```
IF (XACT_STATE()) = -1
BEGIN
    -- The transaction is uncommitable
    ROLLBACK TRANSACTION;
END
ELSE IF (XACT_STATE()) = 1
```

```
BEGIN
    -- The transaction is commitable
    COMMIT TRANSACTION;
END
```

For complex stored procedures, consider encapsulating error handling logic into a separate reusable procedure. This promotes consistency and reduces code duplication across multiple stored procedures. Example:

```
CREATE PROCEDURE HandleError
AS
BEGIN
    DECLARE @ErrorMessage NVARCHAR(4000) =
        ERROR_MESSAGE();
    DECLARE @ErrorNumber INT = ERROR_NUMBER();
    DECLARE @ErrorSeverity INT = ERROR_SEVERITY();
    DECLARE @ErrorState INT = ERROR_STATE();
    DECLARE @ErrorLine INT = ERROR_LINE();
    DECLARE @ErrorProcedure NVARCHAR(200) =
        ERROR_PROCEDURE();

    INSERT INTO ErrorLog (ErrorMessage, ErrorNumber,
        ErrorSeverity, ErrorState, ErrorLine, ErrorProcedure,
        ErrorDateTime)
    VALUES (@ErrorMessage, @ErrorNumber, @ErrorSeverity,
        @ErrorState, @ErrorLine, @ErrorProcedure, GETDATE());

    RAISERROR (@ErrorMessage, @ErrorSeverity, @ErrorState);
END;
```

To utilize this error handling procedure within another stored procedure:

```
CREATE PROCEDURE ExampleProcedure
AS
BEGIN
    BEGIN TRY
        -- Your procedure logic here
    END TRY
    BEGIN CATCH
        EXEC HandleError;
    END CATCH
END;
```

Proper error handling is essential for building resilient database applications. By using TRY...CATCH blocks, leveraging system error functions, and ensuring transactions are correctly managed, you can create stored procedures that respond appropriately to errors and maintain data integrity.

8.6 Introduction to Triggers

A trigger in a database is a special kind of stored procedure that automatically executes or fires when certain events occur on a particular table or view. Triggers can be used to enforce business rules, maintain audit trails, and ensure data integrity by automatically executing predefined actions in response to specific data modifications.

Conceptually, triggers consist of three primary components: the event, the condition, and the action. The **event** determines when the trigger should execute, such as INSERT, UPDATE, or DELETE operations. The **condition** specifies any constraints or criteria that must be met for the trigger to activate. Finally, the **action** defines the actual operation to be performed when the trigger fires.

Triggers are classified into two main types based on their timing in relation to the triggering event:

- **Before Triggers**: These triggers execute before the triggering event. They are often used for validation purposes, such as ensuring that data meets certain criteria before being inserted or updated in the database. If the conditions specified in a BEFORE trigger are not met, the triggering event can be cancelled.

- **After Triggers**: These triggers execute after the triggering event. They are typically used for activities like logging changes, maintaining summary tables, or cascading updates through related tables.

Triggers can also be classified based on their execution context:

- **Row-Level Triggers**: These triggers execute once for each row affected by the triggering event. They are useful for operations that must be performed for every individual row, such as updating related records based on changes in a specific row.

- **Statement-Level Triggers**: These triggers execute once for the entire triggering event, regardless of the number of rows affected. They are advantageous when the action to be performed is independent of the specific rows being modified, focusing instead on the event as a whole.

To illustrate the creation and use of triggers, consider the following example where a trigger is defined to automatically update a timestamp column in a table whenever an UPDATE operation occurs.

Suppose we have a users table structured as follows:

```
CREATE TABLE users (
    user_id INT PRIMARY KEY,
    username VARCHAR(50),
    email VARCHAR(100),
    last_modified TIMESTAMP
);
```

We want to ensure that the last_modified column is updated to the current timestamp whenever a record in the users table is updated. For this purpose, we can create an AFTER UPDATE trigger:

```
CREATE TRIGGER update_user_timestamp
AFTER UPDATE ON users
FOR EACH ROW
BEGIN
    UPDATE users
    SET last_modified = NOW()
    WHERE user_id = NEW.user_id;
END;
```

In this example, the trigger update_user_timestamp is defined to execute AFTER UPDATE on the users table. The FOR EACH ROW clause specifies that this is a row-level trigger, meaning it will execute once for each updated row.

The trigger body, enclosed within the BEGIN and END keywords, contains the SQL statements to execute. The NEW keyword is used to reference the new values of the updated row. Here, the UPDATE statement sets the last_modified column to the current timestamp using the

NOW() function for the row identified by NEW.user_id.

Executing an UPDATE operation on the users table will now automatically fire the update_user_timestamp trigger, ensuring the last_modified column is accurately updated as shown:

```
UPDATE users
SET email = 'new_email@example.com'
WHERE user_id = 1;
```

```
Query OK, 1 row affected (0.01 sec)
Rows matched: 1  Changed: 1  Warnings: 0
```

It should be noted that the usage of triggers should be approached with caution. Improper use can lead to complications such as cascading triggers, where one trigger execution leads to another trigger being fired, potentially causing infinite loops. Performance considerations are also essential, as triggers add overhead to data modification statements. Therefore, thorough testing and performance evaluation are crucial when implementing triggers in a production environment.

8.7 Creating and Managing Triggers

Triggers are a powerful mechanism in SQL databases that allow the execution of a specified set of commands automatically when certain events occur within the database. These events can include modifications to table data through insertions, updates, or deletions. Triggers facilitate automated auditing, data validation, and the enforcement of constraints, thus ensuring data integrity and consistency.

A trigger is associated with a table and is activated, or fired, in response to an event on that table. SQL triggers can be classified into different types based on the timing of their execution and the specific event they respond to. The primary types of triggers are:

- **Before Triggers**: Executed before the triggering event, which allows for preemptive data validation and manipulation.
- **After Triggers**: Executed after the triggering event, used typically for logging, auditing, or cascading changes.
- **Instead of Triggers**: Executed in place of the event, primarily used in views where direct modifications are not allowed.

To create a trigger, the CREATE TRIGGER statement is used. The basic syntax for creating a trigger is as follows:

```
CREATE TRIGGER trigger_name
{BEFORE | AFTER | INSTEAD OF} [INSERT | UPDATE |
    DELETE]
ON table_name
[FOR EACH ROW]
[WHEN condition]
BEGIN
  -- Trigger body: SQL statements
END;
```

In the syntax:

- trigger_name: Specifies the name of the trigger.
- BEFORE | AFTER | INSTEAD OF: Defines the trigger timing.
- INSERT | UPDATE | DELETE: Specifies the event that fires the trigger.
- table_name: Identifies the table to which the trigger is attached.
- FOR EACH ROW: Indicates that the trigger should execute per affected row.
- WHEN condition: (Optional) Specifies a condition for the trigger to fire.

The trigger body contains the SQL statements that define the actions to be performed when the trigger is fired. The BEGIN and END keywords enclose the block of statements.

Example: Creating a Trigger

Consider a scenario where we need to create a trigger that automatically logs any inserts into an employees table into an employees_log table. The employees_log table records the changes with the employee ID, action type, and timestamp.

```
CREATE TABLE employees_log (
  log_id INT AUTO_INCREMENT PRIMARY KEY,
  emp_id INT,
  action VARCHAR(50),
  action_time TIMESTAMP DEFAULT CURRENT_TIMESTAMP
```

```
);

CREATE TRIGGER after_employee_insert
AFTER INSERT ON employees
FOR EACH ROW
BEGIN
  INSERT INTO employees_log (emp_id, action)
  VALUES (NEW.emp_id, 'INSERT');
END;
```

In this example:

- The employees_log table is created to store log records.
- The after_employee_insert trigger is defined to fire AFTER INSERT on the employees table.
- For each inserted row in the employees table, a log entry is inserted into the employees_log table.
- The NEW keyword represents the new data being inserted into the employees table.

Managing Triggers

Managing triggers involves actions such as altering existing triggers, disabling, enabling, and dropping triggers when they are no longer needed or when modifications are required.

Altering Triggers

To modify an existing trigger, the most common approach is to drop the existing trigger and recreate it with the required changes. However, some SQL implementations provide the ALTER TRIGGER statement for specific alterations. Here is a general example of dropping and recreating a trigger:

```
DROP TRIGGER IF EXISTS after_employee_insert;

CREATE TRIGGER after_employee_insert
AFTER INSERT ON employees
FOR EACH ROW
BEGIN
  INSERT INTO employees_log (emp_id, action)
  VALUES (NEW.emp_id, 'INSERT');
```

```
END;
```

Disabling and Enabling Triggers

In scenarios where triggers need to be temporarily disabled, the DISABLE TRIGGER and ENABLE TRIGGER statements are used. This functionality may vary between different SQL database systems.

```
ALTER TABLE employees DISABLE TRIGGER
    after_employee_insert;

-- Perform operations without trigger

ALTER TABLE employees ENABLE TRIGGER
    after_employee_insert;
```

Dropping Triggers

To remove a trigger permanently, the DROP TRIGGER statement is used:

```
DROP TRIGGER IF EXISTS after_employee_insert;
```

Triggers provide an essential mechanism for automating tasks, ensuring data integrity, and maintaining logs. Although powerful, they should be used judiciously due to the potential for adding complexity and overhead to database operations. Proper management and documentation of triggers are essential best practices for maintaining efficient and reliable database systems.

8.8 Using Triggers for Auditing and Validation

Triggers are special types of stored procedures that automatically execute in response to certain events on a particular table or view in a database. They play a critical role in auditing and validation by allowing database administrators and developers to enforce business rules, maintain data integrity, and keep track of changes automatically. There are two main types of triggers: **AFTER** triggers and **INSTEAD OF** triggers.

AFTER triggers execute after an **INSERT**, **UPDATE**, or **DELETE** operation has been performed on a table. These triggers are useful for auditing changes since they can store the old and new values of the data. **INSTEAD OF triggers** execute in place of the operation triggering them, providing a way to validate data and enforce constraints that cannot be expressed using standard methods.

To create a trigger, the CREATE TRIGGER statement is used. Here is the general syntax:

```
CREATE TRIGGER trigger_name
ON table_name
AFTER|INSTEAD OF [INSERT], [UPDATE], [DELETE]
AS
BEGIN
    -- SQL statements
END;
```

The following sections illustrate how to use triggers for auditing and validation through practical examples.

In the context of an employee database, consider the employee table:

```
CREATE TABLE employee (
    employee_id INT PRIMARY KEY,
    name VARCHAR(100),
    position VARCHAR(50),
    salary DECIMAL(10, 2),
    last_modified DATETIME
);
```

We aim to audit changes made to the salary field. An auditing table, salary_audit, can be created to store the old and new values along with the timestamp and user who made the change:

```
CREATE TABLE salary_audit (
    audit_id INT PRIMARY KEY IDENTITY,
    employee_id INT,
    old_salary DECIMAL(10, 2),
    new_salary DECIMAL(10, 2),
    modified_by VARCHAR(100),
    modified_at DATETIME
);
```

Next, an **AFTER UPDATE** trigger ensures that every time the salary of an employee is updated, the old and new values of the salary are recorded in the salary_audit table:

```
CREATE TRIGGER trg_salary_update
ON employee
AFTER UPDATE
AS
BEGIN
    IF UPDATE(salary)
    BEGIN
        INSERT INTO salary_audit (employee_id, old_salary,
            new_salary, modified_by, modified_at)
        SELECT
            i.employee_id,
            d.salary AS old_salary,
            i.salary AS new_salary,
            SYSTEM_USER AS modified_by,
            GETDATE() AS modified_at
        FROM inserted i
        JOIN deleted d ON i.employee_id = d.employee_id;
    END;
END;
```

The INSERTED and DELETED tables are special logical tables used in **AFTER triggers** to hold the new and old values of the table, respectively. In this case, INSERTED contains the new salary values, and DELETED contains the old salary values. The trigger highlights how auditing ensures that every modification is logged with the necessary details for traceability.

For data validation, consider a scenario where you need to ensure that the salary of an employee cannot be reduced. This can be achieved using an **INSTEAD OF UPDATE** trigger:

```
CREATE TRIGGER trg_validate_salary_update
ON employee
INSTEAD OF UPDATE
AS
BEGIN
    UPDATE employee
    SET
        salary = i.salary,
        name = i.name,
```

```
        position = i.position,
        last_modified = GETDATE()
    FROM inserted i
    WHERE employee.employee_id = i.employee_id
    AND i.salary >= employee.salary;

    IF EXISTS (SELECT 1 FROM inserted i JOIN employee e ON i.
        employee_id = e.employee_id WHERE i.salary < e.salary)
    BEGIN
        RAISERROR ('Salary cannot be decreased.', 16, 1);
    END;
END;
```

In this example, the INSTEAD OF UPDATE trigger allows the update only if the new salary is greater than or equal to the old salary. If an attempt is made to decrease the salary, the trigger raises an error, preventing the update and enforcing the business rule.

Triggers can also be used to validate other business rules, such as ensuring that specific fields are not null or maintaining referential integrity in more complex scenarios than those addressable by constraints alone.

Output from the examples provided would resemble:

```
Query OK, 1 row affected (0.01 sec)

Query OK, 1 row affected (0.01 sec)
Inserted 1 row(s) into "salary_audit"

Msg 50000, Level 16, State 1, Trigger trg_validate_salary_update, Line 12 Salary cannot be decreased.
```

These examples demonstrate that triggers are powerful tools in SQL for both auditing changes and enforcing data validation, sustaining the robustness and integrity of the database system without additional application-level logic. Triggers execute in response to defined events, offering a reliable and automated mechanism to monitor and control data effectively.

8.9 Introduction to User-Defined Functions (UDFs)

User-Defined Functions (UDFs) are an essential component in SQL that enable the encapsulation of logic into reusable functions, similar to subroutines in conventional programming languages. UDFs allow the SQL developer to create custom functions to perform operations that are not available by default in SQL. These functions can then be used within SQL statements, providing a higher level of abstraction and modularity in database programming.

Classification of UDFs: UDFs are broadly classified into two categories:

- **Scalar Functions:** These functions return a single value of a specified data type. Scalar functions can be used wherever an expression is valid.
- **Table-Valued Functions (TVFs):** These functions return a table data type. They can be used in the FROM clause of SQL queries, similar to a regular table or view.

Both types of UDFs enhance the ability to write clean, maintainable, and efficient SQL code. By encapsulating repetitive logic in UDFs, developers can avoid code duplication and ensure consistency across various parts of the database application.

Structure of UDFs: The general structure of a UDF consists of the following key elements:

- **Function Name and Parameters:** The name of the function and the parameters it accepts. The parameters specify the input values required by the function.
- **Return Type:** The data type or table schema that the function will return.
- **Function Body:** The SQL statements that define the operations performed by the function. This includes any declarations, conditional statements, and return statements.

Example of Scalar UDF: Consider a scalar function that calculates the square of a number. The function, dbo.CalculateSquare, accepts a numeric input and returns its square.

```
CREATE FUNCTION dbo.CalculateSquare
(
    @Number INT
)
RETURNS INT
```

```
AS
BEGIN
    RETURN @Number * @Number;
END;
```

This function can be used in a SELECT statement as follows:

```
SELECT dbo.CalculateSquare(5) AS SquareValue;
```

The output of the above query will be:

```
SquareValue
-----------
25
```

Example of Table-Valued Function: Let's look at a table-valued function that returns all employees from a specified department. The function, dbo.GetEmployeesByDepartment, accepts a department ID as input and returns a table with employee details.

```
CREATE FUNCTION dbo.GetEmployeesByDepartment
(
    @DepartmentID INT
)
RETURNS TABLE
AS
RETURN
(
    SELECT EmployeeID, FirstName, LastName, Position
    FROM Employees
    WHERE DepartmentID = @DepartmentID
);
```

This table-valued function can be used in a SELECT statement like this:

```
SELECT *
FROM dbo.GetEmployeesByDepartment(3);
```

The output will include all employee records that belong to the specified department.

Advantages of Using UDFs: The main benefits of using UDFs in SQL are:

- **Reusability:** Functions can be reused across different queries and applications, reducing code duplication.

- **Modularity:** Functions help in breaking down complex operations into simpler, manageable units.
- **Consistency:** Using UDFs ensures that the same logic is applied uniformly across various database operations.
- **Maintainability:** Code encapsulated in functions is easier to maintain and update. Changes made to a function are automatically propagated to all queries that use it.
- **Abstraction:** Functions hide the underlying complexity from the user, allowing for simpler and more readable SQL statements.

Performance Considerations: While UDFs provide numerous benefits in terms of code organization and reusability, they may impact performance if not used judiciously. Scalar functions, in particular, can lead to performance bottlenecks when used in large queries because they are executed row-by-row. Table-valued functions may also impact performance depending on their complexity and how they are invoked.

The efficient use of UDFs requires understanding their behavior and the execution environment. Profiling and analyzing queries using execution plans can help in identifying performance issues related to UDFs.

By integrating UDFs effectively into your SQL repertoire, you can greatly enhance the flexibility and readability of your database code, while also ensuring a consistent and maintainable codebase.

8.10 Creating Scalar Functions

Scalar functions are user-defined functions that return a single value. These functions can be used to encapsulate reusable logic, simplifying query expressions and improving code readability. Such functions accept input parameters, perform calculations or operations, and return a result based on these inputs.

To create a scalar function in SQL, the CREATE FUNCTION statement is used. The syntax for creating a scalar function is as follows:

```
CREATE FUNCTION function_name (@parameter1 datatype,
    @parameter2 datatype, ...)
RETURNS return_datatype
AS
BEGIN
```

```
    -- Function body: SQL statements that process input parameters
    -- and compute the return value.
    -- Use RETURN statement to return the final result.
    RETURN some_value;
END
```

Here is a breakdown of the key components of this syntax:

- function_name: The name of the function, which must be unique within the database.
- @parameter1, @parameter2, ...: The input parameters that the function accepts, along with their respective data types.
- RETURNS: Specifies the data type of the value that the function will return.
- BEGIN ... END: Encloses the body of the function, which contains SQL statements for processing the input parameters and computing the return value.
- RETURN: This statement is used to return the computed value from within the function body.

Consider an example where we create a scalar function to calculate the total cost of an order, including tax:

```
CREATE FUNCTION dbo.CalculateTotalCost (@quantity INT,
    @unitPrice DECIMAL(10, 2), @taxRate DECIMAL(4, 2))
RETURNS DECIMAL(10, 2)
AS
BEGIN
    DECLARE @totalCost DECIMAL(10, 2);

    -- Calculate total cost before tax
    SET @totalCost = @quantity * @unitPrice;

    -- Apply tax
    SET @totalCost = @totalCost + (@totalCost * @taxRate / 100);

    RETURN @totalCost;
END
```

In this function:

- The function is named CalculateTotalCost.
- It accepts three parameters: @quantity (the number of items ordered), @unitPrice (the price per item), and @taxRate (the tax rate as a percentage).
- The function returns a DECIMAL(10, 2) value, representing the total cost.
- The body of the function calculates the total cost by first computing the subtotal (quantity multiplied by unit price) and then adding the tax amount.

To use the scalar function in a query, you simply call it by its name and pass the necessary arguments. For instance:

```
SELECT dbo.CalculateTotalCost(10, 15.99, 7.5) AS TotalCost;
```

The output of this query would be:

```
TotalCost
----------
171.89
```

Scalar functions can also be used within other SQL statements such as INSERT, UPDATE, and DELETE. Assume you have an Orders table and you want to insert the total order cost for each record. You can execute the following:

```
INSERT INTO Orders (OrderID, Quantity, UnitPrice, TaxRate,
    TotalCost)
VALUES (1, 10, 15.99, 7.5, dbo.CalculateTotalCost(10, 15.99, 7.5));
```

Using scalar functions can greatly improve maintainability. For recursive operations or complex formulas, encapsulating logic in a reusable function reduces redundancy. This allows for centralized updates and mitigates the risk of inconsistencies if the logic necessitates alteration.

When working with scalar functions, consider the following best practices:

- Ensure that functions are deterministic when possible. A deterministic function always returns the same result for a given set of input values, facilitating predictable performance and potential optimization.

- Minimize the execution time within the function to avoid performance bottlenecks. Extensive computations within scalar functions can slow down query processing.
- Appropriately handle NULL inputs within the function. Use ISNULL or COALESCE to define default behaviors for NULL parameters where applicable.
- Incorporate error handling within the function. Use the TRY...CATCH construct to manage exceptions and maintain reliability.

Effective use of scalar functions enhances query simplicity and code reusability, contributing to more robust database application development.

8.11 Creating Table-Valued Functions

Table-Valued Functions (TVFs) are an essential component in SQL for returning a table data type. Unlike scalar functions that return a single value, TVFs return a table, allowing for more complex and flexible data retrieval operations. TVFs are useful for encapsulating logic that returns row sets and can be utilized in SELECT statements, JOINs, and APPLY operations.

There are two types of Table-Valued Functions: Inline Table-Valued Functions (ITVFs) and Multi-Statement Table-Valued Functions (MSTVFs). ITVFs are defined using a single SELECT statement and are more efficient since they are expanded in the execution plan as views or derived tables. MSTVFs include multiple statements that can process data before reaching the final SELECT statement that defines the table returned.

To create a Table-Valued Function, one must understand the syntax and structure involved. Consider a practical example where we want to create a function to retrieve employee details based on a department ID. The following sections provide detailed steps and explanations for both ITVFs and MSTVFs.

```
CREATE FUNCTION dbo.GetEmployeesByDepartment (@DeptID
    INT)
RETURNS TABLE
AS
```

```
RETURN
(
    SELECT EmployeeID, FirstName, LastName, JobTitle
    FROM Employees
    WHERE DepartmentID = @DeptID
);
```

The code above demonstrates the creation of an Inline Table-Valued Function named 'GetEmployeesByDepartment'. The function accepts a single parameter '@DeptID' of type INTEGER. The 'RETURNS' clause specifies that the function returns a table. The body of the function is encapsulated within the 'RETURN' keyword, followed by a SELECT statement that retrieves employee data filtered by the given department ID.

To use this function, you can simply call it within a SELECT statement.

```
SELECT * FROM dbo.GetEmployeesByDepartment(3);
```

This query will return the rows from the 'Employees' table where 'DepartmentID' equals 3.

Next, we consider an example of a Multi-Statement Table-Valued Function. MSTVFs are more complex as they allow multiple SQL statements and temporary variable manipulation before producing the final table result.

```
CREATE FUNCTION dbo.GetEmployeeDetails (@DeptID INT)
RETURNS @EmployeeDetails TABLE
(
    EmployeeID INT,
    FullName NVARCHAR(100),
    JobTitle NVARCHAR(50)
)
AS
BEGIN
    INSERT INTO @EmployeeDetails
    SELECT
        EmployeeID,
        FirstName + ' ' + LastName AS FullName,
        JobTitle
    FROM Employees
    WHERE DepartmentID = @DeptID;
```

```
    RETURN;
END;
```

In this example, the function 'GetEmployeeDetails' is defined to return a table variable '@EmployeeDetails'. The structure of the returned table is explicitly defined within the 'RETURNS' clause. The body of the function includes an 'INSERT INTO' statement that populates the table variable. The function ends with a 'RETURN' statement, which outputs the populated table.

To invoke this MSTVF, you can use a SELECT statement similar to how you would with a table:

```
SELECT * FROM dbo.GetEmployeeDetails(3);
```

This query retrieves employee details, including a concatenated full name and job title for employees in the department with ID 3.

When using TVFs, it is essential to consider performance implications. ITVFs are generally more efficient than MSTVFs because the former are inline and can be optimized similarly to views. Conversely, MSTVFs can introduce performance overhead due to their procedural nature and the use of table variables.

Using Table-Valued Functions enhances modularity and code reusability. They encapsulate reusable logic, making maintenance more straightforward and enabling complex querying scenarios. Ensure to test the performance and optimize the functions where possible, considering indexing and query refactoring techniques.

Understanding the creation and usage of TVFs expands one's ability to write advanced SQL queries, leveraging the full power of SQL Server's capabilities for data manipulation and retrieval.

8.12 Best Practices for Stored Procedures, Triggers, and Functions

In this section, we focus on best practices for implementing and maintaining stored procedures, triggers, and user-defined functions (UDFs) within database systems. Adhering to these practices enhances code reliability, maintainability, and efficiency, ensuring robust database applications.

1. Naming Conventions: Proper naming conventions improve code readability and maintainability. Use intuitive and descriptive names for stored procedures, triggers, and functions. Prefixes can help identify the type of database object:

- usp_ for user-stored procedures, e.g., usp_GetCustomerDetails.
- trg_ for triggers, e.g., trg_AfterInsertCustomer.
- udf_ for user-defined functions, e.g., udf_CalculateAge.

2. Modular Design: Break complex logic into smaller, modular components, which can be invoked as needed. This approach facilitates easier debugging, testing, and maintenance. For example, a large stored procedure can be decomposed into several smaller procedures, each handling a specific task.

3. Parameter Usage: Use parameters to make stored procedures and functions more flexible and reusable. Always specify default values for parameters when appropriate and use named parameters to enhance clarity:

```
CREATE PROCEDURE usp_GetCustomerOrders
    @CustomerId INT,
    @OrderDate DATETIME = NULL
AS
BEGIN
    -- Procedure logic here
END
```

4. Error Handling: Implement structured error handling to capture and handle exceptions gracefully. Use TRY...CATCH blocks in T-SQL to manage errors:

```
BEGIN TRY
    -- SQL statements
END TRY
BEGIN CATCH
    -- Error handling logic
    DECLARE @ErrorMessage NVARCHAR(4000)
    SET @ErrorMessage = ERROR_MESSAGE()
    RAISERROR(@ErrorMessage, 16, 1)
END CATCH
```

Record error details in an error log table to assist with troubleshooting and diagnostics.

5. Transaction Management: Ensure atomicity of operations by using transactions. Use explicit transaction control statements like BEGIN TRANSACTION, COMMIT, and ROLLBACK to guarantee data consistency:

```
BEGIN TRY
    BEGIN TRANSACTION
        -- Operations
    COMMIT
END TRY
BEGIN CATCH
    ROLLBACK
    -- Error handling
END CATCH
```

6. Performance Optimization: Optimize stored procedures, triggers, and functions for performance. Use indexing wisely, avoid unnecessary computations, and prefer set-based operations over row-by-row processing. Use the EXPLAIN or SHOW PLAN commands to analyze query performance and optimize accordingly.

```
SELECT col1, col2
FROM my_table
WHERE indexed_col = 'value'
```

7. Avoid Side Effects: Especially for UDFs, avoid side effects such as modifying global variables or changing the state outside the function. Functions should be deterministic, providing the same output for the same input without altering the system state.

8. Security Practices: Use the principle of least privilege, granting the minimum necessary permissions to database objects. Use parameterized queries to mitigate SQL injection risks and avoid dynamic SQL execution where possible:

```
CREATE PROCEDURE usp_SafeExample
    @UserInput NVARCHAR(4000)
AS
BEGIN
    DECLARE @SQL NVARCHAR(4000)
    SET @SQL = N'SELECT * FROM Employees WHERE Name =
```

```
        @UserInput'
    EXEC sp_executesql @SQL, N'@UserInput NVARCHAR(4000)',
        @UserInput
END
```

9. Consistent Formatting and Documentation: Consistently format code for readability. Include comments and documentation for complex logic, specifying the purpose of each database object, parameters, return values, and sample usage. Well-documented code is easier to understand, maintain, and extend:

```
/*
    Procedure: usp_GetCustomerDetails
    Purpose: Retrieves details of a specified customer
    Parameters:
        @CustomerId - ID of the customer to retrieve
    Returns: Customer details rowset
*/
CREATE PROCEDURE usp_GetCustomerDetails
    @CustomerId INT
AS
BEGIN
    SELECT * FROM Customers WHERE CustomerId =
        @CustomerId
END
```

10. Testing and Validation: Thoroughly test stored procedures, triggers, and functions to ensure they meet the required specifications and handle edge cases appropriately. Use unit testing frameworks where available, and validate the functionality in a development environment before deploying to production.

By adhering to these best practices, database developers can create efficient, reliable, and maintainable stored procedures, triggers, and functions, enhancing the overall robustness and performance of database systems.

Chapter 9

Database Security and User Management

This chapter addresses the critical aspects of database security and user management. It covers user authentication methods, access control mechanisms, and role-based access control (RBAC). The chapter discusses strategies for encrypting data at rest and in transit, preventing SQL injection attacks, and auditing database activity. It also includes backup and recovery strategies, compliance with regulatory requirements, and best practices for ensuring database security, backed by practical case studies.

9.1 Introduction to Database Security

Database security encompasses a set of policies, procedures, and technologies designed to protect database management systems from unintended activities. These activities can be classified as operational errors, malicious attacks, unauthorized access, and misuse. The focus of database security is to ensure the confidentiality, integrity, and availability (CIA) of data. This is achieved by implementing stringent controls over data access and usage. The field of database security has become increasingly vital as the amount and value of data stored within corporate and personal databases continue to grow.

Securing a database involves multiple layers of defense, which typically include the database environment, the database software, and the data itself. The primary components of database security strategy include:

- User Authentication and Access Control
- Data Encryption
- Auditing and Monitoring
- Backup and Recovery
- Compliance with Regulatory Requirements

These components must work in harmony to create a secure data storage and retrieval system.

User Authentication mechanisms verify the identity of users attempting to access the database. Strong authentication methods, such as multi-factor authentication (MFA), can significantly enhance security by requiring users to provide multiple forms of identification.

Access Control determines which users can access specific data and what actions they can perform. This includes fine-grained permissions, role-based access control (RBAC), and ensuring adherence to the principle of least privilege, where users are granted the minimal level of access necessary for their tasks.

Data Encryption is vital for protecting sensitive information from being accessed by unauthorized users. Encryption techniques are applied not just to data at rest (stored data), but also to data in transit (data being transferred across networks). This dual approach ensures that data is protected both when stored and when communicated between systems.

Auditing and Monitoring involve systematically recording database activities and analyzing these records to detect and respond to security incidents. This includes setting up audit trails, monitoring database user activities, and identifying anomalous behaviors that may indicate a security breach.

Backup and Recovery strategies ensure data availability and integrity by creating copies of the database that can be restored in case of data loss, corruption, or a security incident. This also forms a critical component of disaster recovery planning.

Compliance with Regulatory Requirements necessitates that organizations adhere to relevant laws, regulations, and industry standards concerning data security and privacy. Compliance frameworks such as GDPR (General Data Protection Regulation), HIPAA (Health Insurance Portability and Accountability Act), and PCI DSS (Payment Card Industry Data Security Standard) provide guidelines for safeguarding sensitive data.

User Authentication and Access Control
Incorporating robust user authentication and access control is the first layer of defense in database security. Authentication verifies the identity of the user, while access control defines what an authenticated user is authorized to do. Implementing a combination of strong passwords, biometrics, and login-based tokens can thwart unauthorized access.

```
-- Example of creating a user with specific permissions in SQL
CREATE USER 'db_user'@'localhost' IDENTIFIED BY '
    password123';
GRANT SELECT, INSERT, UPDATE, DELETE ON
    database_name.* TO 'db_user'@'localhost';
```

The example demonstrates how to create a user and assign SQL permissions, thus showcasing the fundamental operations of access control in SQL. This ensures that users can only perform actions that are explicitly granted to them.

Data Encryption Technologies
Encryption methods are crucial to protect data assets through encoding to make them unreadable to unintended recipients. Key encryption methods include symmetric encryption, where the same key is used for encryption and decryption, and asymmetric encryption, which uses a pair of public and private keys.

```
-- Example of enabling transparent data encryption (TDE) on a SQL
    Server database
USE master;
GO
CREATE DATABASE DB1;
GO
USE DB1;
GO
CREATE DATABASE ENCRYPTION KEY
WITH ALGORITHM = AES_256
ENCRYPTION BY SERVER CERTIFICATE MyServerCert;
GO
ALTER DATABASE DB1
```

```
SET ENCRYPTION ON;
GO
```

Implementing Transparent Data Encryption (TDE) in SQL Server, as demonstrated, ensures that data at rest is encrypted, thus enhancing the protection of stored data.

Auditing and Monitoring

Ongoing monitoring and auditing of database activity are crucial to detect potential security breaches and ensure policy compliance. SQL-based audit and logging mechanisms can track user actions and system changes, providing vital information for forensic analysis.

```
-- Example of setting up an audit in SQL Server
CREATE SERVER AUDIT MyAudit
TO FILE (FILEPATH = 'C:\Audits\')
WITH (ON_FAILURE = CONTINUE);
GO
CREATE SERVER AUDIT SPECIFICATION MyAuditSpec
FOR SERVER AUDIT MyAudit
ADD (FAILED_LOGIN_GROUP);
GO
ALTER SERVER AUDIT MyAudit
WITH (STATE = ON);
GO
```

The setup illustrated captures failed login attempts, thus contributing to the identification of unauthorized access attempts.

Backup and Recovery

Reliable backup and recovery solutions safeguard data integrity and availability. Regular backups must be taken, and recovery procedures should be tested to ensure they are effective in restoring data after loss or corruption.

```
-- Example of performing a full database backup in SQL Server
BACKUP DATABASE [DB1] TO DISK = 'C:\Backups\
    DB1_Backup.bak'
WITH FORMAT, INIT, NAME = 'Full Database Backup';
GO
```

The backup command ensures a recoverable copy of the database is available, which is essential for any disaster recovery plan.

Regulatory Compliance
Adhering to regulatory requirements involves implementing and documenting security measures to protect sensitive data. Compliance audits and certifications can demonstrate that an organization meets the necessary legal and industry standards for data protection.

The comprehensive implementation of these measures results in a fortified database environment where data integrity, confidentiality, and availability are preserved.

9.2 User Authentication

User authentication is a fundamental aspect of database security, ensuring that only authorized users can access the system. It involves verifying the identity of a user based on credentials such as a username and password. Other authentication mechanisms include multi-factor authentication (MFA), biometrics, and digital certificates. Proper authentication mechanisms prevent unauthorized access and protect sensitive data.

User authentication can be broadly categorized into three main types:

- **Password-Based Authentication**
- **Multi-Factor Authentication (MFA)**
- **Public Key Infrastructure (PKI)**

Password-Based Authentication This is the most common authentication method in databases. A user provides a username and password, which the system checks against a stored set of credentials. To enhance security in password-based systems, several practices should be followed:

- **Strong Password Policies**: Require users to create passwords that are complex and difficult to guess, typically including a mix of upper and lower case letters, numbers, and special characters.
- **Password Hashing**: Instead of storing plaintext passwords, store hashed passwords using a strong cryptographic hashing function such as SHA-256.

```
-- Example: Storing a password securely by hashing
INSERT INTO Users (username, password_hash) VALUES ('
    user1', SHA2('password123', 256));
```

- **Salted Hashing**: Add a unique salt to each password before hashing to prevent attacks using precomputed hash tables (rainbow tables).

```
-- Example: Generating a salt and storing a salted hash
SET @salt = CONCAT(RAND(), RAND(), RAND());
INSERT INTO Users (username, salt, password_hash)
    VALUES ('user2', @salt, SHA2(CONCAT('password123',
    @salt), 256));
```

- **Account Lockout Mechanism**: Implement mechanisms to lock the account after a number of failed login attempts to prevent brute-force attacks.

```
-- Example: Implementing account lockout after 3 failed
    attempts
UPDATE Users SET login_attempts = login_attempts + 1
    WHERE username = 'user3';
IF (SELECT login_attempts FROM Users WHERE username
    = 'user3') >= 3 THEN
    UPDATE Users SET account_locked = 1 WHERE
        username = 'user3';
END IF;
```

Multi-Factor Authentication (MFA) MFA strengthens security by requiring two or more verification factors. This typically combines something the user knows (password) with something the user has (a device) and/or something the user is (biometric data).

- **SMS OTP**: Send a One-Time Password (OTP) via SMS.

```
-- Placeholder for integration with an SMS OTP sending service
INSERT INTO User_OTP (user_id, otp) VALUES ('user4',
    GENERATE_OTP());
```

- **Authenticator Apps**: Utilize apps like Google Authenticator to generate time-based one-time passwords (TOTP).

```
-- Example: Storing a secret key for TOTP
INSERT INTO Users (username, secret_key) VALUES ('user5',
    'JBSWY3DPEHPK3PXP');
```

- **Biometric Authentication**: Use fingerprints, facial recognition, or iris scans.

```
-- Placeholder for integration with biometric authentication
    system
INSERT INTO User_Biometrics (user_id, fingerprint_hash)
    VALUES ('user6', HASH_FINGERPRINT('
    fingerprint_data'));
```

Public Key Infrastructure (PKI) PKI utilizes cryptographic keys issued by a trusted Certificate Authority (CA). Each user has a pair of keys: a private key and a public key. The private key is kept secret, while the public key is distributed. Authentication is achieved by proving possession of the private key, usually through the use of digital signatures.

- **Digital Certificates**: Issued and signed by a CA, verifying the identity of the user.

```
-- Placeholder for storing a user's digital certificate
INSERT INTO User_Certificates (user_id, certificate) VALUES
    ('user7', 'MIIBIjANB...');
```

- **Digital Signatures**: Utilized to verify the authenticity and integrity of a message or document.

```
-- Example: Verifying a digital signature
IF VERIFY_SIGNATURE('message', 'signature', '
    user_public_key') THEN
    -- Proceed with authenticated action
END IF;
```

A robust user authentication mechanism is essential in safeguarding databases from unauthorized access. Implementing layered authentication methods, keeping up with emerging security standards, and conducting regular security audits are all vital components of an effective security strategy.

9.3 Access Control and Permissions

Access control and permissions are essential elements in ensuring the security and integrity of a database system. They determine who is allowed to access specific data and perform certain operations on that data, thereby minimizing unauthorized access and potential data breaches. Effective access control involves defining, enforcing, and auditing all permissions granted to users and roles within the database.

Access control is generally categorized into three main types: Discretionary Access Control (DAC), Mandatory Access Control (MAC), and Role-Based Access Control (RBAC). Each type offers a different approach to controlling access and is suitable for various use cases.

Discretionary Access Control (DAC): This type of control grants access based on the identity of the user. The owner of a piece of data or an object has the discretion to delegate access rights to other users. DAC is flexible but can be challenging to manage in large systems as it relies heavily on individual users' decisions.

To assign permissions using DAC in SQL, the following commands are commonly used:

```
GRANT SELECT, INSERT ON employees TO alice;
REVOKE INSERT ON employees FROM bob;
```

In this example, the GRANT statement is used to allow the user alice to perform SELECT and INSERT operations on the employees table. Conversely, the REVOKE statement removes the INSERT permission from the user bob.

Mandatory Access Control (MAC): This is a more rigid form of access control where access to data is granted based on policies defined by the system administrator. These policies are non-discretionary and are usually associated with the security labels of the information and the clearance of the user. MAC is commonly used in environments requiring high security, such as government or military applications.

For example, in a SQL-based system that implements labeled security, you might encounter something like this:

```
CREATE POLICY classified_information_policy
FOR ALL TABLES
USING (user_has_clearance(username, 'TOP SECRET'));
```

This example demonstrates creating a policy that ensures only users with the clearance level 'TOP SECRET' can access specific tables.

Role-Based Access Control (RBAC): RBAC is a widely adopted model that assigns permissions to roles rather than individuals. Users are assigned roles based on their job functions, and these roles determine their access rights. This approach simplifies permission management, especially in large organizations.

For instance, consider the creation of roles and their assignment in SQL:

```
CREATE ROLE manager;
CREATE ROLE developer;

GRANT SELECT, INSERT, UPDATE ON employees TO manager;
GRANT SELECT ON employees TO developer;

GRANT manager TO alice;
GRANT developer TO bob;
```

In this scenario, the CREATE ROLE command establishes two roles: manager and developer. The GRANT statements assign specific permissions to these roles, and users alice and bob are then granted the roles of manager and developer, respectively.

Fine-Grained Access Control (FGAC): Beyond traditional access control methods, FGAC allows specific access policies at a more granular level. This can involve implementing policies at the row or column level within a table, such as restricting certain rows based on user attributes.

In SQL, FGAC can be implemented using views or policies, as demonstrated below:

```
CREATE VIEW manager_view AS
SELECT * FROM employees WHERE department = 'Management';

GRANT SELECT ON manager_view TO alice;
```

Here, the CREATE VIEW statement creates a view that only includes employees from the 'Management' department. The GRANT statement allows user alice to SELECT from this view, thereby restricting her access to management-related data only.

Access Control Best Practices: - *Principle of Least Privilege*: Grant users the minimum level of access required to perform their duties. This reduces the risk of accidental or malicious data exposure. - *Regular Audits*: Periodically review and update access controls to ensure they align with current organizational needs and policies. - *Separation of Duties*: Distribute responsibilities among multiple users or roles to prevent any single point of failure or misuse.

Applying these best practices ensures a robust access control framework that can effectively safeguard the database against unauthorized access while maintaining operational efficiency.

9.4 Role-Based Access Control (RBAC)

Role-Based Access Control (RBAC) is a widely adopted access control mechanism that restricts network and database access based on the roles of individual users within an organization. Unlike discretionary access control (DAC) and mandatory access control (MAC), RBAC is more scalable and flexible, catering to the needs of complex and dynamic organizational structures. This section delves into the RBAC model, its components, and the implementation procedures required to enforce RBAC in relational databases.

Primarily, RBAC revolves around three core elements: roles, role permissions, and user-role assignments. A role is a collection of permissions that an organization defines based on job duties. Permissions specify the high-level operations that can be carried out on database objects, such as SELECT, INSERT, UPDATE, DELETE, and EXECUTE. These permissions are then assigned to roles rather than directly to users. Finally, users are assigned roles according to their responsibilities, which indirectly grants them the necessary permissions to perform their tasks.

Roles: In an RBAC system, roles represent the various job functions or titles within an organization. Each role encapsulates a set of permissions aligned with the responsibilities of that position. For example, a database administrator (DBA) role might have permissions to create, modify, and delete databases, while a data analyst role might have permissions to read specific tables and execute analytical reports.

Role Permissions: Permissions are granted to roles rather than individual users. This abstraction simplifies managing permissions because changes are made at the role level, automatically propagating to all users assigned to the role. The granularity of permissions can vary, often defined at the level of tables, views, columns, or stored procedures.

User-Role Assignments: Users are assigned roles based on their job functions. A user can be assigned multiple roles, and consequently, their effective permissions are the union of permissions associated with all their roles.

To demonstrate how RBAC can be practically implemented in a relational database, consider the following SQL scripts. These examples show how to create roles, grant permissions to roles, and assign roles to users in a SQL database management system (DBMS) such as PostgreSQL:

```
-- Creating roles in PostgreSQL
CREATE ROLE dba;
CREATE ROLE data_analyst;

-- Granting permissions to roles
GRANT CREATE ON DATABASE mydb TO dba;
GRANT DROP ON DATABASE mydb TO dba;
GRANT SELECT, INSERT ON ALL TABLES IN SCHEMA public
    TO data_analyst;
GRANT EXECUTE ON ALL FUNCTIONS IN SCHEMA public TO
    data_analyst;

-- Create users
CREATE USER alice WITH PASSWORD 'securepassword123';
CREATE USER bob WITH PASSWORD 'anothersecurepassword';

-- Assign roles to users
GRANT dba TO alice;
GRANT data_analyst TO bob;
```

In the example above, we first create the roles *dba* and *data_analyst*. Subsequently, we grant appropriate permissions to these roles. For instance, the *dba* role is granted permissions to create and drop databases, while the *data_analyst* role is granted permissions to select and insert data in all tables within the *public* schema. Additionally, users *alice* and *bob* are created and assigned the roles *dba* and *data_analyst* respectively, thereby enabling them to perform their designated tasks.

One significant advantage of RBAC is the ease of administration. When an employee's responsibilities change, system administrators can simply adjust the user's role assignments rather than modifying individual permissions. This not only streamlines access management but also reduces the possibility of errors. Moreover, RBAC enhances security by enforcing the principle of least privilege, ensuring users have the minimum necessary access to perform their jobs.

It is pertinent to mention that the implementation of RBAC should be complemented with rigorous processes for role design, approval, and periodic review. Roles should be defined clearly and documented comprehensively. Regular audits should be conducted to verify role assignments and their justifications. This helps in identifying and rectifying any potential discrepancies or excessive permissions granted inadvertently.

```
Roles:
+dba
  + Permissions: CREATE, DROP on database mydb
+data_analyst
  + Permissions: SELECT, INSERT on all tables in public schema, EXECUTE on all functions in public schema
Users:
+alice
  + Role: dba
+bob
  + Role: data_analyst
```

Understanding and implementing RBAC thus necessitate careful planning and execution. Well-defined roles and robust user-role management processes significantly contribute to a secure and manageable database environment.

9.5 Encrypting Data at Rest

Encrypting data at rest is an essential measure to protect sensitive information stored within a database from unauthorized access and breaches. This section delves into the methodologies and practices to ensure confidential data remains secure while it is stored on physical or virtual storage systems.

Storing data at rest under encryption implies converting sensitive data into a secure format that is not readily interpretable without decryption keys. Data at rest encompasses all data in persistent storage, including the database files, backups, and logs. Effective encryption strategies synergize with proper key management practices to maintain the data's confidentiality and integrity.

Encryption algorithms are the cornerstone of securing data at rest. The most commonly used encryption algorithms fall under symmetric and asymmetric cryptography. Symmetric cryptography, also known as secret-key cryptography, uses a single key for both encryption and decryption, while asymmetric cryptography involves a pair of keys—public and private.

AES Encryption:

The Advanced Encryption Standard (AES) is a widely accepted symmetric encryption algorithm used for securing data at rest. AES offers varying key length options of 128, 192, and 256 bits, with larger key sizes providing stronger security. Implementing AES encryption in a database context involves the following steps:

- **Key Management:** Secure generation, storage, and rotation of encryption keys. The use of hardware security modules (HSM) or dedicated key management services is recommended to safeguard encryption keys.
- **Data Encryption:** Applying AES encryption to data before writing to persistent storage. This can be implemented at the application layer or the database layer.
- **Decryption:** Retrieving and decrypting data during read operations using the secure key.

Below is an example of AES encryption in Python using the 'pycryptodome' library:

```
from Crypto.Cipher import AES
from Crypto.Random import get_random_bytes

# Generate a random 256-bit key
key = get_random_bytes(32)

# Create a cipher object using the key
cipher = AES.new(key, AES.MODE_GCM)

# Encrypt the data
data = b'Sensitive data that needs encryption.'
ciphertext, tag = cipher.encrypt_and_digest(data)

# Output the encrypted data
print(f'Key: {key.hex()}')
print(f'Nonce: {cipher.nonce.hex()}')
print(f'Ciphertext: {ciphertext.hex()}')
```

```
print(f'Tag: {tag.hex()}')
```

Transparent Data Encryption (TDE):

Transparent Data Encryption (TDE) is a database-level encryption feature designed to encrypt data at rest without requiring changes to the applications accessing the database. TDE typically encrypts the underlying database files, such as data files and backup files. Implementation steps for TDE include:

- **Enabling TDE:** Activate TDE on the database server or the specific database instance.
- **Encryption Key:** Generate and assign a database master key and a certificate or asymmetric key for TDE.
- **Encryption:** Apply the encryption to the database files, ensuring the data is encrypted on disk.

Example enabling TDE in SQL Server:

```
-- Create a master key
CREATE MASTER KEY ENCRYPTION BY PASSWORD = '
    StrongPassword';

-- Create a certificate
CREATE CERTIFICATE TDECert WITH SUBJECT = 'TDE
    Certificate';

-- Create a database encryption key and encrypt it with the certificate
USE YourDatabase;
CREATE DATABASE ENCRYPTION KEY WITH ALGORITHM =
     AES_256 ENCRYPTION BY SERVER CERTIFICATE
    TDECert;

-- Enable TDE
ALTER DATABASE YourDatabase SET ENCRYPTION ON;
```

Disk-Level Encryption:

Another layer of protection can be provided by disk-level encryption. This approach encrypts the entire storage medium, ensuring all data written to disk is encrypted. Disk-level encryption tools include BitLocker on Windows and LUKS on Linux. Here's an example of setting up LUKS on a Linux system:

```
# Install cryptsetup if not already installed
sudo apt-get install cryptsetup

# Initialize the LUKS partition
sudo cryptsetup luksFormat /dev/sdX

# Open the LUKS partition
sudo cryptsetup luksOpen /dev/sdX encrypted_disk

# Create a filesystem on the encrypted partition
sudo mkfs.ext4 /dev/mapper/encrypted_disk

# Mount the encrypted partition
sudo mount /dev/mapper/encrypted_disk /mnt/encrypted
```

Key Management:

Effective key management is critical in maintaining the security of encrypted data. Key management involves policies, procedures, and technologies to generate, distribute, store, rotate, and revoke encryption keys securely. Best practices include:

- **Use Strong Keys:** Use cryptographically strong keys generated using secure algorithms.
- **Secure Storage:** Store keys in dedicated HSMs or key management services rather than within the application or on the same server as the encrypted data.
- **Key Rotation:** Regularly rotate encryption keys and have mechanisms to re-encrypt data with new keys.
- **Access Control:** Restrict access to keys to authorized personnel and systems only.

Using a managed key service in AWS:

```
import boto3
from botocore.exceptions import ClientError

# Create a KMS client
kms_client = boto3.client('kms')
```

```
# Encrypt data
response = kms_client.encrypt(
    KeyId='alias/your-key-alias',
    Plaintext=b'Sensitive data that needs encryption.'
)

# Decrypt data
ciphertext = response['CiphertextBlob']
response = kms_client.decrypt(
    CiphertextBlob=ciphertext
)

# Output decrypted data
print(response['Plaintext'])
```

Employing these encryption strategies safeguards the data at rest, ensuring that even if unauthorized access to the physical storage occurs, the data remains protected and unreadable.

9.6 Encrypting Data in Transit

Ensuring the confidentiality and integrity of data as it travels across networks is paramount in safeguarding sensitive information from interception and tampering. Encrypting data in transit involves the application of cryptographic protocols to secure data exchanges between clients and servers. This section delves into the mechanisms and best practices for encrypting data in transit, specifically focusing on Transport Layer Security (TLS), configuring secure connections, and utilizing cryptographic libraries.

Transport Layer Security (TLS) is the most prevalent protocol for encrypting data in transit. It supersedes the older Secure Sockets Layer (SSL) protocol, offering enhanced security features and performance. TLS employs a combination of symmetric and asymmetric cryptography to establish a secure communication channel over networks. The typical phases in establishing a TLS connection include:

1. **Handshake Protocol:** This initial phase involves the negotiation of security parameters between the client and the server. The client initiates the handshake by sending a ClientHello message, which includes information about supported TLS versions, cipher

suites, and compression methods.

2. **Server Authentication and Pre-Master Secret Exchange:** The server responds with a ServerHello message, choosing a compatible TLS version and cipher suite from the client's list. The server then sends its digital certificate, verified by a trusted Certificate Authority (CA), followed by the ServerHelloDone message. The client verifies the server's certificate and replies with a ClientKeyExchange message, which contains a pre-master secret encrypted with the server's public key.

3. **Session Key Generation:** Both the client and server independently generate a symmetric session key using the exchanged pre-master secret and randomly generated values. This session key is employed for encrypting subsequent data exchanges, ensuring confidentiality.

4. **Finished Messages:** The client and server exchange Finished messages, encrypted via the session key. These messages contain hashes of the entire handshake process to ensure integrity.

After establishing the secure channel, both parties can exchange encrypted data until the session is terminated. Implementing TLS for encrypting database communications requires precise configuration.

Configuring TLS for Popular Database Systems:

- **MySQL:** MySQL offers support for SSL/TLS from version 4.0 onwards. To enable TLS, configure the server-side settings in the my.cnf file:

```
[mysqld]
ssl-ca = /path/to/ca-cert.pem
ssl-cert = /path/to/server-cert.pem
ssl-key = /path/to/server-key.pem
```

  On the client-side, ensure TLS is enforced by specifying appropriate options:

```
mysql --ssl-ca=/path/to/ca-cert.pem \
      --ssl-cert=/path/to/client-cert.pem \
      --ssl-key=/path/to/client-key.pem \
      --ssl-mode=VERIFY_IDENTITY
```

- **PostgreSQL:** PostgreSQL supports SSL/TLS from version 7.0. Enable SSL via the postgresql.conf file and provide the necessary certificate and key files in the data directory:

```
ssl = on
ssl_cert_file = 'server.crt'
ssl_key_file = 'server.key'
```

  Update the pg_hba.conf file to enforce SSL connections:

```
hostssl all all 0.0.0.0/0 cert
```

- **SQL Server:** For SQL Server, enabling TLS involves installing valid SSL certificates on the server and configuring the server to use these certificates. Use SQL Server Configuration Manager to configure encryption:

```
# Open SQL Server Configuration Manager
# Navigate to SQL Server Network Configuration -> Protocols
    for [YourInstance]
# Right-click 'Protocols for [YourInstance]' and select '
    Properties'
# Enable 'Force Encryption' and specify the path to the SSL
    certificate
```

- **MongoDB:** For MongoDB, enable TLS by specifying the paths to the certificates and keys in the configuration file:

```
net:
  ssl:
    mode: requireSSL
    PEMKeyFile: /path/to/mongodb.pem
    PEMKeyPassword: yourPEMPassword
    CAFile: /path/to/ca.pem
```

  A secure connection can be ensured on the client-side with:

```
mongo --ssl --sslCAFile /path/to/ca.pem \
      --sslPEMKeyFile /path/to/client.pem \
      --host mongodb.example.com \
      --port 27017
```

The use of up-to-date cryptographic libraries ensures robust encryption mechanisms. For instance, OpenSSL, a widely-used library, provides a comprehensive suite of cryptographic functions necessary for implementing TLS. Utilizing libraries such as OpenSSL in applications can significantly simplify the process of securing data in transit.

In multi-tiered application architecture, it is essential to encrypt data not only between clients and database servers but also between all intermediary services. Each connection point in the data flow must be secured to prevent man-in-the-middle (MITM) attacks.

Finally, regular updates and patches to the encryption protocols and libraries are crucial. New vulnerabilities and attacks emerge over time, necessitating prompt action to maintain the security of encrypted communications. Adopting a proactive approach by periodically reviewing and updating the security configurations ensures an up-to-date defense against potential threats.

9.7 SQL Injection and Prevention

SQL Injection constitutes a significant security threat to database systems, arising from improper handling of user inputs in SQL queries. It leverages vulnerabilities in the application code to manipulate database queries, potentially leading to unauthorized access and data leaks. This section elucidates how SQL Injection operates and presents a comprehensive approach to mitigating its risks.

Fundamentally, SQL Injection occurs when unsanitized user inputs are concatenated directly into SQL statements. Consider the following example of a vulnerable SQL query:

```
SELECT * FROM users WHERE username = 'user' AND password
    = 'pass';
```

Here, if the parameters 'user' and 'pass' are derived directly from user input without validation or sanitization, a malicious user could input SQL code instead. For instance:

```
username: admin' --
password: anything
```

This would result in the following query execution:

```
SELECT * FROM users WHERE username = 'admin' -- ' AND
```

```
    password = 'anything';
```

In SQL, the '–' sequence initiates a comment, effectively removing the password condition. The altered query will authenticate the 'admin' user without verifying the password, bypassing security controls.

Techniques for Preventing SQL Injection

1. **Prepared Statements and Parameterized Queries**: The primary defense against SQL Injection is the use of prepared statements and parameterized queries. By separating SQL code from data, the database engine differentiates between code and user input.

```
String query = "SELECT * FROM users WHERE username = ?
    AND password = ?";
PreparedStatement pstmt = connection.prepareStatement(query);
pstmt.setString(1, "user");
pstmt.setString(2, "pass");
ResultSet rs = pstmt.executeQuery();
```

In this example, placeholders ('¿) are used within the SQL query, and the 'PreparedStatement' object securely inserts the user inputs, ensuring they are treated as data rather than executable code.

2. **Input Validation and Escaping**: Validating and sanitizing user inputs is crucial. Input should be checked against a whitelist of acceptable patterns. Characters that could alter SQL command behavior, such as quotes and special symbols, should be escaped or removed.

```
import re

username = re.sub(r"[^\w]", "", username) # Allow only
    alphanumeric characters
password = re.sub(r"[^\w]", "", password) # Allow only
    alphanumeric characters
```

3. **Use of ORM (Object-Relational Mapping) Libraries**: ORM frameworks such as Hibernate (for Java) and SQLAlchemy (for Python) offer an additional layer of security by abstracting database interactions. ORM methods inherently prevent SQL Injection by constructing secure and parameterized queries.

```
from sqlalchemy.orm import sessionmaker

Session = sessionmaker(bind=engine)
```

```
session = Session()

user = session.query(User).filter_by(username='user', password='
    pass').first()
```

4. **Stored Procedures**: Though not immune to SQL Injection, stored procedures can provide a controlled environment by encapsulating SQL code within the database itself. Ensuring that all stored procedure inputs are parameterized can enhance security.

```
CREATE PROCEDURE AuthenticateUser(IN username VARCHAR
    (50), IN password VARCHAR(50))
BEGIN
   SELECT * FROM users WHERE username = username AND
       password = password;
END
```

5. **Least Privilege**: Adhering to the principle of least privilege can mitigate the impact of an SQL Injection attack. Databases should grant the minimum necessary permissions to applications and users, limiting the scope of potential damage.

6. **Web Application Firewalls**: Deploying a Web Application Firewall (WAF) can provide an additional security layer by monitoring and filtering incoming traffic. WAFs can detect and block common SQL Injection patterns.

7. **Regular Security Audits and Penetration Testing**: Conducting regular security audits and penetration tests helps identify and remediate potential vulnerabilities. Automated tools such as SQLMap can be used to test for SQL Injection flaws.

Effective prevention requires a multi-layered approach, combining secure coding practices with robust input validation, least privilege principles, and continuous monitoring. The goal is to create a secure development lifecycle that inherently protects against SQL Injection threats.

9.8 Auditing and Monitoring Database Activity

Auditing and monitoring database activity are fundamental components of an effective database security strategy. This process involves systematically recording and examining the actions taken within a database, providing an empirical basis for ensuring compliance, detecting suspicious behaviors, and optimizing performance. Regular monitoring of database activity helps to uphold data integrity, confidentiality, and availability.

Auditing

Auditing refers to the systematic examination and verification of database records and activities to ensure they comply with established policies and regulatory requirements. It involves capturing detailed records of every access, modification, or potential security breach. The purpose of auditing is multifold:

- **Compliance:** Ensuring that database usage aligns with internal policies and external regulations.
- **Security:** Detecting unauthorized access or anomalous behavior that may indicate a breach.
- **Integrity:** Verifying that data modifications are performed correctly and by authorized users.

The database management system (DBMS) provides mechanisms to facilitate auditing. Let's consider a scenario in MySQL using the AUDIT plugin. Here is an example configuration:

```
INSTALL PLUGIN audit_log SONAME 'audit_log.so';
SET GLOBAL audit_log_policy = 'ALL';
```

This configuration enables the audit log plugin and sets the policy to track all activity. Auditing policies can be customized to focus on specific types of events, such as login attempts or data modifications.

Monitoring

Monitoring involves the continuous observation of database operations to identify and respond to potential issues in real-time. It provides insights into operational performance and security. Monitoring tools collect a wide range of metrics, including query performance, connection statistics, and error logs.

Consider using PostgreSQL's pg_stat_activity view to monitor current activity:

```
SELECT pid, usename, application_name, client_addr,
    backend_start, state, query
```

```
FROM pg_stat_activity;
```

The output of this query provides a snapshot of currently active processes, including information about the user, application, client address, and the state of the query.

```
pid  | usename | application_name | client_addr |    backend_start     | state  | query
-----+---------+------------------+-------------+--------------------+---------+------
8945 | alice   | psql             | 192.168.1.5 | 2022-03-15 12:54:34| active | SELECT * FROM users;
8946 | bob     | psql             | 192.168.1.6 | 2022-03-15 12:55:12| idle   |
```

Combining Auditing and Monitoring

While auditing and monitoring serve different purposes, their integration is crucial for a comprehensive security strategy. Auditors can use monitoring data to correlate events and identify patterns that may indicate potential security risks. Conversely, insights from audits can inform monitoring strategies, ensuring critical activities are scrutinized more closely.

Best Practices

Adhering to best practices can enhance the effectiveness of auditing and monitoring activities:

- **Define Clear Policies:** Establish clear, documented policies outlining what activities must be audited and the retention period for audit logs.
- **Utilize Automation:** Employ automated tools to regularly collect and analyze audit logs, reducing the chances of human error.
- **Access Control:** Limit access to audit logs to essential personnel to prevent tampering and ensure integrity.
- **Regular Reviews:** Conduct regular reviews of audit logs to detect and address suspicious activities promptly.
- **Keep Monitoring Tools Updated:** Ensure that monitoring tools and configurations are regularly updated to maintain compatibility and incorporate the latest security features.

Effective auditing and monitoring of database activity are integral to maintaining robust database security. Through diligent and systematic scrutiny of database operations, organizations can ensure compliance with regulations, detect and mitigate security threats, and uphold the integrity of their data.

9.9 Backup and Recovery Strategies

The fundamental importance of backup and recovery strategies in database management cannot be overstated. These strategies ensure data integrity, availability, and continuity of operations in case of data loss or corruption. Comprehensive backup and recovery plans protect against hardware failures, software bugs, human errors, and various other potential vulnerabilities.

Types of Backups:

There are several types of backups, each with its strengths and limitations.

- **Full Backup:** A full backup captures the entire database at a specific point in time. This type of backup includes all the data, system files, and metadata. Full backups are comprehensive and ensure that all data can be restored, but they are resource-intensive in terms of time and storage.

```
BACKUP DATABASE [YourDatabase]
TO DISK = 'C:\Backups\YourDatabase_Full.bak'
WITH CHECKSUM, STATS = 10;
```

- **Differential Backup:** Differential backups include only the data that has changed since the last full backup. This reduces the amount of data to be backed up compared to a full backup, making the process faster and requiring less storage.

```
BACKUP DATABASE [YourDatabase]
TO DISK = 'C:\Backups\YourDatabase_Diff.bak'
WITH DIFFERENTIAL, CHECKSUM, STATS = 10;
```

- **Incremental Backup:** Incremental backups are similar to differential backups but include only the data that has changed since the last backup, whether it be a full or incremental one. This method reduces both the backup time and storage needs but can make the recovery process more complex.

```
BACKUP DATABASE [YourDatabase]
TO DISK = 'C:\Backups\YourDatabase_Inc.bak'
WITH DIFFERENTIAL, INCREMENTAL, CHECKSUM,
    STATS = 10;
```

- **Transaction Log Backup:** Transaction log backups capture the changes made to the database since the last log backup. This is crucial for databases in full recovery mode because it allows for point-in-time recovery, ensuring minimal data loss.

```
BACKUP LOG [YourDatabase]
TO DISK = 'C:\Backups\YourDatabase_Log.trn'
WITH CHECKSUM, STATS = 10;
```

Recovery Models:

Different recovery models determine how databases maintain transaction log information and in what scenarios backups are necessary.

- **Simple Recovery Model:** In this model, transaction log backups are not maintained, and logs are automatically truncated to manage space. Only full and differential backups are typically used.
- **Full Recovery Model:** All database modifications are fully logged, and transaction log backups are required. This model allows for point-in-time recovery, making it ideal for mission-critical systems where data loss needs to be minimized.
- **Bulk-Logged Recovery Model:** This model captures all changes with minimal logging for bulk operations, balancing between the full and simple recovery models. Bulk operations are log-optimized, reducing log space consumption but still allowing point-in-time recovery for non-bulk operations.

```
ALTER DATABASE [YourDatabase]
SET RECOVERY FULL;
GO
```

Developing a Backup and Recovery Plan:

A robust backup and recovery strategy includes several critical components.

- **Frequency and Scheduling:** Determine the frequency of your backups based on your organization's Recovery Point Objective (RPO) and Recovery Time Objective (RTO). Full backups might be scheduled weekly, differential backups daily, and transaction log backups every few hours.

- **Automating Backups:** Use database management system (DBMS) features or scripts to automate backup processes, ensuring consistency and reliability. SQL Server Agent jobs, cron jobs, or custom scripts can be employed.

```
EXEC msdb.dbo.sp_add_job @job_name = N'Daily Full
    Backup';
EXEC msdb.dbo.sp_add_jobstep @job_name = N'Daily Full
    Backup',
@step_name = N'Backup Step',
@subsystem = N'TSQL',
@command = N'BACKUP DATABASE [YourDatabase] TO
    DISK = ''C:\Backups\YourDatabase_Full.bak'' WITH
    CHECKSUM, STATS = 10;';
-- Schedule the job
EXEC msdb.dbo.sp_add_schedule @schedule_name = N'Daily
    2AM',
@schedule_uid = @MyScheduleUid OUTPUT,
@freq_type = 4,
@freq_interval = 1,
@active_start_time = 20000; -- Set the time for the backup to
    execute
```

- **Testing Backups:** Regularly test backups by restoring them to ensure their integrity and verify that the data can be correctly recovered. This step is crucial to ensure the backups are reliable when needed.

- **Secure Backup Storage:** Store backups in secure locations, preferably offsite or in the cloud, to prevent loss due to disasters at the primary site. Ensure encrypted backup storage to protect against unauthorized access.

```
BACKUP DATABASE [YourDatabase]
TO DISK = 'C:\Backups\YourDatabase_Full_Encrypted.bak'
WITH CHECKSUM, STATS = 10,
ENCRYPTION(ALGORITHM = AES_256, SERVER
    CERTIFICATE = 'BackupCert');
```

- **Documenting Procedures:** Comprehensively document all backup and recovery procedures, including schedules, storage locations, and recovery steps. This documentation is invaluable during an actual recovery scenario and for training purposes.

Recovery Techniques:

Recovery methods can vary depending on the backup strategy employed.

- **Restoring Full Backups:** To restore a full backup, use the following command, which overwrites the existing database.

```
RESTORE DATABASE [YourDatabase]
FROM DISK = 'C:\Backups\YourDatabase_Full.bak'
WITH REPLACE, CHECKSUM, STATS = 10;
```

- **Restoring Differential Backups:** Before applying a differential backup, first restore the last full backup and then apply the differential backup.

```
RESTORE DATABASE [YourDatabase]
FROM DISK = 'C:\Backups\YourDatabase_Full.bak'
WITH REPLACE, NORECOVERY, CHECKSUM;

RESTORE DATABASE [YourDatabase]
FROM DISK = 'C:\Backups\YourDatabase_Diff.bak'
WITH RECOVERY, CHECKSUM, STATS = 10;
```

- **Restoring Incremental Backups:** Make sure to restore the last full backup, followed by each incremental backup sequentially.

```
RESTORE DATABASE [YourDatabase]
FROM DISK = 'C:\Backups\YourDatabase_Full.bak'
WITH REPLACE, NORECOVERY, CHECKSUM;

RESTORE DATABASE [YourDatabase]
FROM DISK = 'C:\Backups\YourDatabase_Inc_1.bak'
WITH NORECOVERY, CHECKSUM, STATS = 10;

RESTORE DATABASE [YourDatabase]
FROM DISK = 'C:\Backups\YourDatabase_Inc_2.bak'
WITH RECOVERY, CHECKSUM, STATS = 10;
```

- **Point-in-Time Recovery:** This recovery type is beneficial for restoring a database to a specific point before a failure or corruption occurred using transaction log backups.

```
RESTORE DATABASE [YourDatabase]
FROM DISK = 'C:\Backups\YourDatabase_Full.bak'
WITH NORECOVERY;

RESTORE LOG [YourDatabase]
FROM DISK = 'C:\Backups\YourDatabase_Log.trn'
WITH STOPAT = '2023-10-01T12:34:56', RECOVERY,
    CHECKSUM, STATS = 10;
```

Backup and recovery strategies form a critical aspect of database management. Implementing structured, regular, and tested backups helps mitigate risks associated with data loss, ensuring data availability and integrity across the organization. Proper documentation and adherence to best practices ensure that recovery processes are efficient and effective, minimizing downtime and operational disruption.

9.10 Compliance and Regulatory Requirements

Compliance with regulatory requirements is a fundamental aspect of database security and management. Various laws, regulations, and industry standards dictate how data must be handled, stored, and protected. In this section, we discuss key regulatory frameworks, the implications for database management, and strategies to ensure compliance.

General Data Protection Regulation (GDPR)

The General Data Protection Regulation (GDPR) is a comprehensive data protection law enacted by the European Union (EU). It sets strict guidelines for data privacy and impacts organizations operating within the EU or handling data belonging to EU citizens. GDPR emphasizes the protection of personal data, granting individuals significant control over how their data is collected, stored, and used.

Key GDPR requirements include:

- **Data Minimization:** Collect only the data that is necessary for the intended purpose.
- **Consent:** Obtain explicit consent from individuals before collecting their personal data.

- **Right to Access:** Allow individuals to access their data and understand how it is being processed.
- **Right to Erasure:** Also known as the "right to be forgotten," individuals can request the deletion of their data.
- **Data Portability:** Allow individuals to transfer their data to another service provider.
- **Breach Notification:** Notify authorities and affected individuals within 72 hours in the event of a data breach.

To ensure GDPR compliance, database administrators must implement robust access controls, encryption methods, and regular auditing to monitor data processing activities.

Health Insurance Portability and Accountability Act (HIPAA)

HIPAA is a regulatory framework in the United States designed to protect sensitive patient health information. It applies to healthcare providers, insurance companies, and their business associates who handle patient data.

Key HIPAA requirements include:

- **Privacy Rule:** Ensures the protection of patient health information and mandates that organizations implement safeguards to protect this data.
- **Security Rule:** Establishes standards for securing electronic protected health information (ePHI). It includes requirements for access controls, audit controls, integrity controls, and transmission security.
- **Breach Notification Rule:** Requires covered entities to notify affected individuals and authorities in the event of a data breach involving ePHI.

To comply with HIPAA, organizations must adopt measures like encryption of data at rest and in transit, access controls, activity monitoring, and ensuring physical security of systems and networks.

Payment Card Industry Data Security Standard (PCI-DSS)

PCI-DSS is a global standard for securing payment card information, applicable to all entities involved in processing, storing, or transmitting credit card information.

Key PCI-DSS requirements include:

- **Build and Maintain a Secure Network:** Install and maintain a firewall to protect data.
- **Protect Cardholder Data:** Encrypt transmission of cardholder data across open, public networks.
- **Maintain a Vulnerability Management Program:** Use and regularly update anti-virus software.
- **Implement Strong Access Control Measures:** Restrict access to cardholder data based on a business requirement-to-know basis.
- **Regularly Monitor and Test Networks:** Track and monitor all access to network resources and cardholder data.

For PCI-DSS compliance, database administrators must ensure encryption, robust access controls, continuous monitoring, and regular vulnerability assessments.

Sarbanes-Oxley Act (SOX)

SOX is a U.S. federal law aimed at improving corporate governance and financial practices. It requires organizations to implement controls to prevent fraudulent activities and ensures the accuracy of financial reporting.

Key SOX requirements relevant to databases include:

- **Accurate Financial Reporting:** Systems must support accurate and complete financial reporting.
- **Internal Controls:** Implement and document internal controls to safeguard financial data.
- **Audit Trails:** Maintain audit trails for all transactions affecting financial data.

Compliance with SOX involves securing financial data, implementing access controls, maintaining audit trails, and ensuring robust data integrity measures.

Federal Information Security Management Act (FISMA)

FISMA is a United States federal law that defines a comprehensive framework to protect government information, operations, and assets against natural or man-made threats.

Key FISMA requirements include:

- **Risk Management:** Agencies must develop, document, and implement an agency-wide program to provide information security.
- **Security Controls:** Provide a set of minimum security requirements for information systems.
- **Continuous Monitoring:** Continuously monitor security controls to ensure effectiveness.

To satisfy FISMA compliance, federal agencies must implement risk management frameworks, establish security controls, and conduct continuous monitoring of information systems.

Aligning Database Security with Regulatory Requirements

To align with these regulatory frameworks, organizations must:

- Conduct thorough risk assessments to identify and mitigate risks.
- Implement encryption for data both at rest and in transit to ensure data confidentiality.
- Establish and enforce access control policies to limit data access to authorized users.
- Regularly audit and monitor database activities to detect and respond to potential security incidents.
- Ensure comprehensive backup and recovery strategies are in place to protect against data loss.
- Provide training and awareness programs for employees on data protection and security practices.

Compliance is not a one-time activity but an ongoing process requiring regular updates to policies, procedures, and technologies to address evolving threats and regulatory changes.

```
-- Enable auditing for SELECT statements on patient_info table
AUDIT SELECT ON patient_info BY ACCESS;
```

```
-- Example output of an audited database access
USER     | TIMESTAMP                  | ACTION  | OBJECT
--------|--------------------------|---------|-------------
DOCTOR1 | 2023-05-14 10:23:45        | SELECT  | patient_info
```

By understanding and incorporating these regulatory requirements, organizations can enhance their database security postures and ensure they meet legal and industry standards. This process involves continuous assessment, applying appropriate safeguards, and maintaining vigilance in protecting sensitive data.

9.11 Security Best Practices

Implementing best practices for database security is essential for the protection of sensitive information and ensuring compliance with regulatory requirements. These best practices provide a comprehensive and systematic approach to minimizing risks and mitigating potential security threats. This section will delve into several essential best practices, including principle of least privilege, regular security audits, strong password policies, encryption, use of secure connections, patch management, monitoring, and training.

Principle of Least Privilege (PoLP): One of the fundamental principles in database security is the principle of least privilege, which states that users should be granted the minimum level of access necessary to perform their job functions. This reduces the potential attack surface and limits the damage that can be done by compromised accounts. For example, a user tasked with querying data should not have access to modify the database schema.

```
-- Example of granting minimal privileges
GRANT SELECT ON employees TO reporting_user;
```

Regular Security Audits: Conducting regular security audits is a critical best practice for identifying vulnerabilities and ensuring compliance with security policies. Audits should be performed by internal teams or external third-party auditors to provide an objective assessment of the database security posture. Regular audits help in detecting unauthorized access attempts, misconfigurations, and potential weaknesses in the security infrastructure.

Strong Password Policies: Enforcing strong password policies is crucial for protecting user accounts from brute-force attacks and unauthorized access. Password policies should mandate complexity requirements, including mixed-case letters, numbers, and special characters. Additionally, policies should require periodic password changes and prohibit the reuse of previous passwords.

```
-- Example of creating a strong password policy
ALTER PROFILE default LIMIT
  FAILED_LOGIN_ATTEMPTS 5
  PASSWORD_LIFE_TIME 90
  PASSWORD_REUSE_TIME 365;
```

Encryption: Data encryption is a vital best practice for protecting sensitive information. Encryption should be applied to data at rest and in transit. For data at rest, this involves encrypting the database files and backups. For data in transit, it requires securing communications between clients and the database server using protocols such as TLS (Transport Layer Security).

```
-- Example of setting up Transparent Data Encryption (TDE)
ALTER SYSTEM SET ENCRYPTION WALLET OPEN;
ALTER TABLESPACE users
  ENCRYPTION USING 'AES256'
  ENCRYPT;
```

Use of Secure Connections: Ensuring that all database connections are secure is another critical security best practice. This involves configuring the database server to accept only secure connections and enforcing the use of protocols such as SSL/TLS for encrypting data in transit.

```
-- Postgres example for enforcing SSL connections
ALTER SYSTEM SET ssl = 'on';
ALTER SYSTEM SET ssl_cert_file = '/path/to/server.crt';
ALTER SYSTEM SET ssl_key_file = '/path/to/server.key';
```

Patch Management: Regularly applying patches and updates is essential to protect the database from known vulnerabilities. Database administrators should monitor vendor release notes and apply security patches as soon as they become available. Automated patch management tools can assist in keeping the database systems up-to-date and secure.

Monitoring: Continuous monitoring of database activity helps detect anomalies and potential security incidents in real-time. Monitoring should include logging of successful and failed login attempts, changes to database schema, and any actions on sensitive data.

```
-- Enabling audit logging in MySQL
SET GLOBAL general_log = 'ON';
SET GLOBAL general_log_file = 'audit.log';
```

Training and Awareness: Providing regular training and raising awareness among all users about security best practices is crucial in mitigating human errors that can lead to security breaches. Training should cover topics such as recognizing phishing attempts, the importance of strong passwords, and how to securely handle sensitive data.

Adhering to these best practices can significantly enhance the security posture of a database system, ensuring that data remains protected from unauthorized access and potential breaches. By following the principle of least privilege, conducting regular security audits, enforcing strong password policies, implementing encryption, securing connections, applying patches timely, setting up continuous monitoring, and supporting user training, organizations can minimize risks and ensure robust database security.

9.12 Case Studies in Database Security

In this section, we explore real-world scenarios that illustrate the significant principles and practices of database security discussed in previous sections. These case studies provide concrete examples of how various security measures can be implemented, challenges that may arise, and strategies to mitigate potential issues.

Case Study 1: SQL Injection Attack on a Banking System

A leading banking institution faced an SQL injection attack on its online banking system, where a malicious actor exploited vulnerabilities in the input fields of the customer login page.

```
SELECT * FROM users WHERE username = 'admin' --' AND
    password = '';
```

In the code snippet above, the attacker injected '–', which is a comment sequence in SQL. This tricked the system into bypassing the password requirement.

The attack exposed several critical weaknesses:

- Poor input validation
- Inadequate use of prepared statements
- Lack of robust error handling

To prevent this, the bank implemented parameterized queries:

```
PreparedStatement ps = connection.prepareStatement("SELECT *
    FROM users WHERE username = ? AND password = ?");
ps.setString(1, username);
ps.setString(2, password);
ResultSet rs = ps.executeQuery();
```

This measure eliminates the risk of an attacker manipulating the SQL query structure. Additionally, they enforced stricter input validation and filtered out suspicious characters.

Case Study 2: Role-Based Access Control (RBAC) in a Healthcare System

A healthcare provider adopted RBAC to manage user permissions efficiently. By defining roles such as ‘doctor‘, ‘nurse‘, and ‘administrator‘, the organization restricted data access based on user roles.

```
CREATE ROLE doctor;
CREATE ROLE nurse;
CREATE ROLE administrator;

GRANT SELECT ON patient_records TO doctor;
GRANT SELECT, UPDATE ON patient_records TO nurse;
GRANT ALL PRIVILEGES ON patient_records TO administrator;
```

RBAC implementation ensured that:

- Doctors could view patient records without modifying them.
- Nurses had the ability to update patient records.
- Administrators had full control over patient records.

This segregation of duties minimized the risk of data breaches and maintained compliance with healthcare regulations.

Case Study 3: Data Encryption and Secure Backup in E-Commerce

An e-commerce company implemented encryption for sensitive customer data, both at rest and in transit.

For data at rest, they employed Transparent Data Encryption (TDE):

```
ALTER DATABASE e_commerce_db SET ENCRYPTION ON;
```

For data in transit, they secured connections using SSL/TLS, ensuring that data transmitted between clients and servers was encrypted.

Regular backups were encrypted using:

```
BACKUP DATABASE e_commerce_db TO DISK = 'backup.bak'
WITH ENCRYPTION (ALGORITHM = AES_256);
```

This strategy ensured that even if an unauthorized entity accessed the backup storage, the data remained unreadable without the encryption keys.

Case Study 4: Auditing and Monitoring in Financial Services

A financial services firm implemented a comprehensive auditing system to monitor database activity and detect suspicious behavior.

They configured audit trails to log activities like logins, data modifications, and administrative actions:

```
CREATE SERVER AUDIT FinanceAudit
TO FILE (FILEPATH = 'C:\\audit_logs\\');
ALTER SERVER AUDIT FinanceAudit WITH (STATE = ON);

CREATE DATABASE AUDIT SPECIFICATION FinanceDBSpec
FOR SERVER AUDIT FinanceAudit
ADD (SELECT, INSERT, UPDATE, DELETE ON database::
    FinanceDB BY [public]);
ALTER DATABASE AUDIT SPECIFICATION FinanceDBSpec
    WITH (STATE = ON);
```

The audit logs were periodically reviewed using automated tools and manual inspection to identify and investigate any anomalies promptly.

Case Study 5: Compliance and Regulatory Requirements in Pharmaceutical Industry

A pharmaceutical company needed to comply with strict regulatory requirements regarding data privacy and integrity.

They adhered to the following security protocols:

- Implemented end-to-end encryption to safeguard patient data.
- Enforced strict access control measures to ensure only authorized personnel could access sensitive information.
- Regularly conducted security audits and vulnerability assessments.

To maintain compliance, they used:

```
CREATE LOGIN auditor WITH PASSWORD = 'complex_password'

CREATE USER auditor FOR LOGIN auditor
GRANT VIEW SERVER STATE TO auditor;
GRANT SELECT ON audit_logs TO auditor;
```

This setup allowed external auditors to review necessary data without risk of unauthorized modifications.

Examining these real-world cases highlights the critical aspects of database security within various industries. Each scenario underscores the necessity of adopting robust security practices and continually monitoring and updating security measures to protect sensitive data and maintain regulatory compliance.

Chapter 10

NoSQL Databases and SQL Integration

This chapter provides an overview of NoSQL databases, detailing their various types such as key-value, document, column-family, and graph databases. It compares NoSQL to traditional SQL databases and discusses use cases for NoSQL. The chapter includes practical guidance on setting up NoSQL databases and performing basic and advanced operations. It explores strategies for integrating SQL and NoSQL databases, using SQL with systems like MongoDB and Cassandra, and the concept of polyglot persistence. Practical case studies in NoSQL and SQL integration are also provided.

10.1 Introduction to NoSQL Databases

NoSQL databases represent a significant departure from traditional relational database management systems (RDBMS). Unlike relational databases that use structured query language (SQL) for defining and manipulating data, NoSQL databases do not rely on a fixed schema. They are designed to handle distributed, large-scale data storage and enable rapid data access while accommodating the need for scalability and flexibility.

The term 'NoSQL' stands for 'Not Only SQL,' emphasizing that these databases can support other data models besides the relational model. NoSQL databases are particularly useful in big data and real-time web applications. NoSQL systems are optimized for the very different workload and data structures, offering different benefits and trade-offs compared to traditional relational databases.

Characteristics of NoSQL Databases

- **Schema-less:** NoSQL databases do not require a predefined schema. This allows the storage of varying data formats in the same database.
- **Horizontal scalability:** Traditional relational databases scale vertically by adding more resources to a single server. NoSQL databases scale horizontally by adding more servers or nodes to distribute the load.
- **Distributed Computing:** Data is distributed across multiple servers, offering greater reliability and availability.
- **Flexible data models:** NoSQL supports various data models, including key-value, document, column-family, and graph.
- **High-performance:** Optimized for specific use cases, NoSQL databases often provide superior performance for read and write operations.

CAP Theorem

The CAP theorem, proposed by Eric Brewer, is a fundamental principle that applies to distributed systems, including NoSQL databases. It asserts that a distributed database system can only achieve two out of the following three guarantees:

- - **Consistency (C):** Every read from the database returns the most recent write.
- - **Availability (A):** Every request receives a response, regardless of the success or failure of the operation.
- - **Partition Tolerance (P):** The system continues to operate despite network partitions.

Given this theorem, NoSQL databases often choose to sacrifice consistency for availability and partition tolerance, reflecting their design goals for strong performance and resilience in distributed environments.

Data Models in NoSQL Databases

NoSQL databases support various data models, allowing them to handle different data storage and retrieval requirements efficiently:

1. **Key-Value Stores:** These databases store data as a collection of key-value pairs. Examples include Redis and DynamoDB. They are highly efficient for simple lookups.

```
# Example of key-value storage in Redis
SET user:1001 "John Doe"
GET user:1001
```

The output would be:

```
"John Doe"
```

2. **Document Stores:** Document databases store data in document formats such as JSON, BSON, or XML. Examples are MongoDB and CouchDB. They are well-suited for semi-structured data.

```
# Example of document storage in MongoDB
db.users.insertOne({"user_id": 1001, "name": "John Doe", "email": "
    john@example.com"})
db.users.find({"user_id": 1001})
```

The output would be:

```
{ "_id": ObjectId("60c..."), "user_id": 1001, "name": "John Doe", "email": "john@example.com" }
```

3. **Column-Family Stores:** These databases store data in columns rather than rows, making them suitable for analytical queries across large datasets. Examples include Cassandra and HBase.

```
# Example of column-family storage in Cassandra
CREATE TABLE users (user_id int PRIMARY KEY, name text,
    email text);
INSERT INTO users (user_id, name, email) VALUES (1001, 'John
    Doe', 'john@example.com');
SELECT * FROM users WHERE user_id = 1001;
```

The output would be:

```
 user_id | name     | email
---------+----------+-------------------
    1001 | John Doe | john@example.com
```

4. **Graph Databases:** These databases use graph structures with nodes, edges, and properties to represent and store data. They are

ideal for applications that involve complex relationships. Examples include Neo4j and OrientDB.

```
# Example of graph storage in Neo4j
CREATE (user:User {user_id: 1001, name: "John Doe", email: "
    john@example.com"})
MATCH (user:User {user_id: 1001}) RETURN user
```

The output would be:

```
{ "user": { "user_id": 1001, "name": "John Doe", "email": "john@example.com" } }
```

Understanding the foundations of NoSQL databases provides a groundwork for exploring their varied data models, performance characteristics, and applicability to different use cases. Their flexibility and scalability make them well-suited for modern applications, particularly those needing to handle large volumes of unstructured data, real-time applications, and distributed architectures.

10.2 Types of NoSQL Databases: Key-Value, Document, Column-Family, Graph

NoSQL databases, which stand for "Not Only SQL," represent a variety of database technologies that were developed to handle the large scale of data that SQL databases struggle with, as well as to incorporate different flexibility needs. This section will delve into the primary types of NoSQL databases: key-value, document, column-family, and graph databases.

Key-Value Databases

Key-value databases are the simplest form of NoSQL databases. In this model, each data item is stored as a key-value pair. This allows for very high performance and flexibility. The keys are unique identifiers, and the values can be any type of data, from simple strings to more complex data structures.

The simplicity of key-value stores makes them ideal for caching and session management. Below is an example of setting and retrieving data using a key-value store in Redis:

```
SET user:1000 "John Doe"
GET user:1000
```

The output of the GET command in Redis would be:

"John Doe"

The unstructured nature of key-value databases comes with a trade-off: while they are highly efficient, they lack the complex querying capabilities of more structured databases.

Document Databases

Document databases store data as documents, typically in a format like JSON or BSON (Binary JSON). Each document is a self-contained unit, which can contain nested data structures like lists and dictionaries. This schema-less design allows for agility, as different documents within a collection can have varying fields.

MongoDB is a popular document database. Here is an example of inserting and querying a document in MongoDB:

```
db.users.insert({"name": "Jane Doe", "email": "jane.doe@example.
    com"})
db.users.find({"name": "Jane Doe"})
```

The output of the find operation might look like:

{ "_id" : ObjectId("5f8d0d55b54764421b7156c2"), "name" : "Jane Doe", "email" : "jane.doe@example.com" }

Document databases are particularly well-suited for content management systems (CMS), blogging platforms, and e-commerce applications, where the flexibility to handle varied and evolving data structures is an advantage.

Column-Family Databases

Column-family databases store data in columns rather than rows, which enables the handling of large data sets with high availability and performance. This type of database is efficient for read and write operations and is structured in a way that allows data to be distributed across many nodes, facilitating horizontal scaling.

Apache Cassandra is a widely used column-family database. Below is an example of creating a table and inserting data in Cassandra:

```
CREATE TABLE users (
    user_id UUID PRIMARY KEY,
    name TEXT,
    email TEXT
);
```

```
INSERT INTO users (user_id, name, email) VALUES (uuid(), 'John
    Smith', 'john.smith@example.com');
```

To retrieve data:

```
SELECT name, email FROM users WHERE user_id =
    12345678-1234-5678-1234-567812345678;
```

Column-family databases are ideal for large-scale applications that require high throughput, such as real-time analytics, logging, and distributed data stores.

Graph Databases

Graph databases use graph structures for semantic queries, with nodes, edges, and properties representing and storing data. They are designed to handle data whose relations are well represented as a graph, and are widely used in social networks, recommendation engines, and fraud detection.

Neo4j is a popular graph database. Below is an example of creating nodes and relationships in Neo4j using Cypher Query Language:

```
CREATE (a:Person {name: 'Alice'}),
       (b:Person {name: 'Bob'}),
       (a)-[:FRIENDS_WITH]->(b);
```

To query the data:

```
MATCH (a:Person)-[:FRIENDS_WITH]->(b:Person)
WHERE a.name = 'Alice'
RETURN b.name;
```

The result might be:

```
"Bob"
```

Graph databases are specialized for scenarios where the relationships between data points are as crucial as the data points themselves, such as social graphs, network topologies, and organizational structures.

The diversity of NoSQL databases ensures that database administrators and developers have the right tools to efficiently and effectively store, query, and analyze data, regardless of its complexity or scale. Each type of NoSQL database has unique features that make it suitable for specific use cases, providing the flexibility to handle various data models and workloads.

10.3 Comparing NoSQL and SQL Databases

The evolution of databases has led to the categorization of database management systems (DBMS) into two major types: SQL (Structured Query Language) databases, commonly known as relational databases, and NoSQL (Not Only SQL) databases. Understanding the fundamental differences between these two types of databases is crucial for selecting the appropriate system for specific applications. This section delves into the key distinctions and similarities between SQL and NoSQL databases, focusing on their data models, scalability, consistency, query languages, and typical use cases.

Data Models

SQL databases utilize a schema-based relational model. Data is organized into tables (relations) consisting of rows and columns, where each row is a unique record and each column represents a specific attribute of the data. The table structure is predefined, and schema enforcement ensures data integrity and adherence to defined types and constraints. The following SQL code demonstrates the creation of a simple table:

```
CREATE TABLE users (
    id INT PRIMARY KEY,
    name VARCHAR(100),
    email VARCHAR(100)
);
```

NoSQL databases, on the other hand, employ a variety of data models, including key-value, document, column-family, and graph models. These databases are generally schema-less, allowing for more flexible data storage. For example, a document-oriented NoSQL database like MongoDB stores data in JSON-like documents, which can have varying structures:

```
{
    "_id": 1,
    "name": "John Doe",
    "email": "john.doe@example.com",
    "age": 29,
```

```
    "preferences": {
        "newsletter": true,
        "notifications": ["email", "sms"]
    }
}
```

Scalability

Traditional SQL databases are designed for vertical scalability, which involves enhancing the capabilities of a single server by adding more resources like CPU, RAM, and storage. While this approach can effectively handle increased loads to some extent, it has limitations due to hardware constraints and cost inefficiencies.

NoSQL databases typically support horizontal scalability, enabling the distribution of data across multiple servers or nodes. This model supports the seamless addition of new nodes to the system, thereby managing growth more effectively. Systems such as Cassandra and MongoDB are designed to handle large-scale applications by partitioning data across distributed architectures.

Consistency, Availability, and Partition Tolerance (CAP Theorem)

The CAP theorem posits that a distributed database can only guarantee two out of the following three properties simultaneously: Consistency, Availability, and Partition Tolerance.

SQL databases often prioritize consistency and availability. They adhere to ACID (Atomicity, Consistency, Isolation, Durability) properties to ensure reliable transactions. In a highly available setting, if partition tolerance is not a requirement, SQL databases guarantee consistent state changes and immediate data availability to clients.

NoSQL databases relax the constraints of consistency in favor of availability and partition tolerance, aligning with the BASE (Basically Available, Soft state, Eventual consistency) model. Eventual consistency allows systems to return operational responses without the need for strong consistency across the entire data set immediately, which is particularly beneficial for applications with high availability requirements and distributed node structures.

Query Languages

SQL databases use Structured Query Language (SQL) for defining and manipulating data. SQL provides complex querying capabilities, joining multiple tables, filtering data based on various conditions, and performing aggregate functions:

```
SELECT users.name, orders.amount
FROM users
JOIN orders ON users.id = orders.user_id
WHERE orders.amount > 50;
```

NoSQL databases often employ query languages or APIs tailored to their specific data models. For example, MongoDB uses a rich query language for document retrieval and manipulation, which includes support for embedded documents, arrays, and aggregation pipelines:

```
db.users.aggregate([
    {
        $lookup: {
            from: "orders",
            localField: "_id",
            foreignField: "user_id",
            as: "user_orders"
        }
    },
    {
        $match: {
            "user_orders.amount": { $gt: 50 }
        }
    },
    {
        $project: {
            "name": 1,
            "user_orders.amount": 1
        }
    }
]);
```

Typical Use Cases

SQL databases are highly suitable for applications requiring complex queries, transactions, and consistency. They are commonly used in financial systems, enterprise applications, and scenarios where data integrity is paramount. Their robust query capabilities and ACID compliance make them ideal for environments where data relationships are well-defined and central to application logic.

NoSQL databases cater to applications needing high performance, flexibility, and scalability. They excel in use cases involving large volumes of unstructured or semi-structured data, real-time analytics, and distributed data processing. E-commerce platforms, content management systems, IoT applications, and social networks often leverage NoSQL databases to handle diverse data types and intensive read/write operations efficiently.

By contrasting SQL and NoSQL databases in terms of data models, scalability, consistency, query languages, and use cases, this section provides a comprehensive understanding of their respective strengths and limitations. This knowledge is essential for making informed decisions on the appropriate database technology for specific application requirements.

10.4 When to Use NoSQL Databases

Understanding when to deploy NoSQL databases instead of traditional SQL databases is crucial for optimizing system performance, scalability, and flexibility. NoSQL databases are designed to address specific challenges that conventional SQL databases may struggle to overcome. These scenarios highlight key conditions under which selecting a NoSQL database is advantageous:

1. High Volume of Unstructured, Semi-Structured, or Structured Data

NoSQL databases excel in handling large volumes of unstructured, semi-structured, or structured data. Traditional SQL databases impose a rigid schema, which can be limiting when dealing with diverse data types. In contrast, NoSQL databases, such as document stores (e.g., MongoDB), can store JSON-like documents, allowing for a flexible data model.

Example:

```
# Python code to insert a document into a MongoDB collection
from pymongo import MongoClient

client = MongoClient('localhost', 27017)
db = client['example_db']
collection = db['example_collection']

document = {
```

```
    "name": "John Doe",
    "age": 29,
    "address": {
        "street": "123 Main St",
        "city": "Anytown",
        "state": "CA"
    },
    "interests": ["reading", "hiking", "coding"]
}

collection.insert_one(document)
```

2. Horizontal Scalability Requirements

Applications needing to scale out across multiple servers can benefit significantly from NoSQL databases. Unlike SQL databases, which often face limitations in horizontal scalability due to their ACID transaction constraints, many NoSQL databases (e.g., Cassandra, HBase) are built for distributed architecture, supporting horizontal scaling with ease.

Example:

Cassandra uses a peer-to-peer architecture with no single point of failure, making it ideal for applications needing high availability and horizontal scalability.

```
# Cassandra CQL command to create a keyspace with replication
CREATE KEYSPACE example_keyspace
WITH replication = {'class': 'SimpleStrategy', 'replication_factor':
    3};
```

3. Flexible Schema Design

Businesses that continuously evolve their data models benefit from the flexible schema design of NoSQL databases. Schema-less databases eliminate the need for predefined tables and fields, allowing rapid adjustments without downtime for schema migrations. This is particularly useful in agile development environments where requirements change frequently.

4. Rapid Development and Iteration

NoSQL databases are advantageous for projects requiring rapid development and iteration cycles due to their flexible and dynamic schema. Document-based databases such as MongoDB allow developers to store complex data structures, which aligns closely with the data handled in modern web applications.

5. High Throughput and Low Latency

Applications requiring high throughput and low-latency responses, such as real-time analytics or e-commerce platforms, are well-suited for NoSQL databases. Examples include Redis for in-memory data structures and queries, or Couchbase, which offers high-speed read and write operations.

Example:

Using Redis for caching to improve application performance:

```
# Python code to set and get cache data in Redis
import redis

r = redis.Redis(host='localhost', port=6379, db=0)

# Setting a value in the cache
r.set('user:1000', 'John Doe')

# Getting a value from the cache
value = r.get('user:1000')
print(value.decode('utf-8'))
```

6. Complex Data Models and Relationships

Graph databases such as Neo4j are specifically designed to handle complex relationships between data entities. These databases are optimal for social networks, recommendation engines, or any system where understanding and querying relationships are paramount.

Example:

Query in Cypher to find friends of friends in a social network stored in Neo4j:

```
MATCH (user:Person)-[:FRIEND]->(friend)-[:FRIEND]->(foaf)
WHERE user.name = 'Alice'
RETURN foaf.name
```

7. Cost Efficiency

NoSQL databases can offer cost efficiency through the use of commodity hardware and open-source software. They often allow for more cost-effective scaling compared to traditional high-end SQL servers. By distributing data across multiple inexpensive nodes, organizations can achieve scalability without significant expense.

8. Handling Big Data and Real-Time Analytics

For systems managing big data and requiring real-time analytics, NoSQL databases provide the necessary performance and scalability. Tools like Apache HBase or Apache Cassandra are engineered to manage large datasets efficiently, offering robust solutions for analytics and real-time data processing applications.

In each scenario, it is critical to evaluate the specific needs and constraints of the application. While NoSQL databases provide numerous advantages for certain use cases, scenarios requiring complex transactions and ACID compliance may still benefit more from traditional SQL databases. By carefully assessing factors such as data volume, structure, scalability needs, and development requirements, the appropriate database management system can be selected to optimize performance and flexibility.

10.5 Setting Up a NoSQL Database

Establishing a NoSQL database environment entails several crucial steps, which vary depending on the specific NoSQL database system being employed. This section outlines a methodical approach for setting up a NoSQL database, ensuring a functional and manageable environment. The examples provided utilize MongoDB, one of the most widely used NoSQL databases.

Step 1: Installation

To begin, download and install MongoDB from the official website. For users operating on different systems, the installation commands vary:

```
# On Ubuntu
sudo apt-get update
sudo apt-get install -y mongodb

# On macOS using Homebrew
brew tap mongodb/brew
brew install mongodb-community

# On Windows
```

```
# Download the installer from the MongoDB website and follow GUI
    instructions.
```

Step 2: Starting the MongoDB Service

Post-installation, start the MongoDB service. This action initializes the database server, enabling connections and data operations.

```
# On Ubuntu
sudo systemctl start mongodb
sudo systemctl enable mongodb

# On macOS
brew services start mongodb-community

# On Windows
# Use the services tool (services.msc) to start the MongoDB service
    or use command line:
net start MongoDB
```

Step 3: Verifying the Installation

Ensure that MongoDB is running correctly by verifying its status. This step helps identify any immediate issues with the database setup.

```
# On Ubuntu
sudo systemctl status mongodb

# On macOS
brew services list

# On Windows
# Use the services tool or:
net start MongoDB
```

Additionally, you can check by connecting to MongoDB using its shell interface.

```
# Connect to MongoDB shell
mongo
```

A successful connection prints the MongoDB shell version and a command prompt ('>'), signifying that the database server is operational.

Step 4: Configuration

Configure MongoDB for enhanced security and performance. Modify the mongod.conf configuration file located typically at /etc/mongod.conf on Linux or installed directory on Windows and macOS. For instance, enable authorization:

```
# /etc/mongod.conf

security:
  authorization: "enabled"
```

Restart MongoDB to apply configuration changes:

```
# On Ubuntu
sudo systemctl restart mongodb

# On macOS
brew services restart mongodb-community

# On Windows
net stop MongoDB
net start MongoDB
```

Step 5: Creating the First User

Once authorization is enabled, initiate the Administrative shell and create the first user. This user will have administrative privileges.

```
# Connect to the admin database
mongo
use admin

# Create an administrative user
db.createUser({
  user: "admin",
  pwd: "secure_password",
  roles: [ { role: "userAdminAnyDatabase", db: "admin" } ]
})
```

Step 6: Basic Operations

Execute basic operations to ensure the database is functioning as expected. These include creating a collection and inserting documents.

```
# Connect with the admin user
mongo -u "admin" -p "secure_password" --authenticationDatabase "
```

```
    admin"

# Switch to test database and create a collection
use test

# Insert a document
db.collection.insertOne({ name: "John Doe", age: 30, job: "Engineer"
    })

# Retrieve the inserted document
db.collection.find()
```

If the insertion and retrieval complete without errors, the MongoDB setup is operational.

Step 7: Backup and Recovery

Establish backup and recovery procedures to safeguard data integrity. Use mongodump and mongorestore for this purpose.

```
# Backup
mongodump --out /backup/directory/path

# Restore
mongorestore --dir /backup/directory/path
```

Regularly schedule these commands through cron jobs or other task schedulers to automate the process.

Adopting these steps facilitates a robust MongoDB environment, laying the groundwork for further advanced operations and integrations.

10.6 Basic NoSQL Operations

In this section, we will explore the fundamental operations performed in NoSQL databases, which include CRD (Create, Read, and Delete) operations. These operations are central to interacting with any database system, facilitating the manipulation and retrieval of data. We will use examples that are representative for key-value stores, document stores, column-family stores, and graph databases, to ensure a comprehensive understanding.

1. Key-Value Stores

Key-value stores utilize a simple yet powerful model that allows users to store values indexed by unique keys. Operations commonly performed in key-value stores include adding a new key-value pair, retrieving a value by its key, and deleting a key-value pair.

- **Create Operation**:

```
import redis

r = redis.Redis(host='localhost', port=6379, db=0)
r.set('user1', 'John Doe')
```

- **Read Operation**:

```
value = r.get('user1')
print(value.decode('utf-8'))
```

```
John Doe
```

- **Delete Operation**:

```
r.delete('user1')
```

2. Document Stores

Document stores, such as MongoDB, emphasize flexible schemas, enabling the storage of semi-structured data. Documents are housed within collections, and common operations include inserting a document, finding documents, and removing documents.

- **Create Operation**:

```
from pymongo import MongoClient

client = MongoClient('localhost', 27017)
db = client.my_database
collection = db.users

user_document = {
    "name": "Jane Doe",
    "email": "jane.doe@example.com",
    "age": 30
}
```

```
collection.insert_one(user_document)
```

- **Read Operation**:

```
user = collection.find_one({"name": "Jane Doe"})
print(user)
```

```
{'_id': ObjectId('...'), 'name': 'Jane Doe', 'email': 'jane.doe@example.com', 'age': 30}
```

- **Delete Operation**:

```
collection.delete_one({"name": "Jane Doe"})
```

3. Column-Family Stores

Column-family stores such as Apache Cassandra use a tabular structure but diverge from traditional relational databases through their column-oriented storage. Operations consist of inserting rows, retrieving rows, and deleting rows.

- **Create Operation**:

```
INSERT INTO users (user_id, name, email) VALUES (1, '
    Alice', 'alice@example.com');
```

- **Read Operation**:

```
SELECT * FROM users WHERE user_id = 1;
```

```
 user_id | name | email
---------+------+-------------------
       1 | Alice | alice@example.com
```

- **Delete Operation**:

```
DELETE FROM users WHERE user_id = 1;
```

4. Graph Databases

Graph databases such as Neo4j use nodes, relationships, and properties to represent and store data. Common operations include creating nodes and relationships, querying node properties, and deleting nodes and relationships.

- **Create Operation**:

```
from py2neo import Graph

graph = Graph("bolt://localhost:7687", auth=("neo4j", "
    password"))

graph.run("CREATE (a:Person {name: 'Bob'})")
graph.run("CREATE (b:Person {name: 'Alice'})")
graph.run("MATCH (a:Person {name: 'Bob'}), (b:Person {
    name: 'Alice'}) CREATE (a)-[:KNOWS]->(b)")
```

- **Read Operation**:

```
nodes = graph.run("MATCH (a:Person)-[:KNOWS]->(b:
    Person) RETURN a.name, b.name")

for record in nodes:
    print(record['a.name'], "knows", record['b.name'])
```

```
Bob knows Alice
```

- **Delete Operation**:

```
graph.run("MATCH (a:Person {name: 'Bob'})-[r:KNOWS
    ]->(b:Person {name: 'Alice'}) DELETE r")
graph.run("MATCH (a:Person {name: 'Bob'}) DELETE a")
graph.run("MATCH (b:Person {name: 'Alice'}) DELETE b"
    )
```

These basic operations—creating, reading, and deleting—are foundational to interacting with NoSQL databases. Understanding these elementary commands enables users to build on more complex operations and queries, facilitating efficient data management and retrieval in NoSQL systems.

10.7 Advanced Queries in NoSQL

Advanced queries in NoSQL databases extend far beyond simple CRUD operations (Create, Read, Update, Delete). These queries leverage the unique capabilities of NoSQL databases to handle unstructured or semi-structured data, allowing for more complex and nuanced data retrieval and manipulation.

NoSQL databases such as MongoDB, Cassandra, HBase, and Neo4j offer various querying mechanisms tailored to their specific data models. This section examines the advanced querying techniques in some of the most popular NoSQL databases to provide a comprehensive understanding.

MongoDB: Aggregation Framework

MongoDB's aggregation framework is a powerful tool for performing data processing and transformation. The aggregation operations group values from multiple documents, operate on grouped data, and produce computed results.

The aggregation framework includes stages that process data and transformation through a pipeline approach:

```
db.sales.aggregate([
  { $match: { status: "A" } },
  {
    $group: {
      _id: "$cust_id",
      total: { $sum: "$amount" }
    }
  },
  {
    $sort: { total: -1 }
  }
])
```

The example above performs the following operations: - $match stage filters documents where the status is "A". - $group stage groups documents by customer ID (cust_id) and calculates the sum of the amount. - $sort stage sorts the results in descending order of the total amount.

Cassandra: CQL (Cassandra Query Language)

While Cassandra primarily uses CQL, akin to SQL, it introduces specific features optimizing queries for its distributed, column-family store nature. Advanced queries often include filtering and allowing secondary indexes:

```
SELECT user_id, first_name, last_name
```

```
FROM users
WHERE age > 25
ALLOW FILTERING;
```

Cassandra's queries leverage:

- ALLOW FILTERING for filtering results post-lookup. - Materialized views for complex query patterns.

Creating a materialized view to query by email might look like this:

```
CREATE MATERIALIZED VIEW users_by_email AS
SELECT *
FROM users
WHERE email IS NOT NULL
PRIMARY KEY (email);
```

HBase: Filter Language

HBase, a column-family NoSQL database, allows complex queries through its filter language. Flters refine scan results by column values, row keys, and other criteria:

```
Scan scan = new Scan();
FilterList filterList = new FilterList(FilterList.Operator.
    MUST_PASS_ALL);
filterList.addFilter(new RowFilter(CompareFilter.CompareOp.
    EQUAL, new BinaryComparator(Bytes.toBytes("rowKey"))));
filterList.addFilter(new ValueFilter(CompareFilter.CompareOp.
    GREATER_OR_EQUAL, new BinaryComparator(Bytes.
    toBytes("value"))));
scan.setFilter(filterList);

ResultScanner scanner = table.getScanner(scan);
for (Result result : scanner) {
    System.out.println(result);
}
scanner.close();
```

The example constructs a scan with a filter list: - Filters rows with rowKey equal to a specified value. - Filters cells with values greater than or equal to "value".

Neo4j: Cypher Query Language

Neo4j, a graph database, uses Cypher as its query language. Cypher excels in pattern matching within graph structures, enabling intricate traversals and transformations:

```
MATCH (p:Person)-[r:ACTED_IN]->(m:Movie)
WHERE p.name = 'Keanu Reeves'
RETURN m.title AS movie, p.name AS actor;
```

This query retrieves movies where Keanu Reeves acted: - MATCH clause patterns the relationships of actors to movies. - WHERE clause filters for 'Keanu Reeves'. - RETURN clause specifies the fields to be returned in the result set.

By harnessing the unique querying capabilities of NoSQL databases — from MongoDB's aggregation pipeline to Neo4j's graph traversals — users can efficiently perform sophisticated data operations tailored to their specific datasets and application requirements. Proper understanding and mastery of these advanced querying techniques can significantly enhance data manipulation and retrieval efficiency in NoSQL contexts.

10.8 Integrating SQL and NoSQL Databases

The integration of SQL and NoSQL databases has become increasingly important in modern data architectures, where leveraging the strengths of both paradigms can provide optimal performance, scalability, and flexibility. This section delves into the methodologies, tools, and best practices for achieving effective integration between SQL and NoSQL databases, ensuring a cohesive strategy that maximizes the advantages of each type.

To begin, consider the distinct characteristics of SQL and NoSQL databases. SQL databases, often called relational databases, are designed around structured data and use a schema-based model. They excel at maintaining data integrity through ACID (Atomicity, Consistency, Isolation, Durability) properties and are ideal for complex queries and transactions. NoSQL databases, on the other hand, are designed to handle large volumes of unstructured or semi-structured data with high scalability and flexibility. They often adhere to the BASE (Basically Available, Soft state, Eventually consistent) principles, making them suitable for distributed systems and real-time applications.

Combining these paradigms can present both opportunities and challenges. Several integration strategies can be employed, ranging from simple data synchronization to more complex polyglot persistence architectures. Below, we explore the primary techniques used to integrate SQL and NoSQL databases, along with relevant examples and practical considerations.

Data Synchronization

Data synchronization involves ensuring that the data between SQL and NoSQL databases remains consistent. This can be achieved using data replication, change data capture (CDC), or scheduled batch processing.

```
-- Assuming you have an SQL table named 'users' and a NoSQL
    collection named 'users_collection'.
-- This example uses a hypothetical ETL tool to perform data
    synchronization.

SELECT
    id,
    name,
    email,
    created_at
FROM
    users
WHERE
    updated_at > :last_sync_time;

-- Pseudocode to represent data update operation in NoSQL
for each record in result_set:
    users_collection.updateOne(
        { _id: record.id },
        { $set: { name: record.name, email: record.email, created_at:
            record.created_at }},
        { upsert: true }
    );
```

Data replication can be either unidirectional or bidirectional. In unidirectional replication, data changes flow from the source database (SQL or NoSQL) to the target database. In bidirectional replication, changes in either database are propagated to the other, ensuring data consistency across both systems.

Change Data Capture (CDC) involves capturing changes made to the SQL database and applying these changes to the NoSQL database. Tools like Debezium or AWS Database Migration Service (DMS) can facilitate CDC.

Scheduled batch processing is a less real-time but simpler approach, where data is periodically transferred from SQL to NoSQL or vice versa based on defined intervals.

Query Translation and Middleware

Query translation involves converting SQL queries into equivalent NoSQL queries and vice versa. Middleware solutions can facilitate this process by acting as an intermediary layer that translates and routes queries between SQL and NoSQL databases. Apache Drill and Apache Calcite are examples of middleware tools that can query both SQL and NoSQL databases.

```
-- SQL Query Example
SELECT name, email FROM users WHERE age > 30;

-- Hypothetical Middleware Translation to MongoDB Query
db.users.find({ age: { $gt: 30 } }, { name: 1, email: 1 });
```

Middleware solutions can abstract the complexities of query translation and provide a unified interface for accessing multiple databases. This approach reduces the need for application-level logic to handle different query languages but must be carefully managed to ensure efficient query performance.

Polyglot Persistence

Polyglot persistence refers to using multiple databases within the same application, each chosen for its suitability to a specific task. This strategy leverages the strengths of both SQL and NoSQL databases by assigning the right database for the right job.

For instance, an e-commerce application might use an SQL database for transactions and product inventory, a key-value store for caching session data, a document database for storing product catalogs, and a graph database for managing social networks and recommendations.

Polyglot persistence provides flexibility and performance optimization but requires careful planning and management to avoid complexity. Consistency models, data distribution strategies, and inter-database communication are crucial considerations.

```
-- SQL for transactional data
INSERT INTO orders (user_id, product_id, quantity, order_date)
    VALUES (?, ?, ?, ?);

-- NoSQL (Key-Value Store) for caching session data
cache.set(user_session_id, serialized_user_data);

-- NoSQL (Document Store) for product catalogs
db.products.insert({
    "product_id": "12345",
    "name": "Smartphone XYZ",
    "description": "Latest model with advanced features...",
    "price": 699.99
});

-- NoSQL (Graph Database) for social network and recommendations
g.V(user_id).out('bought').in('bought').dedup().values('product_id');
```

Practical Considerations

When integrating SQL and NoSQL databases, certain practical considerations must be addressed. These include:

- **Data consistency**: Ensure that the appropriate consistency model is implemented match the application's requirements, whether strong consistency, eventual consistency, or a hybrid approach.
- **Data integrity**: Maintain data integrity across both databases, managing updates, deletes, and transactions effectively.
- **Performance impacts**: Monitor and optimize the performance of both databases, ensuring that synchronization and query translation do not introduce significant latency or resource overheads.
- **Security and access control**: Implement robust security measures and access controls to protect data across both SQL and NoSQL databases.

Integrating SQL and NoSQL databases can offer significant benefits when executed effectively. By leveraging data synchronization, query translation, middleware solutions, and polyglot persistence, applications can harness the strengths of both paradigms to build more scalable, flexible, and performant systems tailored to modern data demands.

Combining these methodologies ensures a comprehensive approach to data management, providing a robust infrastructure that supports the diverse needs of contemporary applications.

10.9 Using SQL with MongoDB

MongoDB, a popular NoSQL database, stores data in a flexible, JSON-like format called BSON (Binary JSON). Despite its NoSQL nature, the demand to leverage the expressive query capabilities of SQL with MongoDB data has led to the development of several tools and extensions. This section explores methods and tools that enable SQL querying on MongoDB collections and illustrates practical examples using these tools.

SQL to MongoDB Translation Layer

The MongoDB Connector for BI (Business Intelligence) is one of the primary tools that facilitates SQL queries over MongoDB data. It translates SQL queries into MongoDB queries and is compatible with existing SQL-based BI and analytics tools. This connector utilizes ODBC or JDBC drivers, making it possible to connect to MongoDB as though it were a relational database.

To use the MongoDB Connector for BI, follow these steps:

1. **Ensure MongoDB and the Connector for BI are installed**. 2. **Start the MongoDB Connector for BI**:

```
mongosqld --mongo-uri mongodb://localhost:27017
```

3. **Configure ODBC or JDBC driver**: Depending on the client application, configure the appropriate ODBC or JDBC driver to point to the MongoDB Connector for BI.

Here is an example of a simple configuration for an ODBC connection:

```
[ODBC Data Sources]
MongoDB BI Connector=MongoDB ODBC Driver

[MongoDB BI Connector]
Driver=/usr/lib/x86_64-linux-gnu/odbc/libmongodbc_sb64.so
ConnectionString=mongodb://localhost:27017
```

4. **Once configured, you can start querying MongoDB using SQL**. Below is an example of an SQL query executed through a BI tool:

```
SELECT name, address.city
FROM myDatabase.myCollection
WHERE age > 30;
```

The Connector for BI will translate the above SQL query into the corresponding MongoDB query.

Third-Party Tools

Another set of tools include SQL Query and Studio 3T. These offer more user-friendly interfaces for executing SQL queries on MongoDB.

Studio 3T provides a full-fledged GUI for connecting to MongoDB and running SQL queries. With SQL Query, it is possible to execute SQL statements directly within the Studio 3T environment.

Example: 1. **Connect to MongoDB using Studio 3T**. 2. **Navigate to the SQL tab within the tool**. 3. **Execute SQL Queries**:

```
SELECT * FROM myDatabase.myCollection WHERE status = '
    active';
```

This is internally translated and executed as a MongoDB query, retrieving corresponding documents.

SQL Aggregation with MongoDB

Advanced MongoDB queries can be performed using the aggregation framework. Certain tools facilitate the execution of these aggregate queries via SQL-like syntax.

Example of translating an advanced SQL aggregation query:

SQL Query:

```
SELECT department, COUNT(*) AS num_employees
FROM employees
WHERE hired_year > 2015
GROUP BY department
HAVING COUNT(*) > 5;
```

The corresponding MongoDB aggregation query:

```
db.employees.aggregate([
  { $match: { "hired_year": { $gt: 2015 } } },
  { $group: { "_id": "$department", "num_employees": { $sum: 1 } }
    },
  { $match: { "num_employees": { $gt: 5 } } }
]);
```

Practical Example

Consider a MongoDB collection customers with the following structure:

```
{
  "customer_id": "C001",
  "name": "John Doe",
  "orders": [
    { "order_id": "1001", "amount": 250, "order_date": "2022-01-15" },
    { "order_id": "1002", "amount": 450, "order_date": "2022-02-20" }
  ]
}
```

To find customers with more than one order using SQL:

```
SELECT customer_id, COUNT(orders.order_id) AS order_count
FROM customers
GROUP BY customer_id
HAVING COUNT(orders.order_id) > 1;
```

Internally, this SQL query is transformed to:

```
db.customers.aggregate([
  { $unwind: "$orders" },
  { $group: { "_id": "$customer_id", "order_count": { $sum: 1 } } },

  { $match: { "order_count": { $gt: 1 } } }
]);
```

Benefits and Considerations

Using SQL with MongoDB bridges the gap between relational and NoSQL databases, making it easier for SQL-savvy users to interact with MongoDB data. This approach simplifies data analytics and reporting processes, allowing the utilization of existing SQL-based tools and expertise.

However, performance considerations should be kept in mind, as the translation layer can introduce overhead. Furthermore, while simple queries translate easily, complex SQL queries may not always map directly to optimal MongoDB queries. Awareness of MongoDB's capabilities and limitations is essential when designing and executing queries through SQL.

Integrating SQL querying with MongoDB extends the versatility of database management, enabling organizations to leverage the sophisticated querying capabilities of SQL alongside the flexibility and scalability of MongoDB.

10.10 Using SQL with Cassandra

Cassandra, a highly scalable and distributed NoSQL database, is well-known for its ability to handle large amounts of data across many commodity servers without a single point of failure. Unlike traditional SQL databases, Cassandra uses a different querying language called CQL (Cassandra Query Language). However, many SQL concepts can be applied or adapted when working with Cassandra. This section will delve into how SQL operations can be translated into equivalent CQL commands and explore the nuances of querying data within Cassandra.

CQL (Cassandra Query Language) is similar to SQL in syntax and semantics, making it easier for those familiar with SQL to work with Cassandra. The following details provide an illustrative guide to perform some basic SQL operations using CQL.

Creating a Keyspace

A keyspace in Cassandra can be likened to a database in SQL. It encapsulates a set of tables and provides options for replication.

```
CREATE KEYSPACE mykeyspace WITH REPLICATION =
{'class' : 'SimpleStrategy', 'replication_factor' : 1};
```

This command creates a keyspace named mykeyspace with a simple replication strategy and a replication factor of 1.

Creating a Table

Creating a table in Cassandra follows a similar structure to SQL:

```
CREATE TABLE mykeyspace.users (
    user_id UUID PRIMARY KEY,
    firstname text,
    lastname text,
```

```
    email text
);
```

In this example, a table named users is created in the mykeyspace keyspace, with user_id as the primary key.

Inserting Data

To insert data into the table, the INSERT INTO statement is used:

```
INSERT INTO mykeyspace.users (user_id, firstname, lastname, email
    )
VALUES (uuid(), 'John', 'Doe', 'john.doe@example.com');
```

This command inserts a new row into the users table with the specified values.

Querying Data

Basic queries in CQL are straightforward and similar to SQL. For example, to select all users from the users table:

```
SELECT * FROM mykeyspace.users;
```

To filter results, the WHERE clause can be used:

```
SELECT * FROM mykeyspace.users WHERE lastname='Doe';
```

It's important to note that Cassandra's query capabilities are limited to the primary key and indexed columns. Efficient querying requires careful schema design.

Updating Data

To update data in Cassandra, the UPDATE statement is used:

```
UPDATE mykeyspace.users SET email = 'john.doe@newdomain.com'
WHERE user_id = some-uuid-value;
```

This command updates the email address for the user with the specified user ID.

Deleting Data

Data can be removed from a table using the DELETE statement:

```
DELETE FROM mykeyspace.users WHERE user_id = some-uuid-
    value;
```

This command deletes the user with the specified user ID from the table.

Using Secondary Indexes

Cassandra supports secondary indexes, which allow for efficient querying on non-primary key columns. Creating a secondary index can be done with:

```
CREATE INDEX email_idx ON mykeyspace.users (email);
```

After creating an index, it's possible to query based on the indexed column:

```
SELECT * FROM mykeyspace.users WHERE email = 'john.
    doe@example.com';
```

Batch Operations

Cassandra allows for batch operations to execute multiple commands as a single atomic operation:

```
BEGIN BATCH
  INSERT INTO mykeyspace.users (user_id, firstname, lastname,
      email)
  VALUES (uuid(), 'Jane', 'Doe', 'jane.doe@example.com');
  UPDATE mykeyspace.users SET email = 'jane.doe@newdomain.
      com'
  WHERE firstname = 'Jane' AND lastname = 'Doe';
APPLY BATCH;
```

This batch operation inserts a new user and updates the email of an existing user in one atomic operation.

Consistency Levels

Cassandra allows the specification of consistency levels on a per-query basis, ensuring flexibility in balancing availability and consistency. Consistency levels such as ONE, QUORUM, and ALL can be defined in CQL queries:

```
SELECT * FROM mykeyspace.users
WHERE lastname='Doe'
WITH CONSISTENCY QUORUM;
```

This command retrieves users with the last name 'Doe' with a consistency level of QUORUM.

These examples illustrate how SQL operations transition into CQL within Cassandra, highlighting both the syntactic similarities and operational differences.

10.11 Polyglot Persistence: Combining Multiple Databases

Polyglot persistence is a data management approach that leverages multiple, diverse database technologies within a single application architecture. This strategy arises from the recognition that no single database can efficiently handle all types of data storage requirements. By combining SQL and NoSQL databases, applications can exploit the strengths of each to optimally manage different data types and workloads.

In polyglot persistence, the application architecture is designed to route data to the database best suited for the specific storage and retrieval requirements. For instance, relational databases (RDBMS) like MySQL or PostgreSQL can be used for structured data requiring complex queries and transactions. In contrast, NoSQL databases such as MongoDB, Cassandra, or Neo4j can handle unstructured or semi-structured data, large volumes of data, and the need for horizontal scalability.

Architectural Design of Polyglot Persistence

The design of an application using polyglot persistence typically involves the following components:

- **Data Source Layer:** This layer encompasses various data stores, including RDBMS and several NoSQL databases (key-value stores, document stores, column-family stores, graph databases).
- **Data Access Layer:** Interfaces or APIs tailored for each data store type facilitate interaction between the application and the databases.
- **Business Logic Layer:** The application logic where decisions about which database to query or write to are made based on data type and use case.

- **Integration Layer:** Middleware or integration frameworks that help to abstract and manage interactions between the application and different databases.

Scenarios for Employing Polyglot Persistence

- **Read-Intensive vs. Write-Intensive Operations:** Traditionally, relational databases are optimized for read-heavy workloads. However, for write-intensive operations, like logging or tracking real-time events, databases like Cassandra are more suitable due to their write optimization and scalability.
- **Different Data Structures:** Applications often handle varied data types. User profiles might be stored in a relational database, while user-generated content, such as comments and messages, might be in a document store such as MongoDB.
- **Graph Relationships:** Social networks or recommendation engines require efficient querying of relationships and connections within data, making graph databases like Neo4j preferable for certain queries.

Implementation Example of Polyglot Persistence

Consider an e-commerce application needing to manage diverse types of data, spanning product catalogs, user profiles, order histories, and social interactions among users. The polyglot persistence design might involve:

- **Product Catalog:** A document store like MongoDB to manage diverse and dynamic product details, where fields may vary greatly between different products.
- **User Profiles:** A relational database like PostgreSQL to maintain consistent, structured user information that supports transactions and complex queries.
- **Order Histories:** A relational database to ensure ACID compliance for financial transactions.
- **Social Interactions:** A graph database like Neo4j to rapidly execute complex queries about user connections and interactions.
- **Real-Time Tracking:** A column-family store like Cassandra for logging and real-time data analytics.

```
import psycopg2

try:
    connection = psycopg2.connect(
        user="username",
        password="password",
        host="127.0.0.1",
        port="5432",
        database="user_profiles"
    )

    cursor = connection.cursor()
    cursor.execute("SELECT * FROM Users WHERE user_id = 123;
        ")
    user_data = cursor.fetchone()
    print(user_data)

except (Exception, psycopg2.Error) as error:
    print("Error while connecting to PostgreSQL", error)
finally:
    if connection:
        cursor.close()
        connection.close()
```

```
const { MongoClient } = require('mongodb');
const uri = "mongodb+srv://username:password@cluster0.mongodb.
    net/product_catalog";

async function run() {
    try {
        const client = new MongoClient(uri, { useNewUrlParser: true,
                useUnifiedTopology: true });

        await client.connect()

        const database = client.db('ecommerce');
        const products = database.collection('products');

        const query = { product_id: "P001" };
        const product = await products.findOne(query);
```

```
        console.log(product);

    } finally {
        await client.close();
    }
}
run().catch(console.dir);
```

```
from cassandra.cluster import Cluster

cluster = Cluster(['127.0.0.1'])
session = cluster.connect('real_time_tracking')

query = "SELECT * FROM logs WHERE event_id = 'E123';"
rows = session.execute(query)

for row in rows:
    print(row.event_data)
```

Data Consistency and Transaction Management

In a polyglot architecture, ensuring data consistency across multiple databases is critical. Techniques such as the following are often employed:

- **Two-Phase Commit (2PC):** A protocol to ensure all databases involved in a transaction either commit or roll back.
- **Eventual Consistency:** Accepting that different parts of the system will become consistent over time, which is often used in highly distributed systems.
- **CQRS (Command Query Responsibility Segregation):** Segregating the read and write operations into different models to improve performance, scalability, and maintainability.

System architects must balance between strong consistency and system performance, depending on the criticality of data and operational requirements.

10.12 Case Studies in NoSQL and SQL Integration

Case studies provide valuable insights into the practical application of integrating SQL and NoSQL databases to solve real-world problems. This section examines specific instances where organizations have effectively combined the strengths of both database models. Through these examples, readers will gain a deeper understanding of the strategies and tools used in such integrations, as well as the challenges and benefits encountered during the process.

Case Study 1: E-commerce Platform Optimization

A leading e-commerce platform faced challenges managing its rapidly expanding dataset, which included product information, user transactions, and activity logs. Initially, the company relied exclusively on a SQL database for its structured data needs. However, as the volume of unstructured and semi-structured data grew, the SQL database alone could not meet performance expectations. The introduction of a NoSQL database provided a solution.

- **System Architecture**
  - **SQL Database:** PostgreSQL
  - **NoSQL Database:** MongoDB
  - **Integration Tool:** Apache Kafka
- **Integration Strategy**

  The SQL database managed relational data, such as user profiles, orders, and inventory. MongoDB stored unstructured data, including user activity logs and product reviews. Apache Kafka facilitated data streaming, ensuring real-time synchronization between the SQL and NoSQL databases. This architecture enabled rapid data retrieval for both transactional and analytical operations.

```
SELECT * FROM products JOIN reviews
ON products.id = reviews.product_id
WHERE reviews.content LIKE '%excellent%';
```

```
Product_Name | Review_Content | Rating
---------------------------------------
Laptop XYZ   | excellent ...  | 5
Phone ABC    | excellent ...  | 4
```

- **Challenges and Solutions**
  - **Data Consistency:** Ensuring consistency between PostgreSQL and MongoDB required careful design. The team implemented event-driven architecture using change data capture (CDC) techniques via Kafka.
  - **Query Complexity:** Combining data from SQL and NoSQL databases for complex queries was challenging. The company developed an intermediary microservice layer to handle composite queries, dividing them into SQL and NoSQL subqueries.
- **Benefits**
  - Enhanced performance and scalability for querying large datasets.
  - Improved user experience due to faster data retrieval times.
  - Flexibility in managing structured and unstructured data.

Case Study 2: Real-Time Analytics for Online Gaming

An online gaming company needed to enhance its real-time analytics capabilities to improve player experiences and optimize game performance. The existing SQL-based data infrastructure could not handle the high-speed data ingestion and complex analytics required.

- **System Architecture**
  - **SQL Database:** MySQL
  - **NoSQL Database:** Cassandra
  - **Integration Tool:** Apache Spark
- **Integration Strategy**

  MySQL stored transactional data, such as player account information and purchase history. Cassandra managed game state data, including player movements and in-game events. Apache Spark processed and analyzed data in real-time, receiving input from both MySQL and Cassandra.

```
SELECT user_id, SUM(purchase_amount)
FROM transactions
GROUP BY user_id;
```

```
user_id | total_purchases
--------------------------
1       | 120.00
2       | 85.50
```

- **Challenges and Solutions**
  - **Latency:** The primary challenge was minimizing latency to provide real-time analytics. The integration of Apache Spark allowed for distributed processing, reducing the time taken for data ingestion and analysis.
  - **Data Volume:** Large volumes of in-game events required a database that could handle high write throughput. Cassandra's scalable architecture efficiently managed the heavy write load.
- **Benefits**
  - Real-time analytics enabled personalized recommendations and dynamic game adjustments.
  - Reduced latency enhanced overall gaming experience.
  - Cassandra's scalability ensured uninterrupted service during peak gaming periods.

Case Study 3: Financial Institution's Fraud Detection

A financial institution faced increasing fraud attempts and needed a robust solution to detect and mitigate fraudulent activities. The existing SQL database was insufficient for handling the real-time data processing required for effective fraud detection.

- **System Architecture**
  - **SQL Database:** Oracle
  - **NoSQL Database:** Redis
  - **Integration Tool:** Apache Flink
- **Integration Strategy**

  Oracle managed customer account data and financial transactions. Redis provided in-memory data storage capable of handling high-speed reads and writes, essential for real-time fraud detection. Apache Flink served as the processing framework, enabling complex event processing (CEP).

```
SELECT account_id, COUNT(*)
FROM transactions
WHERE amount > 10000
GROUP BY account_id
HAVING COUNT(*) > 5;
```

```
account_id | suspicious_count
------------------------------
103        | 6
145        | 8
```

- **Challenges and Solutions**
  - **Real-Time Processing:** The requirement for real-time fraud detection necessitated a system capable of high-throughput, low-latency processing. Redis's in-memory capabilities, combined with Apache Flink's real-time processing engine, provided the necessary speed and efficiency.
  - **Scalability:** The system had to scale seamlessly with the increasing volume of transactions. Redis's distributed architecture ensured consistent performance under load.
- **Benefits**
  - Significantly reduced fraud detection times, enabling quicker response.
  - Enhanced ability to handle large transaction volumes without performance degradation.
  - Improved overall system responsiveness and reliability.

Through these case studies, it is evident that integrating SQL and NoSQL databases can address a variety of data management challenges, leveraging the strengths of both models to create robust, efficient, and scalable solutions.